R

THE

A NEW LOOK AT KRISHNA'S OTHER SONG
THE UDDHAVA GITA

STEVEN J. ROSEN

Foreword by Charles S. J. White

JAICO PUBLISHING HOUSE

Ahmedabad Bangalore Bhopal Chennai
Delhi Hyderabad Kolkata Lucknow Mumbai

Published by Jaico Publishing House
A-2 Jash Chambers, 7-A Sir Phirozshah Mehta Road
Fort, Mumbai - 400 001
jaicopub@jaicobooks.com
www.jaicobooks.com

Originally published in hard cover by Praeger,
an imprint of ABC-CLIO, LLC
Santa Barbara, CA

Published in arrangement with
ABC-CLIO, LLC, Santa Barbara, CA

REDISCOVER THE LOST GITA
ISBN 978-81-8495-252-0

First Jaico Impression: 2011
Reissued: 2013
Originally published as *Krishna's Other Song*

Printed by
Saurabh Printers Pvt. Ltd.
A-16, Sector-04
Noida (U.P.)

Contents

Foreword

The *Uddhava Gita* is virtually unknown in the West. In contrast to its cousin text, the *Bhagavad Gita*, which now claims more than 2,000 translations in some eighty languages (not counting those in various Indian dialects), it exists in only five or six translations, several of which are severely outdated, are written in poor English, with archaic commentaries (irrelevant in the West), and otherwise are inaccessible. In addition, at least three of these efforts are written from the Advaita Vedanta perspective, which tends to neglect the overall tenor of the *Uddhava Gita*'s message, that is, devotion to a personal Deity.

Just as the *Bhagavad Gita* is found in the *Bhishma-parva* section of the epic *Mahabharata*, a text that focuses on the worship of Lord Krishna, the *Uddhava Gita* shines forth from the Eleventh Book of the *Bhagavata Purana*, which emphasizes devotion to the Lord. In lieu of this simple fact, the *Uddhava Gita* properly unfolds only within a *bhakti* (devotional) context, which narrows down the existing translations to two: the work of (1) Bhumipati Dasa and that of (2) Hridayananda Dasa Goswami and the Bhaktivedaṇta Book Trust.

The former work is available mainly in India, and it is directed to an Indian audience, including two dense, traditional commentaries and the original Sanskrit for each verse. It is an unwieldy volume directed primarily to practitioners. The latter translation, completed by Hridayananda Dasa Goswami and his Sanskrit editor Gopiparanadhana Dasa, is the best of the few that do indeed exist. Complete with original Devanagari text, Roman transliteration, word-for-word synonyms, as well as lucid translation and commentary, this edition is recommended for serious students. But *only* for serious students: It is not published as a separate volume but only as part of the larger *Srimad Bhagavatam* (*Bhagavata Purana*)—with the *Uddhava Gita* alone comprising four volumes at some 300 pages each. If the Bhumipati version is unwieldy, this version is downright intimidating.

Enter *Krishna's Other Song: A New Look at the Uddhava Gita.* Here the author augments existing translations by adding context and relevance, readability, and accessibility. This edition does not include the original Sanskrit, already available in other scholarly volumes, nor does it labor to translate each word verbatim. Rather, while giving the reader all of the text's 1,030 verses in plain English, it offers an accessible commentary, especially written for modern students of Hinduism and South Asian studies—as well as for those with a penchant for Indian spirituality.

The emphasis here is not on literal translation but on overall meaning and gist. In cases in which verses speak for themselves, no commentary clutters these pages. But if illumination is needed, in the sense of clarifying concepts, defining obscure Sanskrit words, or unpacking complex philosophical ideas, *Krishna's Other Song* will offer words of wisdom. And so, in this new publication, Steven Rosen again shows that he is in the top rank of contemporary scholars of the Vaishnava-Hindu tradition, sharing with the world fresh and enlightening insights into the teachings of Lord Krishna.

Charles S. J. White
Professor Emeritus of Philosophy and Religion
American University, Washington, D.C.

Introduction

Among ancient India's Sanskrit wisdom texts, the *Bhagavata Purana* stands out in terms of its poetic quality, coherent structure, and philosophical sophistication. The tradition itself sees the *Bhagavata*, as it is sometimes called, as the cream of all Vedic and post-Vedic writings. Accordingly, its twelve massive cantos, or "books," have been foundational for the Vaishnava tradition, and they continue to exert an unparalleled influence on popular Hinduism.

Just as the *Bhagavad Gita*, which is originally part of the *Mahabharata*, often has been published as a separate, stand-alone text, so, too, has the *Uddhava Gita*, which is part of the *Bhagavata*'s Eleventh Book, been published as a separate volume. Despite this special attention, it has never enjoyed the popularity of the *Bhagavad Gita*, especially in the West. Among Vaishnavas and Hindus in general, however, the *Uddhava Gita* is one of the most frequently quoted sections of the *Bhagavata*. It is unmatched in its systematic development of Vaishnava theology on a wide range of topics—from the importance of detachment and the contemplative life to passionate love, from the organization of society to a theology of nature that is spiritually informed. Ultimately, it teaches the secrets of love of God.

The *Uddhava Gita*[1] is a profound philosophical dialogue between Lord Krishna, who is viewed in the Vaishnava tradition as God, and His intimate devotee Uddhava. The book is one of the many "*gitas*" associated with the pan-Hindu theistic tradition. Though the *Bhagavad Gita* is arguably the most famous of these *gitas*, the tradition offers us *Gita Govinda, Gopi Gita, Venu Gita, Bhramara Gita*, and many others. *Gita* simply means "song," and within the context of India's sacred literature, it refers to particularly mellifluous and blessed songs of divine truth, uttered by great devotees or by the Lord Himself.

Many say that the *Uddhava Gita* picks up where the *Bhagavad Gita* leaves off. At the very least, it augments the teachings of the *Bhagavad Gita*—one might even say that it functions as a cap on the *gita* tradition, with culminating knowledge and esoteric nuance not found in other wisdom texts. As His Divine Grace A. C. Bhaktivedanta Swami Prabhupada writes,

> Undoubtedly, the *Bhagavad Gita* was spoken by the Lord on the Battlefield of Kurukshetra just to encourage Arjuna to fight, and yet to complete the transcendental knowledge of *Bhagavad Gita,* the Lord instructed Uddhava. The Lord wanted Uddhava to fulfill His mission and disseminate knowledge that He had not spoken even in *Bhagavad Gita.*[2]

It is not that Prabhupada is minimizing the significance of the *Bhagavad Gita,* which he elsewhere praises as being among the most spiritually uplifting and otherwise edifying works known to man. But he is saying something about the unique importance of the *Uddhava Gita.*

In fact, the *Uddhava Gita* may be the most important of the genre, for it focuses on Lord Krishna's final instructions before leaving the earthly plane. More, these instructions are delivered to Uddhava, who is recognized by the tradition as *mahabhagavata*, or "greatest amongst the devotees," and as *mukhyam krishna-parigrahe*, "foremost of those who are intimate with Krishna" (*Bh.P.* 3.4.24). He is also Krishna's cousin, and practically His twin.

In addition, as opposed to the *Bhagavad Gita*, which Krishna originally spoke for Arjuna's benefit on the eve of what was to be a devastating battle, the *Uddhava Gita* was relayed to Uddhava for the purpose of enlightening sages—he was to go to the Himalayas and, once there, to brighten the light of those who already were set ablaze with transcendental knowledge. They, in turn, were to share this knowledge with the world.

For these reasons and others, it is curious that the *Uddhava Gita* has never enjoyed the fame of its cousin text, the *Bhagavad Gita*, with which it shares several verses in common. In certain ways, the *Uddhava Gita* goes beyond the *Bhagavad Gita*, illuminating its central teaching of devotion to Krishna and emphasizing the importance of seeing Krishna everywhere, in everyone, and at all times.

Who Is Uddhava?

In the epic *Mahabharata* (*Adi* 186.18) we are introduced to Uddhava but without specifics. We are told that he was present at the marriage of Draupadi and, later (*Adi* 218.11), that he was an important guest at another celebration convened at Mount Raivata. We are told that he was a disciple of Brihaspati (the teacher of the gods) and that he possessed unequalled intelligence. It was he who brought the dowry for Subhadra's marriage to Arjuna and was a central figure at the wedding in Indraprastha (*Adi* 220.30). And when the power-mad Salva besieged Krishna's city of Dvaraka, Uddhava was the valiant hero who saved the day (*Vana* 15.9).

Moreover—and perhaps more relevant to our subject at hand—the great epic tells us that Uddhava was present just before Krishna left the mortal world, before the destruction of Dvaraka, the Lord's city. At that time, the

Yadavas—with whom Uddhava was aligned—went to live at Prabhasa Tirtha, located on the western seacoast of India. The journey to Prabhasa is also described in the *Bhagavata Purana*, in the chapter immediately preceding the *Uddhava Gita*.

Anticipating Dvaraka's impending cataclysm, Uddhava left the Yadavas' association, knowing that Krishna was planning to terminate His own activities in the world of men (Mahabharata, *Mausala*, Chapters 3 and 4). Still, although Uddhava is directly mentioned in the epic, he usually is discussed as part of a group, and his individuality is not yet developed.

It is not until we come upon the *Bhagavata Purana* that the personality of Uddhava really comes to life. We first cross his path in the Third Book—in a story that actually occurs out of sequence. (The *Bhagavata* rarely tells stories in chronological order.) Here, Uddhava meets Vidura, Dhritarastra's brother and supremely intelligent advisor, who asks Uddhava about his conversation with Krishna (*Uddhava Gita*), found later in the Eleventh Book, and also about Krishna's associates and family members.

Uddhava and Vidura meet on the bank of the Yamuna, a significant river in Vaishnava theology. At this point, the *Bhagavata* informs us of Uddhava's single-minded devotion, telling us that from the age of five he was absorbed in Krishna and nothing more (*Bh.P.* 3.2.2). It tells us of Uddhava's spirituality in terms of bodily symptoms, that is, that he visibly cried tears of love and that divine ecstasy emanated from his very being (*Bh.P.* 3.2.4–6). Clearly, Uddhava is no ordinary player, even in this most transcendental of dramas.

Uddhava begins to answer Vidura's questions by poetically telling him that "the sun of the world, Lord Krishna, has set, and our house has been swallowed by the great snake of time" (*Bh.P.* 3.2.7). After this, he recounts Krishna's many loving activities in Vraja (Braj), many of which took place near the very river where Vidura and Uddhava now sit. He further describes for Vidura the many divine activities that took place in Mathura and in Dvaraka as well.

Though Vidura, at this point, wants Uddhava to be his spiritual master—for the latter has proven to be well-versed in the science of Krishna—Uddhava is concerned about proper etiquette. Vidura is senior to him, and so, ultimately, he sends him to Maitreya, a wizened sage in whom Uddhava has great confidence.

According to the *Bhagavata*, Maitreya was present while Uddhava received instructions from Krishna, and so Maitreya, too, heard truth directly from the lips of the Lord. Hence Uddhava's certainty that Maitreya could ably guide Vidura. More important, in this portion of the *Bhagavata*, two significant verses about Uddhava (*Bh.P.* 3.4.30–31) are attributed to Lord Krishna Himself:

> My work here is complete, and so I will now depart for My supreme abode. Know for certain that Uddhava, the foremost of My devotees, is the only one who can be directly entrusted with knowledge about Me. Uddhava is not inferior to Me in any way because he is never affected by

the modes of material nature—goodness, passion, or ignorance. He is always transcendentally situated. Therefore, he may remain in this world to disseminate specific knowledge about Me.

Uddhava-sandesh

With the above as an introduction to Uddhava (in the Third Book of the *Bhagavata Purana*), we do not hear of him again for much of the remainder of the *Bhagavata*. However, when we come to the Tenth Book—the life story of Krishna himself—we are confronted with a telling incident in which Uddhava is a central player.

Consider the following background: The demon-king Kamsa had invited Krishna back to Mathura, the Lord's place of birth, sending the noble Akrura to Braj to escort Him. During this period of the Lord's manifestation on earth, He was spending endless days in pastimes of love with the cowherd maidens known as the *gopis*, considered His most intimate devotees, and with other family members and friends. He relished living as a simple cowherd in the bucolic atmosphere of rural Braj, a little village nestled among famous temples in northern India to this day. Still, Krishna indeed took that journey with Akrura to Mathura and, although He promised to, never again returned to Braj. Venturing out of Braj country was not easy for Krishna, for He so loved His devotees there, but it was even harder on the devotees, who loved Him more than life itself.

The evil Kamsa's secret plan was to kill Krishna while He was in Mathura, but Krishna reversed the course of events. After destroying Kamsa and establishing Himself among the Yadavas in Mathura, Krishna sent His chief devotee, Uddhava, back to Braj to comfort and console the devotees whom Krishna had ostensibly turned His back on—particularly, His parents, Nanda and Yashoda, and, above all, the *gopis*, the cowherd women who experienced untold sorrow when He went away. Uddhava's message to the people of Braj is known as *Uddhava-sandesh*. It follows in a long line of *duta-kavya* or "messenger" literature. In later Vaishnava tradition, Uddhava's message as found in the *Bhagavata Purana* was eventually retold, with esoteric details, in a work by Rupa Goswami, a great scholar-saint-poet from sixteenth-century India. His retelling also bears the name *Uddhava-sandesh*.[3]

In the *Bhagavata* version, Uddhava speaks first with Nanda and Yashoda, reminding them that Krishna is eternally present with them, and within them, stating that He dwells in the hearts of all living beings—not least in the hearts of devotees such as these. Then, the next day, he delivers a similar message to the *gopis*, who, when they see Uddhava for the first time, are struck by his resemblance to Krishna, both in terms of his physical appearance and in his apparel. This visual similarity, of course, increases their sense of separation from their beloved. Before speaking to them, Uddhava listens to their outpouring of love: he hears them lament with aching hearts, bemoaning their intolerable situation, their vacant world in Krishna's absence (*Bh.P.* 10.47.4–21).

Uddhava, overcome by their unmotivated and uninterrupted devotion, praises them as the best of all devotees. He conveys the Lord's message of His all-pervasiveness, and how the *gopis* are always united with Him in love.

But these words, true though they are, ring hollow in the presence of the *gopis'* passionate longing for the love of their lives. Still, Uddhava tells them that they must cultivate the ability to see Krishna spiritually, in their heart of hearts. It is for this reason that He remains separate from them—so that they might develop a deeper vision, understanding Him to be united always with them in a love whose intensity cannot be shaken by mere physical absence.

Though the *gopis* accept all that Uddhava says in terms of philosophical accuracy, they are adamant that union is better than separation, and they inquire about Krishna's dealings with the women of Mathura, and whether He still remembers them, the *gopis*, his faithful Braj companions.

While their pain is somewhat assuaged by Uddhava's presence—after all, as we have learned, Uddhava, in many ways, is nondifferent from Krishna—they ultimately are inconsolable in their unrequited love.

Uddhava is amazed by their unwavering devotion, and he again praises them as true models for all Krishna devotees. So moved is he that he prays to be reborn as a shrub, creeper, or herb on Braj ground, so that he might perchance catch the dust kicked up by their feet (*Bh.P.* 10.47.61–63). These deeper teachings about love greatly affect those of the *Uddhava Gita*.

Other Braj traditions are about Uddhava: It is said that he was indeed reborn as a creeper at Sakhi-sthala, near Govardhana, and, further, that Vajranabha, Krishna's great-grandson, came to him at that time for instruction, allowing him to fulfill his role as the one who was qualified to carry on Krishna's message. But these stories take us too far adrift from the subject at hand. Let us now begin to absorb the presence of the actual *Uddhava Gita*, first by exploring the details of its setting and then with a brief overview of its contents. After this, we can dive deep into the ocean of its nectarean verses.

A Taste of the *Uddhava Gita*

The setting of the *Uddhava Gita* is the last night of Krishna's manifest pastimes on this planet. He is planning to leave at a predetermined time, and His loving devotee Uddhava, knowing Krishna's plan, approaches Him: "O Lord Keshava [Krishna], my dear master, I cannot tolerate the thought of Your departure—of giving up the association of Your lotus feet even for a fraction of a moment. I urge You to take me along with You to Your spiritual abode" (*Bh.P.* 11.6.43).

Krishna, of course, naturally is inclined to comply with His devotees' wishes. Still, He has a higher mission for Uddhava: to stay and to sing His glories again and again for the benefit of others. Krishna explains the importance of detachment and tells Uddhava to roam the world as a renunciant, specifically to go to Badarikashram, high in the Himalayas, and to tell the sages there of His mission and teachings.

Just to be clear on what these teachings are, Krishna explains in great detail the philosophy summarized earlier in the *Bhagavad Gita.* He begins by emphasizing the principle of nonattachment, explaining that the material world is ephemeral, leading to pain, and that God and the soul are eternal. He explains the distinction between the body and the self, just as He does to Arjuna in the earlier text. But here He adds more in-depth logical arguments and alternate analogies to enhance His conclusions.

Krishna then stresses the importance of approaching a guru, but He also says that one can observe many truths by heeding the "spiritual master" known as nature. He enumerates for Uddhava twenty-four "natural teachers" gleaned from the world around us, including the earth, the air, and the sky. From the wind, for example, one can learn to come in touch with sense objects while remaining unaffected by them. The text itself asserts, "As the wind carries different aromas but never mixes with them for any length of time, so, too, should a wise person be equal-minded as good and bad dualities come and go, never allowing them to disturb him" (*Uddhava Gita* 1.41).

Krishna goes on to explain the importance of sexual restraint, relating it to the notion that we are not our bodies—preoccupation with sex is a distraction, He says, that cripples our enthusiasm for spiritual life. He talks about how to see this distraction in perspective and how to work toward conquering the senses, thus allowing one to overcome the addiction to sensual indulgence.

This leads into a discussion of the three modes of material nature—goodness, passion, and ignorance—and how to become free from their influence. To help one rise beyond the modes, Krishna points out the importance of keeping company with devotees, giving elaborate details on how to identify who is truly advanced in spiritual life, and who is not.

The same analysis is applied to various kinds of scriptures, with Krishna identifying those that are directed toward people with self-centered motives, and those that lead more serious practitioners to transcendence. Part of this discussion involves the *Vedas*, the sacred scriptures of ancient India. Here, Krishna explains that most portions of the Vedic literature are directed toward those who want to attain godly delights on heavenly planets, which He juxtaposes with the kingdom of God, a superior destination. He explains how to identify scriptures that focus on divine love, minimizing or even eschewing the inferior sacred texts that focus on superficial rules and regulations instead of devotion to the Supreme.

Krishna next explains the complexities of karma, action, and reaction, giving vivid examples of just how entangling karma can be. He recommends only pure works, done on His behalf—and He describes this as the perfection of yoga. He also outlines the entire process of Raja-yoga, over the course of two chapters, sharing its various virtues and traditions. This includes a description of the yogic *siddhis,* or the mystic powers one can develop through yogic practice. He offers that such powers are meant to be an asset, but are more often a deficit, distracting practitioners from the path of devotion.

After this, Uddhava asks Krishna to list His divine attributes, so that devotees will have substance for meditation and contemplation. Krishna is pleased by the request, praising Uddhava as expert in asking appropriate questions: "On the Battlefield of Kurukshetra," Krishna says, "Arjuna . . . asked me the same question" (*Uddhava Gita* 10.6). After this reference to his conversation with Arjuna, Krishna explains how He can be seen in the world and, nearly echoing His own words in the *Bhagavad Gita's* Tenth Chapter, enumerates His opulences as the Absolute Truth: "I am the ultimate goal . . . I am the three-lettered *omkara* . . . I am the Gayatri mantra . . . I am the Himalayas," and so on. He adds several that are not in the *Bhagavad Gita,* such as "Among jewels, I am the ruby, and among flowers the lotus."

He reiterates how important it is that He be seen in everything and in everyone, and He elaborates on how one might accomplish this.

Two chapters also detail the ancient social and spiritual system known as Varnashram Dharma. Krishna makes it clear, as He does in the *Bhagavad Gita*, that one fits into this system according to quality and work, not according to birth (as in the modern-day caste system). The original system is meant to help practitioners use their God-given talents and inclinations to gradually become spiritually mature, at which time they can give their lives over to love of God.

At this point, the Lord summarizes Sankhya-yoga, wherein He enumerates the material elements at length, showing how they differ from the spiritual element, thus facilitating the realization of one's existence beyond the body. He then describes the nature of happiness and distress, elucidating their source and resolution.

He conveys to Uddhava the art of meditation, explaining that meditation reaches its perfection when one learns how to meditate on Him directly. This is best effected by Deity worship, which is the next subject. This is a formal technique of contemplating specific divine images, serving to focus one's attention on the Lord. These subjects culminate in an elaborate discussion of Jnana-yoga, or how to use one's mind and intelligence in the Lord's service, and finally Bhakti-yoga, the science of devoting oneself to God in mood of loving surrender.

For the sake of thoroughness, let it be said that two miniature *Gitas* are embedded in the larger one: the *Hamsa Gita* and the *Aila Gita*. The former appears in Chapter Seven of the *Uddhava Gita*, when the four Kumaras, youthful sages, ask Lord Brahma, the creator of the universe, how one might conquer the desire for sense gratification. Unable to answer, Brahma turns to Vishnu, the Supreme Lord, who appears before him as a great swan (Hamsa Avatar). The Avatar answers that one must learn to distinguish between the body and the self—that the desire for sense gratification stems from identification with the body. To help the Kumaras understand this, Hamsa Avatar summarizes both Sankhya-yoga and Raja-yoga. He also identifies Himself as Supreme.

The *Aila Gita* (Chapter Twenty) centers on the life of King Pururava, whose wife, to whom he was desperately attached, left him, making him miserable. Eventually, his lamentation transforms into detachment, and he realizes how he had wasted his life enamored by his wife's external beauty. This leads to the realization of his existence beyond the body. Thus, through the pain of material life, the King gradually comes to understand his eternal identity as a servant of the Lord.

The stories of the prostitute Pingala (Chapter Two) and the Avanti Brahmin (Chapter Seventeen) might also be considered *Gitas* in their own right. The story of Pingala is particularly poignant: Although initially making her livelihood as a woman of the night, engulfed in the bodily concept of life, she gradually comes to understand the futility of material existence, conquering her material desires with the wisdom of transcendence. The Avanti Brahmin, for his part, was once a wealthy man who became a wandering mendicant. Although harassed by numerous people, he remains steadfast in his devotion. His understanding of detachment and the illusory nature of the material world catapult him into a world of inner awareness, fostering deep realizations about the nature of happiness and distress.

Different Instructions for Different Students

As the *Uddhava Gita* comes to a close, Krishna again emphasizes the importance of Bhakti-yoga, or devotion to Him, and makes two additional points: First, He asks Uddhava to try to see the Supreme Soul, Krishna Himself, in all living beings and at all times. There is a spiritual oneness to all things, Krishna tells Uddhava, and yet He—God—remains a distinct and transcendent individual as well. This is the great mystery of theistic spirituality. Second, Krishna tells Uddhava to renounce the world and accept the life of a mendicant. Students of the *Bhagavad Gita* will notice that this instruction seems diametrically opposed to that given to Arjuna. In the *Bhagavad Gita,* Krishna tells Arjuna to unhesitatingly fight on behalf of the righteous. In other words, Krishna tells him to work in the world for a divine purpose, on God's behalf, not to renounce all action and to sit on his laurels like a would-be *yogi.*

Is Krishna contradicting Himself by telling Uddhava to become a renunciant, to shy away from worldly activities? Not in the slightest. Arjuna was a warrior, in the middle of a battle, and many were depending on him to do his duty. But Uddhava's temperament was different. He was inclined to the mood of the *gopis,* as expressed in the *Bhagavata*'s earlier Tenth Book, including the *Uddhava Sandesh.* Thus, the Vaishnava teachings of India's sages, as expressed in both the *Bhagavad Gita* and the *Uddhava Gita,* take each person's unique psychophysical makeup into account, celebrating the diversity of creation and the special way in which each of us is meant to serve God.

Krishna's Other Song

Before exploring the *Uddhava Gita*'s actual verses, let it be said that this edition is not meant to be a literal translation of the Sanskrit. Rather, it is meant to convey the essence of each verse and its internal meaning as explained by Vaishnava sages throughout history, such as Srila Vishvanath Chakravartipada, Srila Sridhara Swami, Srila Bhaktisiddhanta Sarasvati Thakur, and His Divine Grace A. C. Bhaktivedanta Swami Prabhupada, whose commentaries on the text are now classic.

While benefiting from the insights of these sages, I hope to communicate the teachings in plain, everyday English, so that the modern reader will imbibe an overall sense of what Krishna is teaching to Uddhava and how it affects our lives in the twenty-first century. That is to say, in this edition, the text will not be interpreted in a vacuum—a mere, mechanical translation from Sanskrit to English—but rather as it is received by a living tradition.

Those who know Sanskrit literature and its categories, then, might refer to my work as a *bhavanuvada*—a text that gives the essential idea of each verse as opposed to its literal meaning. I will be paraphrasing the text according to the sages and their realized perceptions. Now, it is true that in Sanskrit literature, the term *anuvada* (literally, "reiteration") has fallen into ill repute. This is because the genre has been abused by a long line of personally motivated or uninformed translators. *Anuvadas* can easily stray from the original intent of the text, serving as little more than an outlet for an author's personal views. This work will be different, however, in that it solely represents the great teachers mentioned above, explaining the text according to their mood, intention, and insights, if also in terms of modern sensibilities.

This is easier said than done. Many of the teachings require background information—that is, knowledge of philosophical systems prevalent in ancient India and a working knowledge of Vaishnava culture. To this end, I offer brief commentary, drawing, as I do, on the stalwarts of the tradition and on my more than thirty years of personal study. I have also made use of the few English translations that exist today, namely, those of Swami Ambikananda Saraswati, Swami Madhavananda, M. S. Venkatachalam, Vasu K. Brown, Bhumipati Dasa, and Hridayananda Dasa Goswami. All have been useful, and all have contributed to this work. My main inspiration, however, comes from the original Sanskrit text and from the insights gleaned from my teacher, Srila Prabhupada (1896–1977), who, in many ways, was like a modern-day Uddhava, having received knowledge directly from Krishna in no uncertain terms.

Notes

1. The *Uddhava Gita* originally occupies Chapters Seven through Twenty-nine of the *Bhagavata Purana*'s Eleventh Book. In *Krishna's Other Song*, however, the *Bhagavata*'s seventh chapter will be called "Chapter One," with the following chapters proceeding from there. In this way, the *Uddhava Gita* stands alone as a separate text.

According to classical commentator Shridhar Swami (*Bhagavata Purana* commentary 11.1.1), the introduction to the *Uddhava Gita* starts in the sixth chapter of the *Bhagavata*'s Eleventh Book. Then, writes Shridhar, in the twenty-three chapters that follow, Krishna's teachings to Uddhava actually begin. Thus, some say that Uddhava's song actually begins with the last ten verses of the *Bhagavata*'s prior chapter (Chapter Six). But this is really just preliminary material setting the stage for the *Uddhava Gita* proper.

2. See His Divine Grace A. C. Bhaktivedanta Swami Prabhupada, *Srimad-Bhagavatam* (Los Angeles, CA: Bhaktivedanta Book Trust, 1972, Canto Three, Chapter Four, Text Thirty-two, purport).

3. For an excellent translation of Sri Rupa's *Uddhava-sandesh*, see Jan Brzezinski, *Mystic Poetry* (San Francisco, CA: Mandala Publishing Group, 1999).

Sri Uddhava Gita

Chapter 1

Krishna's Instructions to Uddhava

1. The Supreme One [Krishna] said: O greatly qualified Uddhava. You have understood My desire—I want to withdraw from earth and to return to the spiritual world. Be it known: Brahma, Shiva, and all other intergalactic rulers are requesting Me to resume My original station in that supreme abode.

Commentary

Krishna's identity as the Supreme Being is indicated in this initial verse of the *Uddhava Gita.* Similarly, the subservient position of the demigods, such as Brahma and Shiva—highly posted universal rulers, on other material planets—is pointed out as well, at least implicitly. All cosmic administrators throughout the universe are conscious of Krishna's activities, because He is their Lord and His actions invariably affect their service.

Why are these highly posted souls asking Him to return to His abode? To understand their request, one must know the backstory of Krishna's appearance in the material world. He was asked by these very same demigods to appear on our planet some 5,000 years ago, to assuage the burden of the earth. The earth was "burdened" for the following reason: The current age, Kali-yuga—an epoch of quarrel and hypocrisy, which began just after Krishna walked the earth—was precipitated by the birth of various demons, who sought to wreak havoc and gain control of our planet's riches. According to the *Bhagavata,* the demigods could not tolerate these deplorable circumstances and pleaded for Krishna Himself to appear and to rectify the situation. This He did, with feelings of love and compassion, eventually ridding the world of its most formidable demoniac elements. Consequently, His mission completed, He was now able to return to His abode, and the demigods are here encouraging Him to do so.

Apropos of this, in this first verse, Lord Krishna confirms His intention of winding up His earthly pastimes, and He also indicates that the demigods are directly concerned about what He might choose to do. Uddhava understands these facts and Krishna praises him for it.

2. **It was because of Brahma, in fact, that I came to this material world. When I appeared here, I came with My other incarnations and expansions. Once having manifested on earth, We performed various activities to help the demigods in universal administration. But now I have completed My work and have chosen to leave.**

3. **By divine arrangement, the Yadu dynasty will perish through in-house fighting, and within one week the ocean will rise up and inundate Dvaraka city.**

Commentary

Krishna proceeds to explain how He will orchestrate His departure from the earth. The royal dynasty in which He appeared—with its many constituents, along with His opulent dwelling place, Dvaraka—will perish by His divine will. This will set the stage for His own departure, for, after this, He, too, will leave the world.

4. **Thus, O saintly Uddhava, in the near future I will take leave of planet earth. After that, because of the onset of the age of Kali, the earth will deteriorate and sinfulness will engulf the land.**

Commentary

When Krishna leaves the planet, it inevitably dries up, like a flower denied essential nutrients. The Lord's departure, in fact, signals the beginning of Kali-yuga, the fourth age cycle, as mentioned above, in which degradation and general negativity are commonplace.

According to ancient Indic texts, four world ages are repeated again and again like seasons. Thus, the Indic concept of time is cyclical: Satya-yuga, which is full of harmony and light, lasts 1,728,000 human years; Treta-yuga, which darkens slightly, is 1,296,000 years; Dvapara-yuga, in which Krishna appears, goes on for 864,000 years; and finally Kali-yuga, the present age of degradation and iniquity, endures for 432,000 years, 5,000 of which have already elapsed.

5. **My dear Uddhava, once I leave this world, you, too, should go, for it would be in your best interest to do so. My dear devotee, you are without sin, and so Kali-yuga would be distasteful to you—the people of this age will be addicted to nefarious activities. Therefore, be wise, and do not stay here.**

6. **With this in mind, please give up all attachment to family and friends, focusing your mind on Me alone. Thus, being always**

conscious of Me, you should see all things equally and wander the earth in this enlightened state.

Commentary

Interestingly, Krishna first tells Uddhava to leave the world, because with the Lord's departure it will quickly become a hellish place, and then He tells Uddhava to wander the earth in an enlightened state. Accordingly, the Vaishnava tradition teaches that whether one goes to the spiritual world or stays in the world of three dimensions—both are the same for one who has transcendental knowledge. That is to say, for one who has attained spiritual perfection, there is no difference between spirit and matter, for such a perfected *yogi* uses both in the Lord's service.

The next instruction relates to giving up worldly attachments. This is not meant to minimize one's affection for family and friends, as a superficial reading of this verse might suggest. Rather, the instruction is a reminder that God and the spiritual pursuit should come first, and that only by developing love of God can one truly love all living entities and indeed all creation as emanating from one divine source.

Therefore, Krishna here instructs Uddhava "to see all things equally," which is a veiled reference to *Bhagavad Gita* 5.18: "The humble sage, by virtue of true knowledge, see with equal vision a Brahmin, a cow, an elephant, a dog, and a dog-eater." And also 6.29: "A true *yogi* sees Me (God) in all beings and all beings in Me." The idea is to develop divine vision, whereby one can love all living entities equally—but this is a vision that comes only to those who develop an enhanced sense of spirituality. For such a person, there is no question of minimizing affection for family and friends. Rather, one's affection becomes *spiritualized*, as one learns to see everything as part of God. This is a theme that the *Uddhava Gita* will repeat in various ways throughout its many verses.

7. Please be aware, O Uddhava, that the perceived material universe is like an illusion, taking shape according to the dictates of the senses and as a result of conditioning. My deluding energy, known as *maya*, makes it seem real, though it is not. You should further be aware that all material things are temporary, which is part of their illusory nature.

Commentary

Both the *Bhagavad Gita* and the *Bhagavata Purana* are clear that the spiritual world, our real home, is ultimate reality and that the material world is like a shadow, or a perverted reflection, meant for wayward souls. The latter world is created by our desire to enjoy separately from the Lord—a desire that manifests as the reality we see around us, a "holding cell" known as the material world. Here, we attempt imitation Lordship, fabricating an existence in which we are the center.

Our desire to be God, say the texts, is often subliminal, but it fosters an atmosphere in the external world that allows us to play out our aberrant fantasy. Life after life, we "create our reality" as the center of attention, until we realize the futile nature of trying to be God. At that time, by the Lord's grace, we come in contact with a pure devotee, who guides us, purifies us, and gives us further association with spiritually gifted beings. We then gradually become free of illusion and see the world as it is. This is the first step toward ultimate spiritual reality.

8. **Bewildered by such illusion, people in this world naturally perceive diversity in material objects, not realizing the essential oneness of material things as the energy of God. Because of this, people discriminate between good and evil, and yet they are shackled by such conceptions. Absorbed in material duality, worldly people contemplate the performance of desirable actions and how those actions differ from those that are forbidden.**

Commentary

All material things share a certain oneness in the sense that they are all part of God's energy—everything is created by Him and emanates from His divine person. That being said, all facets of material nature have different purposes and function in different ways. These differences are as real as the inherent oneness that engulfs all. Krishna is here making the point that it is helpful to see the oneness of all things in creation, since a sense of duality often leads to misconception. Moreover, ethical principles and moral codes—as limited as these concepts are in terms of ultimate truth—rise to the fore because people discriminate based on observed reality.

As the *Uddhava Gita* goes on, however, it becomes clear that duality, when filtered through spiritual knowledge, is even more representative of the true nature of things than oneness is. Ultimately, the difference between God and the living entities—and the love that is made possible by this difference—is where the text hopes to take its readers.

9. **To perceive ultimate truths, one should bring one's senses under control, thus subduing the mind and its illusory misperceptions. One should learn to see the entire cosmos as situated within the body of God, which is expanded everywhere, and to see oneself as part of that divine existence.**

Commentary

The *Uddhava Gita*, like the *Bhagavad Gita*, teaches that all living beings are part and parcel of God. We are like sparks emanating from the ultimate divinity, who is the sum total of all existence, and we are simultaneously one with and different from His divine essence. Such truths are perceived by the grace of God, usually with the help of *sadhana*, or spiritual practice. The specifics of such practices are later revealed in the *Uddhava Gita* and in other spiritual texts, although the essence is mentioned in this verse: gaining control of the senses and subduing the mind. Spiritual practices to achieve these ends allow the living entity to break free from the shackles of *maya* and to perceive reality as it is. Then, with the help of God and His pure devotees, one gradually achieves spiritual perfection.

10. For one who studies sacred literature, and by methodical spiritual practice enters into that literature's true meaning, the pure self is easily understood, giving satisfaction to the mind. Such a person becomes dear to all living beings and experiences no disturbance in life.

Commentary

One who becomes accomplished in spiritual life is naturally happy, with a peaceful mind and a fulfilled heart. Because of this, such a person exudes a loving kindness that is attractive to all living entities.

Sometimes, however, unfortunate beings, because of negative conditioning and degrading habits, will not respond to spiritual adepts. They cannot perceive the light coming from these beings, nor do they realize the advantages of such holy association. Still, even these unfortunate men and women can become fortunate if they have regular association with an advanced soul, whose spiritual potency inevitably penetrates all inauspiciousness and saturates everything in proximity.

As a side issue, children, animals, and plants, all relatively innocent, often can perceive a saintly person's virtues, relishing his or her association. This truth is also suggested in Verse 10, when it is said that the experienced practitioner becomes "dear to all living beings." In other words, all creatures—whether spiritually advanced or not—can sense saintliness when they are confronted with it. Such perception does not require training or external education. If one has an open heart, spiritual truth will work its way in.

11. Having transcended good and evil as commonly understood in the material world, such a person automatically acts in compliance with religious injunctions, naturally avoiding morally unacceptable activities. The spiritual adept does this spontaneously, as second nature, and not because of concern for mundane virtues.

Commentary

When one begins to realize that life is more than material existence, he or she naturally engages in spiritual practice according to their means. Their chosen path may be dictated by birth, environment, mental disposition, conditioning, or a host of other factors. Usually, this path—whether it is a form of traditional religion or some independent process constructed within a seeker's mind—will involve moral codes and ethical principles, which, ideally, are meant to help a person graduate from the modes of ignorance and passion into the light of goodness.

As one truly advances in spiritual practice, however, such ordinary religious concerns become secondary, and service to God takes prominence. Direct spiritual service is enunciated by saints and by the sacred verses of established religious texts. This service usually involves a series of contemplative exercises and practical meditation techniques that are meant to establish remembrance of God and our original life in the spiritual world. Properly executed under a spiritual adept, these exercises and techniques lead to love of God.

Once established on this higher echelon of spiritual endeavor, one behaves "properly," that is, according to the morals and ethics of the material world, as a matter of course, not as a result of conscious endeavor. The analogy often given is that of a fledgling poet as contrasted with an expert poet: When one begins writing poetry, one has to be mindful of appropriate grammar, the conventions of whatever poetry style one happens to be using, and the rules established by predecessor poets. As one becomes accomplished, however, one need not consciously observe poetry's rules and conventions. Rather, one's work takes on a natural ease of its own, even if, without being aware of it, such a poet complies with the rules of good poetry. So it is with a spiritual adept, too, in the sense that he or she naturally will follow the laws of proper human behavior, even if their conscious mind is focused on the Supreme.

12. Those who are true benefactors of all living beings, who are peaceful and well established in both knowledge and realization, see Me in everything. Such an enlightened being never again takes birth in the material world.

Commentary

A central and recurring teaching of the *Uddhava Gita* is that God should be seen everywhere—in all natural phenomena and in the hearts of all living beings. That is to say, He is omnipresent, and part of that omnipresence is His immanence in creation. The literal meaning of immanence is "to be within" or "near"—and this certainly describes God in relation to the world around us, since His essence is always present within the created universe (even while being distinct from it). This truth is expressed in various ways throughout the *Uddhava Gita*. We see it, for example, in this verse, as well as in 5.42–45, 6.14–15, 6.17, 8.45, 9.10–15, 9.36, 10.2, 10.41, and in many others, too.

In a sense, what's being described is a form of pantheism, which teaches that God is all. In other words, for one in knowledge, God's presence permeates every aspect of existence. And yet, in another sense, the teaching of the

Uddhava Gita is more like panentheism—or the teaching that God is an indwelling spirit, animating and thus giving special meaning to everyone and everything. Actually, panentheism also teaches, perhaps more commonly, that everything exists within the reality of God. Thus, He is not only within everything but outside of everything as well.

There is a sort of "Advaitic Theism" pervading the *Bhagavata Purana*'s text. The juxtaposition of these two words is interesting: *Advaita* refers to a certain oneness between God and everything else, with no Supreme Being as a separate entity, whereas "theism" generally refers to the worship of a personal God. In a sense, the words are opposites. And yet the *Bhagavata* indeed conveys the idea that divinity is not limited by either conception—we are one with the Lord in a certain respect, and still He reserves the right of existing as a distinct entity, worthy of our worship.

The *Uddhava Gita* endorses all of these views—and more. Ultimately, it points to Bhagavan realization, in which one not only sees God everywhere but worships a personal divinity, Krishna, with intimacy and love. Still, the goal of life, it teaches, is to see the Supreme as the essence of everything that exists, at all times, and it hopes to bring such vision to its readers.

Most religious scriptures, in fact, concur that God is everywhere. For example, in the Judeo-Christian tradition, King David proclaims, "If I ascend up into heaven, Thou art there: if I make my bed in hell, behold, Thou art there, too" (*Psalm* 139.8). Or, to cite another example, the Lord Himself says, "'I am a God at hand,' saith the Lord, 'and not a God who is far off. Can any hide himself in secret places that I shall not see him?' saith the Lord. 'Do not I fill heaven and earth?' saith the Lord" (*Jeremiah* 23.23, 24). In Islam, the same truth is extolled: God is said to be "in Heaven" (*Koran* 67:16) but also "in the heavens *and the earth*" (*Koran* 66:3)—He is also said to be "nearer to man than his jugular vein" (*Koran* 50:16).

In short, though conditioned beings are unable to see Him, He is existence itself, slightly covered by a veil of illusion. If we would just learn how to lift this thin veil, through the art and science of spiritual practice, we would detect His presence everywhere. Without doubt, God is fundamentally present in every aspect of the natural order of things—at every level of cosmic causality, in every fully conscious moment, and underlying everything that happens. This can be understood in terms of logic and reason. But to actually see His form, to feel it—as He interpenetrates all people, places, and things—this requires higher realization, and a vision bestowed by His own grace.

13. [The original speaker of the *Bhagavata Purana*] Shukadeva Goswami said: Lord Krishna, the Supreme One, thus philosophized with His intimate devotee Uddhava, who lovingly listened to everything the Lord had to say. Afterwards, Uddhava offered his deepest respects to Krishna and spoke the following words.

14. Saintly Uddhava said: My dear Lord Krishna, I know for a fact that You alone award the results of religion and of yogic practice—by Your kindness, You bestow the perfection of spiritual life upon Your ardent devotee. In fact, You are the Supreme achievement—*the goal of both religion and yoga*—and You are the origin of all mystic potency as well. How wonderful, then, that You stand before me and personally explain the nature of material existence, with specifics of how to renounce material attachments through the process of detachment.

Commentary

The last of these three verses is a summation, by Uddhava, of the *Uddhava Gita* up to this point: Krishna is Supreme, the goal of religion, and the source of variegated energies. Yet He stands as a person before His loving devotee to impart eternal wisdom, beginning with the need for renunciation—a need that stems from seeing material things as they are: temporary and limited.

15. My dear Lord, Uddhava continued, people who have no devotion, who see no virtue in the spiritual pursuit, and who are attached to sense gratification, can never know the freedom of renunciation. For them, material enjoyment is nearly impossible to give up.

16. O Krishna, I am also guilty of the illusions of the common person, because my consciousness is absorbed in the material body and its relations, which, I know, are simply products of Your illusory energy. Because I am ensconced in this illusion, I am thinking, "I am this body, and my relatives have some kind of real, abiding relationship with me." Therefore, O Lord, please correct my misconceptions and squelch my illusions. This will enable me to carry out Your instructions.

Commentary

Here, for the benefit of conditioned souls, saint Uddhava poses as one who is not fully enlightened, showing ordinary men and women how to pray. Uddhava mentions the fundamental illusion that underlies all the rest: the bodily conception of life. All other material illusions have this one misconception at their base. If the Lord will elaborate on the foolishness of misconstruing the body for the self, Uddhava reasons, then all who subsequently hear this discussion—either through Uddhava relating it to them at some subsequent retelling or through reading the *Bhagavata Purana*—will become free of material illusion and begin their journey back to the spiritual world.

17. My Lord, You are the Eternal Truth, and You lovingly reveal Yourself to the sincere at heart. Because of Your perfect knowledge,

only You can explain perfect knowledge to others. Thus, a teacher like You is not to be found even among the demigods, or among the highest of exalted beings. Indeed, each and every one of them, including Lord Brahma, is subject to Your illusory energy, and while these highly qualified beings may be exceptional in various ways, they are subservient to You, for they have limited knowledge. They are conditioned souls, who accept material bodies, life after life, and many of them even accept the body as the self.

Commentary

Uddhava is reinforcing the truth of Lord Krishna's supreme position, adding that Krishna is also the most qualified of teachers, being supreme. Comparatively speaking, says Uddhava, the demigods, as teachers, would be poor substitutes, for they are often subject to the same illusions that plague ordinary mortal souls. Uddhava thus wisely expresses his gratefulness for having the perfect teacher, encouraging the Lord to bestow knowledge and wisdom on his eager devotee.

18. Therefore, my dear Krishna—since I am exhausted from the great torment of material life—I surrender unto You, for You are perfect and unlimited. As the omniscient Supreme Lord, whose spiritual abode is free from all anxieties, You are known as Narayana (Vishnu), the true friend of all souls. I approach You for shelter.

Commentary

Uddhava repeats his earnest desire to surrender his life to God. This he does in the mood of a conditioned soul, again, to teach others how such surrender is properly articulated and accomplished—the same can be said of Arjuna, in the *Bhagavad Gita*, who, although an eternal associate of the Lord, posed as one in need of instruction.

It is appropriate for a conditioned soul to admit the pains of material life when praying, and to assure the Lord that he or she is ready to move on to more spiritual concerns, such as pure devotional service (Bhakti-yoga). Uddhava also identifies Krishna with Vishnu, which is an important point in the *Bhagavata Purana*—Krishna is the Supreme Lord, Vishnu, who has multifarious forms and yet remains one. In the vision of the *Bhagavata*, He is the same one Supreme God worshiped in the great monotheistic traditions, despite His numerous manifestations. This is a point that will be repeated again and again in the *Uddhava Gita*.

19. The Supreme One began to reply: If one carefully observes the visible world with even a little sensitivity and intelligence, one is able to rise beyond gross material gratification.

20. Such a person, by looking at the state of the world and applying inescapable logic, can realize quite a bit through his own intelligence. In this way, one sometimes acts as his own teacher (*guru*).

Commentary

There are numerous kinds of people in the world, all at varying degrees of spiritual evolution. Among these people, there are those who—usually after many lifetimes of spiritual inquiry and practice—reach a certain level of ontological awareness, or inner perception. Such people are able to see through the gross illusions of everyday life. By analysis, experience, and sensitivity, they ascertain certain fundamental truths of existence, such as the futility of sense gratification, the need for ethics and morals, and even the existence of a nonmaterial particle that distinguishes living bodies from dead matter. In this sense, they serve as their own teachers (or *gurus*), for they naturally engage in activities that enhance their innate spiritual awareness. The *Uddhava Gita* here expresses appreciation for the lengths to which one can act as one's own *guru*.

The text teaches that one eventually reaches a point at which intuition, learning, and experiential knowledge will not suffice. At that point, one must search out a spiritually perfected being and inquire submissively, rendering service and thus acquiring true transcendental knowledge. Only at the feet of such a master—for Uddhava, it is Krishna Himself—can one learn about realities beyond the material world.

Throughout the text, one will see appreciation for various *gurus*—*gurus* ranging from oneself, as mentioned in Verse 20, to the gurus found in material nature and in everyday experience. But, ultimately, the *Uddhava Gita* directs spiritual practitioners to approach a bona fide spiritual master—someone other than oneself—coming in a recognized traditional lineage, for higher knowledge.

21. When one actually reaches the human form of life—after first having incarnated in innumerable other species and then into less evolved human forms—one tends to engage in spiritual practices. If such a person sees the wisdom in controlling his senses and focusing on the Supreme, he gradually becomes expert in Sankhya-yoga—the spiritual science of analytical discernment and devotion to God. If one is so fortunate as to become involved in this discipline, and to achieve some modicum of accomplishment in it, he can become blessed with a true vision of Me, in My original form, and also understand My variegated potencies.

Commentary

Sankhya, derived from the Sanskrit word meaning "to count," or "to enumerate," is a philosophical system usually associated with the ancient Indian sage known as Kapila and with the writings of Ishvara Krishna (a sage, not to be confused with the Supreme Lord, who is often known by the same name). Properly studied, it focuses on twenty-four material elements, the first being the *mahat*, or the very principle of material nature. After this, Sankhya considers the mind, intelligence, and bodily identity, along with the five gross elements—earth, water, fire, air, and ether—the five sense objects, the five knowledge-acquiring senses, and the five working senses. Sankhya acknowledges the soul, which is not material at all, as the twenty-fifth element. This listing is amended in various ways according to the particular school of Sankhya one subscribes to. The main principle, however, is to determine how the various material elements interact with the living being, or the soul, and to use this in one's pursuit of the spirit.

Ultimately, the goal is to distinguish the twenty-fifth element, the soul, from all other elements of matter. The entire point is to develop discriminatory ability such that one can discern proper identity: The living being is not body, mind, or intelligence, nor is it some imaginary conception of the self. Rather, it is spirit-soul. This can be ascertained through the process of Sankhya philosophy.

Sankhya-yoga is elaborated on in Chapter Six of the *Bhagavad Gita*. As explained there, it is a form of spirituality that focuses on self-analysis and a deep understanding of material nature. The Sankhya path centers on overcoming suffering through cultivating philosophical discrimination and by releasing the soul (*purusha*) from its entanglement in matter (*prakriti*). Western theologians probably would refer to it as a form of metaphysics. It is a preliminary step toward Bhakti-yoga, or the yoga of loving devotion to the Supreme. Here, Krishna is emphasizing the importance of Sankhya, since it is often seen as a subdivision of *bhakti*, or as one of the many roads leading to the ultimate goal of life.

22. **The created world manifests numerous types of material bodies. There are one-legged creatures; others with two, three, four or more legs; and some bodies are not equipped with any legs at all. But know for certain, O Uddhava, that the human form is especially dear to Me.**

23. **Why is human life special? Because even though I, as the Supreme Lord, can never be understood by mere sense perception, human life is like a gateway through which one might understand My essential nature. The human body affords a special benefit: intelligence that prompts living beings to directly search for Me, guiding them to practices that bring them closer to Me.**

Commentary

Lord Krishna echoes the famous first words of the *Vedanta Sutra*: "Now, having finally attained a human form, one should inquire about divinity." This is the sole prerogative of the human species. Other living beings, who have not yet attained a human form, cannot accommodate spiritual truths. After a long evolution through numerous species, however, one finally incarnates as a human, the bodily form of which is properly utilized only by inquiring into higher spiritual reality.

24. **To show that this is so [that the human form is equipped with special intelligence], sages often refer to a famous conversation between the greatly powerful King Yadu and an extremely eccentric holy man (*avadhuta*), who was also very intelligent—a Brahmin.**

Commentary

This is Krishna's segue into the historical narrative of King Yadu and the *avadhuta*. The basic lesson of the story will show that a rational mind and properly directed intelligence can lead to the process of Bhakti-yoga.

25. **As the story goes, King Yadu one day saw in his midst a strange holy man, an *avadhuta* Brahmin, young and learned, who, without shelter or possessions, wandered about without fear. Yadu observed the eccentric holy man for some time and became intrigued by his behavior. Since the holy man seemed genuinely accomplished in terms of spiritual vision, the king wanted to make the most of his association and inquired from him as follows.**

26. **O learned Brahmin, began King Yadu, you don't seem to engage in any conventional religious practice, and yet you exude a certain wisdom, with insight about people and the way of the world. Please tell me, O great one, how did you come to be the way you are, with extraordinary intelligence, and why are you able to travel freely without a care in the world?**

27. **Generally, people exert great effort to cultivate religiosity, or, according to their taste and level of spiritual attainment, they also work hard for economic development, sense gratification, and so on. Their usual motive is longevity, or they desire to acquire fame and material enjoyment.**

28. **But it all seems to come to you quite naturally, without endeavor. You are learned, expert, handsome, and eloquent, and yet you don't seem to do anything, nor do you desire the usual opulence of the material world. Rather, you often appear unconscious and unfocused, as if haunted by ghosts.**

29. Although people of this world are burning with lust and greed, those flames cannot penetrate the ice-like fortress of your consciousness. You are just like a regal elephant who avoids a forest fire by standing within the cooling waters of the Ganges.

30. O Brahmin, you obviously have no desire for material enjoyment as you travel throughout the kingdom without companions or family members. You have no need for anyone or anything. Therefore, I earnestly inquire from you: Please tell me how you achieved this exalted inner state and what causes the great ecstasy you obviously feel in your heart.

31. [At this point, Lord Krishna interrupts the story to comment as follows:] The wise King Yadu, always respectful to priests and intellectuals, waited with bowed head for a response from the *avadhuta*. Being pleased with the king's attitude, the humble Brahmin began to reply.

32. The *avadhuta* Brahmin said: My dear King, I have many spiritual masters, and by utilizing my intelligence in their service, I have developed a deep understanding of reality. Because of the knowledge they impart, I now wander the earth in a fully liberated condition. If you listen closely, I will describe them to you.

33–35. In summary, O King, I have taken shelter of twenty-four extraordinary teachers, who appear in the following forms: the earth, air, sky, water, fire, moon, and sun; also, I accept as guru the pigeon and the python, as well as the sea, the moth, the honeybee, the elephant and the one who steals honey; add to these entities the deer, the fish, the prostitute Pingala, the *kurara* (hawk) bird and the child, as well as the young girl, the arrow maker, the serpent, the spider and the wasp. My dear King, by studying the actions of these people, entities, and phenomena, I have learned the science of the self.

Commentary

The *avadhuta*'s response is unusual. Traditionally, when considering the subject of spiritual masters, one thinks of the *diksha guru* (who initiates into a particular lineage with mantras) or the *shiksha guru* (who instructs in the science of the self). The latter can be the same person as the *diksha guru*, or it might be any number of helpful and experienced practitioners who are advanced in the science of divinity. Additionally, the *chaitya guru*, or the Lord in the heart, guides sincere practitioners with inspiration from within.

However, rarely do we hear of natural phenomena as one's guru. Nor do we hear of a particular prostitute (Pingala), insects, or animals as the guru. The *avadhuta* is making an important point about how a sincere soul can learn from everyone and everything around him, and, when properly guided by purified intelligence, can even accept these people, creatures, and phenomena as teachers, of sorts, from whom or from which one might receive knowledge and guidance.

36. O greatly qualified King Yadu, please pay close attention as I explain exactly what I learn from each of these teachers in a general way.

Commentary

The *avadhuta* Brahmin will now reveal his twenty-four gurus over the next three chapters, ending with the twenty-third verse of Chapter Three. Because his revelation of these gurus is spread out, separated by many verses of his own explanations and elaborations, a clear overview of the twenty-four teachers would be useful. Here is a brief description of who they are and what one might learn from them.

1. Earth: One who is wise will never be distracted from progress on the path of the spirit, even if harassed by other living beings. Such harassment is inevitable, because people act according to a predesigned plan, which is controlled by material nature. Instead, a wise person is steady and unswerving, like the earth. Furthermore, like the mountain and the tree—also part of the earth—one should dedicate oneself to the service of others.
2. Air (or wind): A spiritual practitioner, like everyone else, inevitably will be subjected to material objects that embody both good and bad qualities. But he should see them as nondifferent, since they are both material—and, like the wind, he should never allow them to entangle him in their dualistic web. As the wind carries different aromas but never mixes with them for any length of time, so, too, should a wise person be equal-minded as good and bad dualities come and go, never allowing them to disturb him.
3. Sky: Though the sky extends everywhere and everything has its resting place within it, the sky still remains distinct. It is never implicated or affected by the blowing action of the wind. In the same way, the living entity is never truly affected by material circumstances, even though it is encased in a body made of material elements. The wise person sees this and thus transcends the misconceptions of material involvement.
4. Water: The saintly person must endeavor to be like pure water, free from all contamination and gentle, flowing with the ups and downs of life. By seeing, touching, or hearing such a saintly person, all living beings are cleansed, just as one is cleansed by coming in contact with pure water.
5. Fire: If a sincere spiritual practitioner consumes contaminated food by chance, he is not affected, for he is like fire, which burns to ashes all

contaminated substances. Like fire, too, a saintly person is sometimes concealed, that is, his spirituality is not obvious to one and all, and sometimes apparent. When he takes the position of being one's guru, he burns to oblivion the past and future sins of his disciples, if they follow his instructions.

6. Moon: The moon famously waxes and wanes, and yet it is still the moon, unaffected by these superficial changes. Similarly, the living entity should not be affected by bodily changes from birth to death, and even when rebirth takes place.
7. Sun: Just as a saintly person can accept nearly any material item and, at the appropriate time, award it to someone else, so can the sun evaporate water and return it to earth as rain, for the benefit of all. Like the sun, too, a saintly person is reflected in many objects, or situations, in various ways, but is never divided—he is one and single-minded in purpose.
8. Pigeon: The *avadhuta* tells the story of a pigeon and his family, living peacefully in their nest when a hunter comes along and systematically dismantles their happy home, killing them all, one by one. The lesson here is the sorrow of excessive attachment, which, of course, is a quality that should be avoided.
9. Python: The python is known in India as a creature that does not make arrangements for his own food, but rather waits for food to come to him. The peacefulness and patience that this requires are qualities that saintly people embody and fledgling practitioners should develop.
10. The sea: A saintly person, being a repository of practically applied knowledge, is never disturbed—he is always tranquil, like the sea.
11. The moth: One who avoids spiritual practice is foolishly captivated by a woman's charms (or a woman by a man's charms), just like a moth is captivated by the very flame that burns it in the end.
12. The honeybee: In traditional India, renounced ascetics generally beg food from different houses by going door to door—this is called *madhukari*, or "honeybee," for it is reminiscent of the bee who takes nectar from different flowers. Another aspect of the honeybee can be found in saintly people: They take the essence of different scriptures. A truly wise person accepts truth wherever he finds it, never limiting himself to one tradition.
13. The elephant: One should take heed of how hunters capture the great bull elephant with the allure of a she-elephant—a trap that causes him to fall into a ditch. Saintly people, therefore, are always cautious when in proximity to the opposite sex.
14. The honey thief: Renunciants and celibate students are entitled to make use of the wealth of hardworking householders, just as a honey thief takes away honey from the nests of busy bees.
15. The deer: When the hunter's horn makes its bewitching sound, deer come running, as they are shot, one by one, with his gun. Noting this, the spiritual practitioner should never allow himself to get lost in mundane sound vibration: nonspiritual music and words of material interest should be approached with caution, if at all.

16. The fish: Because of their uncontrolled tongues, fish are soon caught on the fisherman's hook. Therefore, the spiritual practitioner controls his senses, beginning with the tongue, so he does not fall prey to the "hook" of material life.
17. Pingala: This was a specific prostitute whose life of ill repute gradually became untenable, both because it was a difficult way to make a living and because it was morally reprehensible. Accordingly, she gave up her business and, through gradual purification, was able to remember Krishna, allowing her to become peaceful and happy once again.
18. The *kurara* bird: One day, a hawk was carrying some food for its own personal consumption when a group of larger hawks came along, wanting the edible for themselves. The initial hawk gave up his food spontaneously, fearing for his life, as he flew off. Relinquishing his much desired meat and saving himself in this way, he felt more happiness than he possibly could have if he had eaten the food. The lesson: quick pleasures offer minimal rewards; long-term pleasures are more valuable.
19. The child: A child is happy due to ignorance, and yet in this way he is similar to a saintly person, who is happy due to having surrendered to God.
20. The young girl: One day, a young girl of marriageable age received some suitors at her home. Only she was there, as her parents were away. Dutifully, she went into the kitchen to prepare food for the young men. While making rice, her bracelets started to bang together, making a sharp noise. Noticing the sound, she feared that the young men in the next room would hear it as well, and would think her family poor because she was doing the cooking herself, without servants. To remedy this, she broke all the bracelets except two on each arm, but even these made the same jangling noise. She then removed two others, leaving only one on each arm. Thereafter, she worked in silence. The lesson: When many people live together, a clashing of interests and in-house fighting become inevitable. It is, therefore, ideal to live alone, especially if one wants to pursue deep meditation and other spiritual practices that require concentration.
21. The arrow maker: Once, a king and his retinue were passing by the dwelling of a humble arrow maker, but the latter was so absorbed in his work of making a straight arrow that he did not see the king. Similarly, the devotee should be so absorbed in the Lord that he remains undisturbed by the duality of the material world.
22. The snake: It is observed that snakes make no special home for themselves, but rather that they take over the homes of others, having eaten them. A sage should similarly exert no special effort for his own shelter, focusing instead on serving God with full faith that provisions will be made for his well-being.
23. The spider: God is comparable to the spider because He creates a cosmic network from His own energy and then withdraws it into Himself, just as a spider does with his web.

24. The wasp: Once, a wasp trapped a weaker insect in its lair. Out of intense fear, the lesser insect took on the mentality of a wasp—for it could only think of its captor and nothing else—and thus it became a wasp in its next life. This teaches us that we attain our future births based on that which our minds are fixed upon in this one.

37. The earth teaches me that one should just go on doing what he or she was born to do, even if aggressors manhandle you or harass you in various ways. Indeed, aggressors are acting helplessly under the control of God, according to their own conditioning. Even if raped or pillaged, the earth is never distracted from its duties; nor should we be distracted from ours.

38. Further, we should learn from the mountain to devote all our efforts to the service of others, which is reminiscent of the tree, too—always dedicated to others, even if neglected or abused.

Commentary

As the great apostle of devotional love Sri Chaitanya Mahaprabhu (1486–1533) taught to his followers: A true spiritual seer should be more tolerant than a tree, willing to give shade and shelter to all, no matter what the circumstances. The *avadhuta*'s instruction on what one might learn from the earth, the mountains and trees is a precursor to Mahaprabhu's famous mantra on tolerance, in which he, too, specifically evoked the analogy of a tree.

39. One who is truly enlightened should take solace in the simple things of life, without overly endeavoring for sense gratification. Put simply: one should care for the material body and for one's day-to-day life but only in a secondary way—always being mindful that higher knowledge and self realization come first.

Commentary

Modern society tends to prioritize in favor of material sense gratification. Here, the *Uddhava Gita*, through the words of an enlightened *avadhuta*, tells us that it should be the other way around: Spiritual practice should come first, and we should maintain our bodies and social life in the service of that ultimate pursuit, which is God.

40. A spiritual practitioner, like an ordinary materialist, is also surrounded by sense objects and material temptations, which naturally possess both good and bad qualities. Nonetheless, those who have transcended the dualities of the material world—and those who are trying to do so—will avoid the distracting phenomenon

known as sense gratification, even when confronted with the world around him. Such a person, in fact, behaves like the wind.

41. **Just as the wind carries numerous aromas but does not actually mix with them, so, too, does a self-realized soul live in various material bodies throughout his material sojourn. Though he or she will experience their various qualities and functions, such a soul never becomes entangled or engrossed in the world of illusion.**

42. **Thus, a contemplative and realized person, even while residing in a material body, understands himself to be pure spirit soul. In addition, it is important to note that the spirit soul enters all kinds of bodies, within each and every species of life, both moving and nonmoving; in this way the individual souls are all-pervading. This all-pervasiveness, furthermore, is enhanced by the presence of the Supreme, who accompanies all spirit souls as the Supersoul [God's panentheistic feature]—so both the soul and the Supersoul are simultaneously present within all beings. The nature of the individual soul in relation to the Supersoul can be grasped with reference to the sky: although the sky extends everywhere and everything rests within the sky, this same sky does not mix with anything, nor can its existence as the sky ever be compromised.**

Commentary

The *Uddhava Gita* here echoes the words of its sister text, the *Bhagavad Gita* (13.23), which underlines the distinction between God, as He appears in each individual's body, and the finite soul—you and I—the main proprietor of the body. The ancient Upanishads, appended to the *Vedas*, describe this dynamic by way of a familiar analogy: two birds sitting in the same tree. One bird is enjoying the fruits of the tree, and that bird is the ordinary soul. The other bird merely accompanies him, as his constant companion and friend—and that is God.

Spiritualists who sense the presence of God in one's body tend to overemphasize the oneness between God and the living entity. They confuse the Lord and His partial manifestation as the individual soul, thinking both are the same. Therefore, sacred texts such as the Upanishads, the *Bhagavad Gita*, and the *Uddhava Gita* highlight the distinction between the two by comparing them to two birds, as expressed above.

43. **Again, a strong wind may blow clouds and storms across the sky; but the sky remains as it is, fundamentally unaffected when all is said and done. In a similar way, the individual soul is never really affected by contact with material nature, although, for a time, it**

may appear to be so. The living being finds itself in a body made of earth, water, and other material elements, and, because of this, is compelled to act according to the three modes of nature (goodness, passion, and ignorance). Ultimately, however, the soul's eternal spiritual nature is never actually affected.

Commentary

Several of these preceding verses, again, are reminiscent of the *Bhagavad Gita*. Chapter Fifteen, Verse 8, for example, compares the living soul to air, telling us that just as air carries various aromas, so, too, do living entities carry various conceptions of life. Even so, the text tells us, souls remain unchanged by these conceptions, which may touch them in day-to-day life but not in an ultimate spiritual sense.

44. O King, please know this to be true: If one is saintly, he is, commensurately, just like pure, natural water, for he is free from all contamination. Such souls are gentle by nature, and even their words create wonderful sensations, which, again, resemble cascading, flowing water. If one merely sees, touches, or hears such a saintly person, purification is guaranteed, just as one is inevitably cleansed by contact with unpolluted water. In this way, a saintly person is just like a holy place, purifying all who come into contact with him. This is largely because he always chants the glories of the Lord by engaging in *kirtan* (call-and-response singing).

Commentary

Here is the *Uddhava Gita*'s first glorification of *kirtan*, the recommended process of God-realization for the current age. In previous ages, deep, contemplative meditation techniques, elaborate temple worship, and Hatha-yoga were recommended. But in this age, when life is short and memory weak, when we tend to easily succumb to bodily appetites and fall into illusion, the preferred means of practice is chanting the holy names in the association of like-minded souls, and results are attained easily.

It is difficult in this age to achieve perfection by engaging in other forms of yoga, which, even if perfected, only serve the purposes of those directly practicing it. *Kirtan*, however, is blissful and easy to perform, benefiting not only the practitioner but also anyone within earshot. It is open to all, whether plant or animal, child or accomplished spiritualist—any living being can either call out to his Maker with heart and soul or hear that calling on some level, thus achieving the perfection of yoga.

Kirtan is outstanding as a yoga practice because it does not require withdrawal of the senses. Most forms of yoga involve the grueling task of shutting oneself off from material life and focusing the mind and senses in a strict way. With *kirtan*, however, even if one does not have the senses under control, one can still remain fixed in practice. In other words, even if the mind wanders, the person who engages in chanting performs spiritual activity, and will make gradual advancement on the path, while one who engages in silent meditation with a wandering mind has no recourse but to return to material life.

45. The potency of saintly individuals emerges due to their consistent practice of austerities. Their focus is single-minded and they avoid mundane enjoyment in the material world. They only eat food that comes of its own accord, without making a huge endeavor to secure their lot in life. If, by chance, they happen to ingest unholy food, or something undesirable, they remain unaffected, just like fire, which burns up all unwanted substances that fall in its path.

46. A saintly individual is in many ways just like fire, which is sometimes hidden and sometimes apparent, unnoticeable in ash or ablaze in full-blown flame. To help those who are not enlightened, he often becomes a spiritual master, to relieve the suffering of ordinary living entities. In such a position, he burns to ashes all the sinful reactions of his disciples, mercifully accepting their karma (results for their past deeds) and their ritual offerings.

Commentary

People who are spiritually advanced feel for the suffering of ordinary souls, who, due to conditioning, often are addicted to bad habits. Ordinary souls, too, because of their karma, are forced to enjoy or suffer in a temporary world of untold sorrow. Even their enjoyment invariably leads to a state of misery, either because of innate dissatisfaction, the death of a loved one, or their own inevitable demise.

Indeed, material desire and its resultant "happiness" fall into one of three categories: (1) You aspire for something and you do not achieve it. This causes misery. (2) You aspire for something, you do achieve it, but it does not live up to your expectations. This also causes misery. (3) You aspire for something, you achieve it, and it lives up to your expectations. But you lose it after some time.

Thus, due to the temporary nature of the material world, all mundane enjoyment will ultimately lead to misery.

Not so for spiritual pleasure, which is eternal and unending. Those souls who are blessed with this variety of happiness, because of spiritual practice and the mercy of the Lord, want nothing more than to share it with others. This is the inherent quality of those who are saintly—in addition to being like fire, as this verse tells us, they are an ocean of compassion. Mixed metaphor intended.

The water analogy, two verses prior, explains that they are pure. Now they are being compared to the opposite—fire—for with their purity they burn away the sinful reactions and the pain of conditioned souls. But they are only able to do this if the conditioned soul surrenders to them and follows their instructions. In this way, great souls adopt the position of spiritual master (*guru*) to extend their causeless mercy.

The *Bhagavad Gita* (4.34) encourages all serious seekers to humbly approach a teacher of spiritual science, adding that they should be fully ready to offer menial service and to inquire about spiritual matters. The traditional Hindu guidebook for life, the *Manu-samhita*, tells us much about the guru-disciple relationship: the disciple should revere and serve the bona fide teacher with heart and soul (12.83). In addition, he should not argue with him (4.179–180) and always occupy a lower seat (2.198). He should never mock his teacher, nor should he abandon him, unless there is an extreme situation wherein the guru himself abandons his spiritual practices (2.199 and 11.60). A true disciple will not associate with his teacher's opponents (3.153) and quickly dismiss himself from the company of those who mock him (2.200). Finally, Manu tells us that the guru is responsible for his disciples' karma, meaning that he willingly absorbs all reactions to his disciples' previous activities and burns them to ashes (8.316–318). This latter point corresponds to the teaching in this verse of the *Uddhava Gita*.

47. Fire manifests in various ways according to the size and characteristics of the substance burned: When setting wood ablaze, for example, flames can be mild or ferocious, depending on the size and quality of the wood itself. Similarly, the omnipotent Supreme Godhead enters the bodies of both higher and lower forms of life, which He creates by His own potency. And, mystically, He appears to assume the identity of each.

Commentary

Although the previous verse compares saintly people to fire, here, the *avadhuta* Brahmin compares the Supreme Lord to that same element. His point is this: Greatly empowered beings, like demigods from higher planets, reflect the Lord's qualities to a great degree, while humans may not. In animals, plants, and other organisms, the Lord's presence may be less obvious still. But despite this fact, He is present in all living entities as their well-wisher, as their source, and as their constant companion. He accompanies them through their sojourn in the material world because of a profound sense of compassion and love.

48. Though living beings go through various phases of life, from birth to death, these are all just permutations of the body and have no relation to the soul. In a similar way, the waxing and

waning of the moon does not actually affect the moon itself. Such changes are external and illusory, enacted by the imperceptible movements of time.

Commentary

The *Uddhava Gita* strongly asserts a metaphysical truth that is proclaimed throughout the Vedic literature and especially in the *Bhagavad Gita*: We are not our bodies. Though the soul is temporarily encased in a material shell, which goes through numerous changes because it exists within time, and though the identification with the body is strong, due to lifetimes of conditioning, the actual living being, as part of God, transcends matter and has a separate existence. The entire project of the spiritual pursuit, or self-realization, is to uncover this original identity and to become reestablished in our relationship with the divine.

49. Fire is constantly in flux, appearing and disappearing with the passage of time, and yet, although this is the case, most people won't notice it. In a similar manner, time moves in waves, like a mighty river, instigating birth, growth and death for all material bodies. Even still, the soul, who is subject to these changes while within a material body, cannot perceive the effects of time and its illusory nature.

50. With its intense rays, the sun evaporates large quantities of water, and, in due course, returns that water to the earth in the form of rain. Along similar lines, a saintly individual may accept material things just like anyone else, utilizing his senses as if an ordinary soul. Yet, without attachment, he willingly returns such material objects at the right time and right place—to the appropriate person. Thus, he knows how and when to accept and reject the objects of the senses, thus avoiding material entanglement.

Commentary

Despite the common misconception about what it means to be spiritually advanced—that is, that one must be a renunciant, an ascetic, leaving aside all material things—a sincere practitioner may use the accoutrements of this world in a positive, spiritual way. What distinguishes him is not that he does not use these things—a car, a computer, a telephone, to cite several common examples—but that he is unattached to them. He may use them in spiritual service, and, when the time is right, he willingly relinquishes them to the appropriate person, who will then use these same things in a similarly appropriate way.

51. The sun is reflected in various objects, and yet it remains undivided. The sun does not merge into its reflection, either. Indeed,

it would be rather foolish to think of the sun in this way. A similar phenomenon: Even though the soul is reflected in different material bodies, at different times, it remains undivided and nonmaterial in all circumstances.

52. It is crucial that living entities never feel excessive affection for any person, place, or thing, nor should they be overly concerned about anything material. If they allow themselves this luxury, they will experience untold suffering, just like the foolish pigeon I am about to describe.

Commentary

This teaching (and the one that follows about the pigeon who loved his family) should be understood in context. The operative expression here is "*excessive* love" (*ati-sneha*), with an emphasis on the word "excessive" (*ati*). It is not that one should renounce love of family and friends and all things material but rather that one should see this love in proper perspective. Ideally, it should be seen as subservient to love of God and the spiritual element.

In fact, selfless love—true love—is only possible if one transcends the bodily concept of life. Otherwise, "love" is usually motivated by self-interest or extended self-interest, not always, but for the most part. That is to say, love in the material world is generally about self-love or, at best, it is about love for those who have some relation to our material bodies—family, friends, countrymen. The plain fact is this: In the ultimate analysis, love in the material world tends to be self-centered.

There are rare exceptions, when one actually comes out of oneself and genuinely cares for another, without expectation of return. But, usually, if one looks deeply, penetrating the inner depths or motivating factors of this love, it is usually based the desire to "pat oneself on the back" or to better one's self-image. At the end of the day, if one does not cultivate higher loving sentiments, which stem from a spiritual sensibility or the realization of one's existence beyond the material body, one's love will necessarily fall short. At best, it will be tied to various positive conceptions of the self: "I am a good person; I am altruistic." With such self-conceptions, one tends to act properly, attempting to fulfill deeply rooted personal needs and ideas about how one is supposed to act.

Even so, it is not until we can go beyond ourselves, seeing life as something greater—focusing on love of God and the spiritual bonding we all know as creatures of God—that real love manifests in the hearts of living beings. Moreover, mundane "love" tends to end in disappointment, abuse, and depression, for even when it approaches true love, selfless love, as in a parent's love for her child, the temporary nature of the material world imposes death upon all, abruptly taking away the object of one's affections—and that is if our beloved does not leave of his or her own accord long before death makes its appearance. Mundane love thus carries with it pain and frustration, whereas spiritual love is fulfilling and ecstatic.

This is a central teaching in all religious traditions. Take Christianity, for example. Jesus says, "He who loves father or mother more than me is not worthy of me; and he who loves son or daughter more than me is not worthy of Me" (Matthew 10:37). At times, he expresses it more harshly: "If anyone comes to me and does not *hate* his father and mother, his wife and children, his brothers and sisters—yes, even his own life—he cannot be my disciple" (Luke 14:26).

These are not the most popular or commonly quoted verses in modern Christendom. But they are clearly in the scripture. So what are they trying to convey? What can Jesus possibly be saying here, given the fact that he has already instructed that we are to love even our enemies (Luke 6:27)? And he also quotes the Old Testament, "Honor your father and your mother" (Exodus 20:12), which is a commandment he fully endorses (Ephesians 6:1–3; Colossians 3:20). So the verse asking us to "hate" is not what it appears to be. Obviously, he is directing us toward proper priorities, toward a sense of what should come first. Jesus is communicating that our supreme love must be for God alone. All other love is secondary or rather a manifestation of that love, if indeed it is love at all.

The same teaching is found in the Torah (the Old Testament), in the story known as "The Binding of Isaac," which is about Isaac and his son (Genesis 22:1–24). Here, God asks Abraham to sacrifice his son Isaac on Mount Moriah. According to the story, Abraham sets out to obey God's command without question. After Isaac is bound to an altar, however, an angel stops Abraham at the last minute. So the killing did not take place. But the test was to see whether Abraham's love for God superseded his love for anything else, including family.

What are we to learn from this?

The Judeo-Christian tradition is known as a tradition of love and hope, of faith and light. It is a tradition of morals and ethics, of universal love and family values. Apropos of this, the above is properly interpreted within a wholesome and loving context. This is also true in the Vaishnava tradition.

Naturally, harsh scriptural statements can lead one toward otherworldliness and renunciation, inculcating callous attitudes toward family and loved ones. But this, again, is not the point of the texts. While it is true that scriptures and saintly people hope to give practitioners a sense of realism, underlining the clear facts of material existence—that this world is a temporary abode of misery wherein repeated birth and death take place—they also hope to convey a deeper view of reality, wherein love reigns supreme and compassion is the rule, where loved ones are seen as precious servants of the Lord and life is valued as the greatest of gifts.

53. The story of the pigeon begins like this: Once upon a time, there was a pigeon who loved his wife dearly and, together, they lived

in the forest in their humble nest. Theirs was a happy home, in a beautiful tree, where they lived for years on end.

54. The two pigeons tended their household duties with great satisfaction. On a daily basis, they enjoyed each other's loving glances, bodily forms, and general disposition. In this way, they were completely enthralled with each other.

55. Without thinking of the future, they engaged in the normal, everyday acts of a loving couple, deeply appreciating their tranquil home in the picturesque forest.

56. Whenever the she-pigeon desired something, she would get it. Indeed, she knew how to lovingly manipulate her husband to obtain her ends, and he in turn would accommodate her by faithfully doing whatever she wanted. Thus, he was totally dedicated to her in every way.

57. In due course of time, the she-pigeon became pregnant and, as fate would have it, numerous eggs appeared within the happy couple's nest.

58. Soon, the eggs hatched, and baby birds, with soft limbs and light feathers—as only the Lord can create—brightened the lives of these already blissful pigeons.

59. The baby birds began their awkward chirping, which sounded adorable to the parents, increasing their affection with each moment. Because of this, love permeated that little nest all the more, as the happy couple raised their beautiful offspring without any worries at all.

60. The parent-pigeons felt great satisfaction when looking at the soft wings of their newborn birds, and they deeply relished their innocent chirping and youthful, tentative movements. Watching the little ones jump up and attempt to fly, the parents were overwhelmed with joy.

61. Completely and fundamentally bewildered by the illusory energy of the Lord, the two pigeons were blinded by mundane affection, and in this way they spent their days taking care of their young offspring.

62. Then, one day, the two parent-birds went out looking for food to bring back for their little ones. With their baby-pigeons' hunger in mind, they spent much time wandering the forest attempting to find something suitable to eat.

63. While they were out, a hunter happened upon the nest and saw the vulnerable young pigeons sitting there by themselves. Using a large net, he captured them all.

64. At that exact moment, the two parent-pigeons returned from their food-gathering adventure.

65. As they approached their nest, the mother-pigeon was the first to see it: her dear ones were trapped in a hunter's net, crying piteously. Her heart practically stopped, and she screamed in pain as she rushed toward them. She heard their little voices calling out to her, too, in desperation.

66. The ropes of maternal affection had tied her to an irrational love, and she could not see beyond them. Bound by the intricate knots of the Lord's illusory energy, completely given to material attachment, she charged head first toward her helpless progeny, and in this way, she, too, became entangled in the hunter's net.

67. The father-pigeon now saw his young ones, who he loved more than life itself, along with his life's partner, his wife, horribly bound in the hunter's net. Feeling helpless, the poor male pigeon began to cry from deep in his soul.

68. He uttered the following words: My life is now totally devoid of purpose! What a fool I was, to get so distracted by family life, allowing myself to become obsessed with it. Indeed, I allowed it to get in the way of my spiritual practices, which is what life is really all about. No satisfaction comes from materialistic obsession, even if that obsession is for finer material things, like family. Nor does it allow one to fulfill the real purpose of life. My dear family members, who were the basis of my spiritual path—as well as the source of my enjoyment and the reason I worked so hard to earn a living—are now evaporating like smoke.

Commentary

Obviously, the analogy of the pigeon and his obsessive love for family is beleaguered by limitations and inaccuracies. For example, the idea of "earning a living" is something peculiar to humans, as is the need for "spiritual practices." Indeed, even the feeling of "love for family," in general, might, no doubt, be seen as a bit of a stretch for pigeons. But the author of the *Uddhava Gita* is trying to convey a basic message that speaks to the heart—about the foolishness of obsessive attachment and misplaced or excessive love—and the use of a defenseless "pigeon family" can be quite effective in the regard.

69. My wife and I were perfectly suited to each other, the male-pigeon continued, and, what's more, she always faithfully listened to my words, treating me like her Lord and Master—so high was her regard for me. But now, witnessing the plight of her children,

she abandoned me to be with them—she opted to leave me behind, preferring instead to accompany our lovable children to heaven.

70. **As a result, I am destined to be miserable, living in an empty home, a mere shell of what it once was. My wife and children are dead. Why would I possibly want to go on? This situation has caused such anguish that life itself has become synonymous with suffering.**

Commentary

Again, the *Uddhava Gita* is not saying that family life is not desirable, nor is it saying that one should avoid it or disregard family and friends in any way. Rather, if one chooses a path that includes wife and family, teaches the *Uddhava Gita*, one should do so with eyes wide open. In other words, death is inevitable. Either we die and the family suffers because of our separation, or they die, and we suffer, because of separation from them. Therefore, to avoid this, at least to some extent, our involvement in family life should be pursued with proper perspective. That is to say, family life can be an asset on the path to God, or, conversely, it can be detrimental, depending on how it is used. If it becomes the center of our lives, and we obsessively make it our prime focus, eclipsing even our love for God, then it becomes a distraction resulting in misery. But if family and friends serve the central function of pursuing the spirit, and we see them as eternal spirit souls and love them in that capacity, they become an indispensable asset on the path of transcendence.

71. **Feeling his desire to live being pulled from his heart, the father-pigeon helplessly watched as his unfortunate wife and children, trapped and dying, struggled for their lives. Looking on in horror, his mind lost all focus, and he fell unconscious, thus allowing the hunter's net to engulf him as well.**

72. **Having now achieved his goal—to capture the entire family of pigeons—the cruel hunter set off for his own home.**

73. **The point should be clear: If one becomes improperly attached to love and family in the material world, undo misery will arise as a natural result. If, like the pigeon, we try to find pleasure in a life separate from God, focusing on sexual attraction and its natural results—family and friends—we will invariably live a life of suffering in due course.**

74. **Human life is achieved after taking birth in multifarious species, each with a type of family and associated sense pleasure. Therefore, human life is meant for something greater. But if a human**

being simply devotes his time to love and family like the foolish bird in this story, then he has misused his human form. He is like the person who has climbed to a high place only to once again fall down and start his journey all over again.

Commentary

The final verse of this chapter brings to mind *The Myth of Sisyphus.* In the original Greek tale, Sisyphus was a king who was cursed to roll a huge boulder up a hill, only to watch it roll down again. At which point, he was destined to roll it up yet again, repeating this frustrating process throughout eternity. Existentialist philosopher Albert Camus popularized the story, opining that life in the material world is often tragic and absurd in the same debilitating way. The word *sisyphean* has come to mean, "endless and unavailing, as in useless labor or task." According to the *Uddhava Gita*, when one allows material conditioning—desire and attachment—to consume one's life, it is not unlike the story of Sisyphus, resulting in pointless aggravation and endless misery.

Chapter 2

The Lesson of Pingala

1. **[The overarching dialogue, between Lord Krishna and Uddhava, continues through the words of the *avadhuta* Brahmin, who expresses his profound realizations to King Yadu:] O King, said the Brahmin, all conditioned souls naturally feel out of place in the material world, and they experience misery, no matter where they are—in heaven or in hell. Just as this misery comes of its own accord, so, too, will happiness occur, even without one's seeking it. For this reason, people who are truly intelligent do not make separate endeavors for material happiness.**

Commentary

Here the *avadhuta* Brahmin continues with his explanation of what one can learn from "gurus" that appear in nature—specifically from nine gurus beginning with the python (*ajagara*), as we will learn in the next verse. This teaching is instructive, especially because materialists tend to strenuously endeavor for sense pleasure, not knowing that one is allotted only a certain amount according to karma (one's previous actions) and conditioning, which allow one to enjoy or acts as a barrier to enjoyment according to past mental impressions and psychophysical makeup.

The spiritual practitioner knows this and thus takes the entire enterprise of material enjoyment in stride, focusing instead on the spiritual pursuit. "I do not endeavor for calamity," he or she reasons, "and yet calamity certainly occurs in due course. In the same way, I need not go out of my way for pleasure—it will naturally manifest when the time is right. Rather, let me devote my endeavors to worthwhile spiritual action, being fully aware that material pleasure and pain will arise according to my past deeds."

2. **This is the example of the python: He does not overly endeavor for personal maintenance, and he only accepts food that comes of its own accord, not caring if such food is delicious or tasteless, ample or meager. A wise soul will follow this example.**

3. **A saintly person will simply fast if food is not readily available. Such a soul sees no need to make an elaborate endeavor just to acquire edibles. His vision is as follows: If, by God's arrangement, food is not forthcoming, there must be some unseen reason for this, and I will accept His desire graciously. Thus, following the example of the python, a saintly person remains peaceful and patient, never hankering for food and amenities.**
4. **When one can thus remain peaceful and materially detached, maintaining his body without significant endeavor—this is true saintliness. The point is this: Despite being quite capable, with adequate physical, mental and intellectual strength, a saintly person does not become enchanted by material gain but rather always remains focused on spiritual practices.**
5. **Externally, a saintly person is happy and pleasing in demeanor. But internally he is generally grave and thoughtful. Because he is deep, with profound knowledge, he is never disturbed. In all situations, he is like the tranquil waters of a calm and unfathomable ocean.**
6. **When the rainy season rears its head, the pounding rivers rush into the ocean. By contrast, in the summer, dry weather causes shallow rivers with much less water. Even so, the ocean does not generally overflow during the rainy season, nor does it totally dry up in the hot summer. Similarly, a saintly person whose life is devoted to transcendence will sometimes, by providence, receive great material opulence, and other times he will find himself with few material assets. Be that as it may, he does not rejoice when flourishing, nor does he hang his head in sorrow when poverty-stricken.**

Commentary

The saint is equal-minded in happiness and distress. This is a major teaching in the *Bhagavad Gita*, too, to be noted by all aspiring spiritual practitioners: The quality of equanimity should be cultivated by everyone. True, a saintly devotee will have mastered the art, but unless one practices throughout one's life, the requisite qualities of detachment and indifference to worldly phenomenon will not develop. This is so because one becomes equal-minded through practice.

The *Bhagavad Gita* highlights the importance of developing this quality:

> One who is not envious but is a gentle friend to all living entities, who does not think himself a proprietor and is free from all egoistical notions, who is equal in both happiness and distress, who is tolerant, always satisfied, self-controlled, and engaged in devotional yoga with determination, his mind and intelligence fixed on Me—such a devotee is very dear to Me. (12.13–14)

Or, again,

> One who is equal to friends and enemies, who knows equipoise in honor and dishonor, heat and cold, happiness and distress, fame and infamy, who is always free from impure thoughts, always contemplative and satisfied with anything, who doesn't care where he lives, who is fixed in knowledge and engaged in devotional yoga, is very dear to Me. (12.18–19)

In other words, one should consider happiness and distress equally (*sama duhkha sukham*), knowing both to be the mercy of the Lord. We should endure all karma, good and bad, aware that it is our due, embracing it graciously. Being equal in happiness and distress, we learn tolerance of suffering (*kshami*), helping us first to transcend the bodily concept of life and, ultimately, to develop love for Krishna.

7. **Failing to control one's senses in this way, one helplessly feels attraction upon seeing a member of the opposite sex. This attractive feature is created by the illusory potency of the Lord just to test people regarding their spiritual practices. When a woman, for example, speaks with enticing words, smiling seductively and moving her body in just the right way, a man's mind can easily be captured, thus luring him into the dark well of material existence. In such an instance, he is just like a moth maddened by fire, rushing blindly into its flames.**

8. **Beautiful women, who are decorated with fine ornaments, suggestive clothing, and other cosmetic attractions, tend to arouse men with little spiritual sense and underdeveloped abilities to discriminate. Being eager—if even on a subliminal level—for attention and ego-gratification, such a foolish man loses his intelligence and causes his own undoing, just like the moth who rushes into a blazing fire.**

9. **Instead, a saintly person avoids such material interests and, even in terms of eating, accepts only enough food to keep body and soul together. He also goes door-to-door, begging little morsels of food from each family. In this way, he should be like the honeybee, who goes from flower to flower.**

Commentary

The *Uddhava Gita*, written in India, millennia ago, naturally suggests going door to door, begging morsels of food to keep body and soul together—this was the custom for monks and holy people at that time. The overarching principle, however, is simply this: One who wants spiritual realization should not be preoccupied with bodily concerns, whether in terms of attracting the opposite sex, accumulating money, or even securing food. As life goes on, the physical dimensions of reality and social interaction arise of their own accord, and, with due discretion, one might indulge them to a certain extent, but it should never be an emphasis.

The principle of begging door to door is a humbling experience, reminding practitioners that they own nothing and that they are at the mercy of others. If one finds alternative, more modern means of accomplishing this end, that is, of developing a sense of humility and detachment, the same result would be achieved. The *Uddhava Gita* is after ultimate spiritual results, not a particular method of attaining them.

That being said, the practice, called *madhukari*, which means "like a bee," is still enacted today at Govardhana and other areas of sacred India, where renunciants travel without money or possessions, depending only on pious Brahmin families who specifically cook for them, offering sparse edibles and various items for their nourishment and well-being. The basic idea is this: Just as the bee takes a little from each flower and then moves on to the next, the saintly person takes only a little life-sustaining food from each family, moving from one to the other without attachment, as indicated in the next verse.

10. Honeybees take nectar from all flowers, large and small. Similarly, an intelligent human being should take the essence from all religious scriptures.

Commentary

The *Uddhava Gita* describes the Saragrahi Vaishnava, that is, one who looks for the essence—a spiritual practitioner who is universal in his thinking and nonsectarian in his approach.

The Vedic literature teaches that religion is like a human being. Just as all humans have a body and a soul, so, too, does religion. The body of religion refers to its external principles—its customs, rituals, and dogma. People who emphasize this aspect of religion think in terms of "us and them," and they are the cause of interreligious bickering and even religious wars. The soul of religion, however, is embraced by the mystics, or by people who appreciate the inner core of a given spiritual tradition. Such saintly people are nonsectarian and see harmony in all spiritual truth. The *Uddhava Gita* encourages this kind of spirituality.

11. Those who are actually advanced on the spiritual path do not think, "I will eat this food tonight and horde this other food for tomorrow." In other words, a saintly person is not preoccupied with food or material amenities. Rather, he lives simply, often using his own hands as a plate and eating whatever fits on them.

His stomach is his only storage, without concern for his future stock of food. In essence, he does not imitate the greedy honeybee, who anxiously collects more honey than needed in a particular day.

Commentary

The traditional commentators mention two types of honeybees—those that collect nectar from flowers and those that manufacture honey in the beehive. Here, the *Uddhava Gita* refers to the latter kind of bees, who are known to greedily collect so much honey that they often trap themselves in their own hive. The analogy is quite fitting, for materialistic people, too, become engulfed in the unnecessary accumulation of material amenities, trapping themselves in their day-to-day world of spiritual forgetfulness.

The aspiring spiritual practitioner is advised to be aware of such excessiveness, and to avoid this pitfall on the path to transcendence.

Of course, the great Gaudiya-Vaishnava master, Srila Bhaktisiddhanta Sarasvati Thakur (1874–1937), commenting on this verse, points out that one should be bold in one's pursuance of spiritual life, accumulating whatever one needs without worry of material attachment. Everything—even material amenities—can by used in a spiritual way, thus divesting it of its negative material influence. The art and science of using matter for spiritual purposes must be studied under an adept who is expert in such procedures. Once trained in this way, the practitioner can accumulate the honey of the material world without getting trapped like the unfortunate honeybee mentioned above.

12. **A spiritually realized person should not be contemplating that which he will eat later in the same day, and certainly not in the next day. If he sets aside this proscription and, like the foolish honeybee, accumulates more food than immediately necessary, his simple edibles will be his ruination.**

13. **Those who are spiritually advanced know the dangers of touching someone of the opposite sex. Therefore, sages will never touch a young girl, even those whose sexual organs are not yet developed. In fact, they will not even let their feet rub against a wooden doll in the shape of a female. Be it known: Bodily contact with a member of the opposite sex leads to degradation and illusion, reducing the level of a spiritual practitioner to that of an elephant who is captured because of his desire to touch the body of a she-elephant.**

Commentary

The Vaishnava tradition explains the connection between these two verses: There is a straight line between the tongue, the belly, and the genitalia. If one eats whatever one pleases, as often as one pleases, the senses become unrestrained, fostering a mood of sense gratification. This state of affairs quickly leads to sexual desire and the need to indulge one's bodily longings. Left unattended, it is suicide for the aspiring spiritualist.

The elephant analogy is easily understood by those raised in India and in similar countries. The trick usually employed for capturing elephants is as follows: A deep hole is dug and then camouflaged with grass, mud, twigs, and so on. On the other side of the hole, a she-elephant is paraded about, which makes the male-elephant race toward her, hoping to satisfy his sexual desire. In this way, he falls into the disguised pit and is captured. The *Uddhava Gita* is teaching that wise souls should not be like the elephant, who causes his own downfall—literally and figuratively—by desiring the opposite sex.

14. Those with adequate intelligence will never try to exploit the opposite sex for sense gratification. Among other problems that arise from such exploitation, a person can be killed by competing suitors. Consider the elephant yet again: In the same way that a male-elephant might try to enjoy a she-elephant without competition—but is often killed by other bull elephants who are also trying to enjoy her—a human man searching out illicit sexual connection with the opposite sex can easily be killed by her other lovers.

15. Because of greed, one may accumulate vast quantities of wealth, often with great struggle and pain. However, even if one goes through untold hardships for this purpose, one might not actually secure their desired amount. What's more, whatever amount one does get is usually squandered in due course. Even still, if one does manage to procure a desirable amount of money and use it wisely, it is not always possible to get what one wants out of it, nor to give it away in charity as one might like. All connection with money, then, tends to end in disappointment or frustration. In fact, the greedy man is like the bee that produces a large quantity of honey but then finds it stolen by someone wanting to enjoy it personally (or to sell it to others). Indeed, no matter how carefully one protects his hard-earned wealth or tries to prevent others from stealing it, there are those who are expert in detecting the whereabouts of valuable things, and they will claim it as their own, in one way or another.

16. In the same way that a hunter or gatherer may abscond with the honey produced by hard-working honeybees, saintly renunciants will naturally enjoy the property of ordinary people who are addicted to family enjoyment.

Commentary

In Vedic culture, celibate students and renounced monks are entitled to share the assets of those who live and work in the world. This is as much a benefit to the worldly person as to the renunciant.

In working hard to accrue material amenities, the householder builds up karma and will ultimately enjoy and suffer according to his karmic debt. By sharing the fruits of his work with those who are dedicated to God, the householder burns away his residual karma and advances in spiritual pursuits. In return, the renunciant shares his knowledge and blesses the householder in various ways. Consequently, both benefit from a mutually enriching exchange.

17. If a person renounces the world to live in the forest, he should never listen to materialistic songs or music borne of passion. Instead, such a saintly person should take heed of the deer, who is disoriented by the charming music of the hunter's horn and is thereby captured and killed.

Commentary

Sound vibration is more powerful than most people think. Just as mantras and especially *kirtan*—call-and-response chanting of God's names—can lead to liberation and spiritual awakening, mundane sounds, borne of goodness, passion, and ignorance, can bind one to the material world. Even when conveyed with beautiful and mellifluous melodies, such lower-echelon sound vibrations can infect the consciousness with mundane attachments, bringing listeners into an ever deepening state of conditioned existence.

18. Even the great sage Rishyashringa, son of Mrigi, became a victim of worldly singing, dancing and musical entertainment, and, as a result, became just like a pet animal.

Commentary

The story of King Mrigi is retold in the *Mahabharata*. Briefly, the king raised his son, Rishyashringa, to have boy-like innocence, never touching a woman and avoiding all the usual shackles of material life. In much the same way that the Buddha was kept in his kingdom as a youth, just to protect him from the outside world, Rishyashringa became a powerful *yogi*, because his father sheltered him and kept him pure.

As time passed, however, a neighboring kingdom found itself suffering from drought, and its leaders were informed that the unfortunate climate would lose its sway only if Rishyashringa stepped foot in their court. To this end, the military chiefs of this kingdom devised a plan—they would send a beautiful seductress to lure Rishyashringa out of his protective lair and into their domain.

Their plan succeeded, and the once-powerful sage lost all potency, becoming yet another conditioned soul. He became a servant of his senses, the text tells us, like a helpless animal.

19. As is well known, the fisherman's hook easily catches its prey, for fish anxiously try to taste the worm dangling there. In similar fashion, a foolish person, hooked on sense gratification, is easily deceived by the urges of the tongue, which lead to his inevitable demise.

20. Those who are wise abstain from eating certain foods and instead practice regulated eating. Such souls can quickly bring all their senses under control—except the tongue. Fasting often causes an increased desire to gratify the sense of taste.

Commentary

Fasting is not being criticized here, but it is clearly indicated that by foregoing the pleasures of the tongue, one will not necessarily achieve the expected result. By abstaining from certain foods, at certain times, one will, of course, gain mastery over the senses, to a certain degree. But hunger and a desire to eat will remain. Therefore, the *Uddhava Gita*, coming squarely in the Vaishnava tradition, teaches that one must conquer the tongue not by fasting but by honoring *prasadam*, that is, vegetarian food that has been offered to Krishna with love and devotion. This is the Vaishnava way of mastering the senses—by engaging them in God's service.

21. If one has not conquered the dictates of the tongue—even if he has mastered all the other senses—he should be understood as a slave of his desires. However, if he simply learns to control the tongue, he has truly mastered them all.

Commentary

Vaishnavas teach that one must eat only *prasadam*, as mentioned above, and also use one's tongue to glorify the Lord. If one speaks about Krishna to those who are near and dear, chants the holy name in a regulated way (*japa*), and also sings the Lord's praises (*kirtan*)—in addition to taking *prasadam*—one is understood to have conquered the tongue. After some time of using the tongue in this way, all the other senses become subdued, and one feels purified from within. The body then becomes a true temple of the Lord, with each of the senses illumined by divine knowledge.

22. The kings of the past knew well about the city of Videha, where there was once a prostitute named Pingala. Now please listen intently as I reveal what I learned from her.

23. According to her profession, she would stand in her shadowy doorway nightly, showing her beautiful form to all who passed by. Her intention was to find suitable customers to bring into her home.

24. Anxious to get money, she carefully observed all passersby, thinking, "Hmm, this one is surely capable of paying my price, and this one is not." She had no other focus as various men walked down her darkly lit street.

25–26. In this way, she watched as many men came and went, passing by her house. Prostitution was her only means of income, and so she was anxious about which customers would have the appropriate amount of money and which ones would not. Her worries about finding just the right men, with suitable funds, became pathological, causing her to nervously pace back and forth in her doorway, unable to find the right clients and unable to just go home and go to sleep.

27. Because so many nights passed in this way, Pingala, who was completely absorbed in trying to find men who could sexually and financially accommodate her, gradually became severely depressed, and her face lost its natural beauty. In due course of time, overwrought with anxiety and disappointment, she lost all desire to find men and to go on with her business—she began to feel detachment and a strange happiness entered her heart.

28. She began to feel disgust for her career as a prostitute and gradually lost all attraction for it. Her sense of detachment acted just like a sword, cutting to pieces all of her previously held hopes and desires. As she came to numerous realizations about her material situation, she began to sing the following truths.

29. O King, just as the vast majority of conditioned souls never desire to give up their false sense of proprietorship in the material world, a person who has not developed detachment, through inner realization, never gives up the bondage of the material body.

30. How intense was my illusion! Simply because I could not control my mind, I worked so hard to extract various pleasures from insignificant and pathetic men.

31. Fool that I am, I have given up the spiritual service of that transcendental person who, being eternally situated within my heart, is actually most dear to me, although I had forgotten. That most dear one is the Supreme Lord, who is our real benefactor,

awarding us love and happiness according to our capacity. Indeed, He is the source of all prosperity, even though I foolishly looked for it elsewhere. How stupid I was to have completely neglected Him in favor of insignificant men who could never satisfy my inner desires and ultimate longings. Indeed, these poor substitutes in the material world have simply brought me misery, fear, anxiety, and illusion.

32. I have senselessly tortured myself, selling my body to lusty, unfortunate men. Totally engulfed in the lowest profession of all—as a prostitute—I hoped to enjoy money and sex.

33. This material body, Pingala continued, is like a house in which I, the soul, am living. The bones, including those making up my spine, ribs, arms and legs, are like the beams and pillars of this house, allowing it to have structure and form. The entire house is ghastly, covered, as it is, with skin, hair and nails. Moreover, the nine doors leading into this house tend to excrete foul substances, like stool and urine. When I think about it, what fool but me could devote herself to this material body, the external shell of the soul, thinking that she might find pleasure and love here?

Commentary

Pingala's words resound throughout the Vedic literature, and the "nine doors" she refers to is common imagery in these texts. In the *Bhagavata Purana,* or *Srimad-Bhagavatam,* Canto Four, Chapters Twenty-four through Twenty-nine, for example, one finds an elaborate allegory focusing on "the City of Nine Gates." The central character in the allegory is a king named Puranjana—the Sanskrit word *puran-jana* means "one who enjoys bodily existence." This refers to the soul. King Puranjana, we are told, departed from the spiritual world through misuse of independence, as do many souls, and journeyed to the material world, accompanied by Avijnata Sakha ("the unknown friend"). This friend, of course, is none other than the Supersoul—the expansion of God who accompanies all beings during their material sojourn.

And so, Puranjana arrives in Nava Dvara Puri, the City of Nine Gates (that is, the material body). He finds pleasure at each of the city's entrances—two eyes, two nostrils, two ears, mouth, anus, and frontal genitalia. Moreover, as Puranjana wanders through the gardens of the city, he encounters an extremely beautiful woman. He is attracted to her, and she to him. She becomes his Queen (Mahishi)—in reality, she is the subtle material element, intelligence, which is needed both to enjoy the city in any effectual way and also to renounce it in due course.

The allegory is developed with numerous other characters, too: There is a serpent with five hoods—this is *prana* (breath), which, as yoga texts reveal, is composed of five kinds of air. Avijnata, God, also manifests as our conscience, which we tend to neglect. The attacking "*gandharvas*" are days and nights, which, as we know, have the cumulative effect of taking our lives. Accordingly, Kala Kanya is the terrible maid of time, which comes crashing down all around us, as Prajivara is the embodiment of disease, to which we all must succumb, in one way or another.

In the end, the helpless Puranjana, on his deathbed, thinks only about his treasures, kingdom and other belongings. He says to himself: "The poor queen—who will take care of her when I'm gone?" While dying, Puranjana forgets his good friend Avijnata. Steeped in ignorance, he suffers agony for countless years. Mentally clinging to his wife even at his hour of death, he is then born as a most beautiful princess in the kingdom of Vidharba. The story goes on to his next birth as the princess, but the main teaching is to understand the distinction between body and self, which is Pingala's main point.

34. In this entire city of Videha, I must be the most foolish of its citizens. I chose to ignore the Supreme Lord, the awarder of all that is true and good, and instead I desired to enjoy my senses in the company of many men.

35. In the ultimate analysis, God is the most dear of all living beings, because He is everyone's well-wisher, benefactor and the Supreme witness in everyone's heart. Fully realizing this, I will now offer Him my complete surrender, and by paying this price, I will relish His love, just as His eternal consort does.

36. Some say that men are naturally suited to provide sense gratification for women. But each of them, from the lowest man to the demigods in heaven, is temporary and limited, with a beginning and an end. They will all be destroyed by time. Considering this, how much actual pleasure or happiness could any of them ever give to someone else?

37. And so, even though I stubbornly tried to enjoy the material world, I was fortunate enough to be unsuccessful, allowing detachment to rise up in my heart. This, indeed, brings me an even greater happiness. Because of my detachment, I know that the Supreme Lord Vishnu will be pleased with me. Indeed, I must have unconsciously performed some pious activity, thus warranting His attention and satisfying Him in some way.

38. A person who suffers will soon become detached and indifferent to the material world, and this can lead to freedom from the bondage of material society, friendship and love. It has actually worked that way in my own life, and I witnessed detachment blossoming in my heart. For this reason, I do not see myself as unfortunate but rather as someone who has attained the supreme

fortune due to unfortunate circumstances. That is to say, I am in fact fortunate for having received the mercy of the Lord. In this way, I take great solace in knowing that He must somehow or other be pleased with me.

39. **Though some might take it as ill fortune, I feel deep gratitude for that which the Lord has bestowed upon me. As a result, I have given up my sinful ways and now take shelter of Him, the Supreme Friend of all living beings.**

40. **What's more, I am now completely satisfied, which increases my faith in the Lord's mercy. He has given me the realization to maintain myself with whatever comes of its own accord, and so I live like a saintly person. God, I have come to understand, is the real source of love and happiness, and my life is now His.**

41. **This is difficult for most people to realize, for their intelligence is stolen away by their own actions—by the activities of sense gratification. Such behavior causes one to fall into the dark well of material existence, where the deadly serpent of time imposes death upon all. No one but the Supreme Lord could save people from the hopelessness of material life.**

42. **Sometimes God gives ordinary souls a glimpse of truth, allowing them to see that the entire universe is consumed by the serpent of time. When such vision is bestowed on limited beings, they become more serious about the purpose of life and detach themselves from the material world. In that blessed condition, living entities are able to protect themselves with spiritual practices.**

43. **The *avadhuta* Brahmin concluded: In this way, Pingala made up her mind to renounce all her sinful desires. No more would she enjoy sex with her lovers, or look for new ones. Rather, she became perfectly peaceful.**

44. **Material desire, which comes from forgetfulness of God, is the root of all sadness, and freedom from such desire situates us in the sphere of ultimate happiness. Pingala tasted this higher pleasure and was thus able to leave her prior life behind, including her desire to have sex with lusty men, her vain attempts at raising money, and leading a materialistic life.**

Commentary

In the *Bhagavad Gita* (2.59), Lord Krishna also expresses the need for acquiring a higher taste: "The embodied soul should restrict himself from sense enjoyment, even if the taste for sense objects remains. But this is difficult. However, if such a person ceases enjoyment by experiencing a higher taste, he will be fixed in consciousness and thus more easily perform his duties." In other words, unless one is transcendentally situated, it is not possible to truly abandon sense enjoyment. The process of restricting the senses by rules and regulations is something like restricting a diseased person from eating certain types of food. The patient neither likes such restrictions nor loses his taste for opulent eating. Rather, these restrictions will only truly work if the person develops a higher taste. Similarly, one who has tasted the nectar of Lord Krishna as he advances in spiritual life will no longer have a taste for mundane pleasures. This is the main teaching in the story of Pingala.

Chapter 3

Detachment from All Things Material

1. The *avadhuta* Brahmin continued: All people in this world have preferences due to their conditioning, and they develop attachments accordingly. These attachments cause misery in due course. If one can understand this simple truth, he could avoid untold frustration and sadness.

2. Learn from the hawk: There was once a group of large hawks, unable to find food. They therefore attacked a smaller, weaker hawk, who had in its mouth some meat. As the larger hawks flew toward the smaller bird, he relinquished his meat and, by this spontaneous renunciation, experienced actual happiness.

3. A related point is this: In general, people become ensnared in family life and are always concerned about home, children and reputation. By design, I have nothing to do with these things. I have no family about which to worry, and I do not care about honor and dishonor. My life is merely about the soul, and my love for everyone is on the spiritual platform. In this way, I walk the earth like a child.

4. In fact, there are two types of people who may be considered free from all anxiety: those who are mentally handicapped or childlike and those who are absorbed in the Supreme.

5. There was once a young girl, of marriageable age, who was left alone in her house. Her parents not available to watch over her and her relatives nowhere to be found, several men arrived at her home, specifically desiring to marry her. She was gracious, hospitable, and received them with great respect.

6. The girl went off to a private area and started to make food preparations for her male guests. She began by vigorously beating some rice, preparing it from its husk. As she worked in this way, her

conch bracelets, which were plentiful on her forearms, started to collide, making a loud noise.

7. **She didn't want the men who had come for her hand in marriage to hear her cooking, for she feared they would think she was poor—why else would she be busily engaged in the menial task of husking rice? Using her intelligence, the shy girl broke the shell bracelets from her arms, leaving just two on each wrist. This caused much less noise.**

8. **Still, as she continued to work with the rice, her remaining bracelets continued to bang together and make noise. To remedy this, she took one bracelet off each arm, and with the remaining ones there was hardly any sound.**

9. **I want you to know, said the *avadhuta* Brahmin, that I have traveled extensively to learn about the nature of the world, and I personally witnessed the lesson conveyed by this young girl.**

10. **The teaching from the girl and her bracelets should be clear: When many people live in one place it inevitably leads to disagreement and argument. In fact, even if there are only two people living together, like two bracelets, in due course they will clash. Therefore, the best way to avoid conflict is to live alone, and this is what we learn from the example of the diminishing bracelets.**

11. **Staying alone, one can learn to focus on the Supreme through yoga and other established processes without distraction. Having thus perfected yogic sitting postures and techniques of yogic breathing, one can make the mind steady through detachment, enabling one to meditate on God. In this way, one should carefully focus the mind on the goal of life: yoga practice, or linking with the Supreme.**

Commentary

The Brahmin recommends yoga because this was the prescribed means of self-realization in previous ages, when kings practiced strenuous *asanas* (sitting postures) and *pranayama* (controlled breathing) to master the body and mind, both of which were then used to focus on the Supreme. King Yadu, to whom the Brahmin was speaking, would have been familiar with these methods. Of course, the recommended process of self-realization in the current age is *kirtan*, or chanting the name of God. Moreover, as the *Bhagavad Gita* tells us: "Of all *yogis*, that person who always abides in Me [Krishna] with feelings of faith, worshiping Me in a mood of service, is most intimately related to Me as the highest of all *yogis*" (6.47). Thus, the yoga practice mentioned here attains perfection in Krishna consciousness.

12. This is the proper way to control the mind: by focusing it on the God. Thus, if one can subsist in a solitary, stable place, the mind can easily become free from distractions and material desires. In this way, the mode of goodness gradually increases, while passion and ignorance diminish. As time goes on, one can even transcend material goodness, establishing oneself on the spiritual platform. In other words, when the mind is released from the dictates of the modes of material nature, one's involvement in mundane existence is virtually extinguished. At this time, one enters into direct relationship with the Supreme Lord, achieving the perfection of yoga.

13. When one attains this level, totally absorbed in God, one no longer sees the world in terms of material duality. To understand this, consider the arrow maker, who was so focused on making a straight arrow that he neglected to notice the king himself, who was standing right beside him.

14. If one wishes to attain saintliness, he should live alone and act demurely, so he is not recognized or noticed by others. Limiting the number of people he interacts with, he should minimize verbal exchanges and social intercourse.

15. To be sure, when living in this temporary material body it is virtually impossible to maintain a happy situation or to construct a stable household. The snake, however, enters someone else's home and prospers without attachment.

Commentary

Snakes are known for slithering into another's home. They do not construct their own dwelling but rather travel here and there, making use of the labor of others. The *Uddhava Gita* is not arguing that practitioners should avoid responsibly by exploiting someone else's dwelling for their own sense gratification. No. Rather, it is telling us that saintly people should not have to be distracted by such mundane considerations. Ordinary people should help them by giving them facility, which in turn will allow them to focus on the Supreme. This will benefit all of society, including the people who work hard in the material world.

16. Be alone in life, like the Lord: Narayana is worshipable, the source of all living entities. Without any outside help, He creates the universe and destroys it, using little more than His own potency known as time. Thus, in due course, He withdraws into Himself the cosmos, including all conditioned living entities, and leaves subtle matter, *pradhana*, the basis of all things, in an

unmanifest state. In this way, in the aftermath of annihilation, the Lord stands alone.

Commentary

Generally, Vaishnava texts explain that the Lord is always accompanied by His devotees and that the spiritual world is a celebration of divine love, with numerous kinds of living beings interacting with Krishna in a mood of intimacy and devotional service. When contemplating the Lord's pastimes, however, two things are considered: *rasa* ("esoteric rapture") and *siddhanta* ("philosophical conclusion"). *Rasa* refers to the sweet nature of the Lord's inner activity, the manifestation of His desire for love. It is from this perspective that He is seen as the reservoir of pleasure, enjoying endless exchanges of love with His eternal associates. That being said, in terms of *siddhanta*, which refers to ontological reality, the Lord is always alone—the Supreme One from whom everything emanates. It is this philosophical perspective that is called on in this verse.

17–18. When God, in the form of time, transforms His material potencies, such as the mode of goodness, into a neutral condition (*pradhana*), He remains Supreme, even as He governs that neutral state. He is the supreme worshipable object for liberated souls and demigods, too, even as He is for ordinary conditioned souls. Be it known: He is eternally free from any limitation, and He is the ultimate manifestation of spiritual bliss, which one experiences upon seeing His form. By His association, then, one fully understands the word "liberation."

19. At the time of creation, the Supreme Lord expands to awaken His material energy, *maya*, which is composed of the three modes of material nature. In this way, He creates the *mahat-tattva*, or the basis of all matter.

20. The *mahat-tattva* is also known as *sutra*, and it spawns, in addition to the three modes, the entire material cosmos. Indeed, all of material existence, it is said, is resting within that *mahat-tattva*, and because of this expansion of the Lord, all living entities undergo their material sojourn.

21. The Lord issues forth and eventually withdraws cosmic manifestation, much like the spider expands thread through his mouth, plays with it for some time and, eventually, swallows it.

22. Whatever you contemplate—whether due to love, hate or fear—know for certain that your object of focus will become your

destination. If your mind and intelligence center on a particular bodily form, that is the sort of form you'll attain without fail.

23. **O King, listen to this story: A large wasp once forced a lesser insect into his hive and kept him trapped there. The smaller insect, with intense fear, naturally meditated upon his captor, wondering what he would do to him. Then, surprisingly, even without giving up his own body, the small insect gradually achieved the same state as the wasp, developing similar features. Thus one achieves a state of existence according to one's consistent concentration.**

Commentary

The secret of reincarnation is here revealed. Because of absorption in a particular kind of material life, one takes on an appropriate body, commensurately. The focus at the time of death, especially, determines where we go in our next birth. As the *Bhagavad Gita* says, "Whatever state of being one remembers when he leaves his body, O Arjuna, that state he will attain without fail" (8.6).

With this verse, the *avadhuta* Brahmin concludes his description of his twenty-four gurus, each of which has been summarized for readers in Chapter One, Verses 33–35 (commentary).

24. **These are the spiritual masters I advise you to learn from, for they have given me great wisdom. Now please be attentive as I explain what I learned from my own body, my final teacher.**

25. **I've learned detachment from my material body, and because of this I regard it as one of my many gurus. The body is born and dies, inevitably coming to a painful end. With this understanding, I use my body to acquire knowledge and to make progress in spiritual life. But I always remember that it will ultimately be consumed in due course of time. Thus, remaining detached, I move about in this world.**

26. **As a result of bodily identification, one accumulates money with great struggle. In this way, he hopes to expand his interests, working hard to secure and protect his wife, children, property, relatives, friends, and so on. This is all extended sense gratification, and, ultimately, he does this due to attachment to his own body. Because of this, inadvertently, he assures himself future births: As a tree produces the seed of a future tree before it passes away, the dying body of a human being manifests the seed of his next material body in the form of accumulated karma—for all material actions invariably carry with them material reactions.**

Thus, by assuring its own continuation through attachment and karma, the material body diminishes and finally dies.

27. Just as a man with many wives must accept countless responsibilities, working hard for their maintenance and happiness—as they pull him in different directions, each struggling for her own gratification—similarly, the material senses beleaguer the conditioned soul, pulling him in many different directions at once. The tongue beckons him to arrange for tasty food, just as thirst pushes him toward suitable drink. In the midst of this, his sex organs demand satisfaction, and his sense of touch has him moving about, looking for soft, pleasant objects to feel. His stomach, too, harasses him until it is satisfied; his ears listen here and there for pleasing sounds; his sense of smell has him sniffing for pleasant aromas; and his ever-wandering eyes look the world over for wonderful things to see. In this way, his bodily senses, organs and limbs, all constructed to desire satisfaction, pull him in diverse directions, driving him mad.

28. The Supreme Lord, by using His material energy, created innumerable species of life—various kinds of bodies—just to house conditioned beings. But these various forms of trees, reptiles, animals, birds, snakes, and so on, were not satisfying to Him. And so He created human life, which is a gateway, of sorts, allowing conditioned souls the intelligence to perceive the Absolute Truth. Thus, the human body, if utilized properly, is a secret way of exiting material life, especially prepared by the Lord.

29. It takes many births to achieve the precious human form of life, and, although it is temporary, it allows for the highest perfection. Having attained this rare form, then, a human being should not waste his time. Rather, he should seriously endeavor for the ultimate purpose of life—the spiritual pursuit—while he is of sound body and mind. After all, sense gratification is available in all the lower species as well, whereas the path of spiritual perfection is only possible for a human being.

30. Having learned from my many spiritual masters, I was able to attain realization of the Supreme Person, which fostered in me a sense of renunciation and enlightenment. Because of this, I am able to wander the earth without attachment or false ego.

31. Though the Absolute Truth is One, various sages and scriptures have described Him in many different ways. For this reason, an aspiring spiritual practitioner would do well to learn the perspectives of numerous spiritual masters, rather than just hearing from one.

Commentary

The tradition ultimately teaches that one should surrender to a *diksha* guru, or one who initiates into spiritual science. Such a teacher often becomes the central focus of a student's life, and one can make great progress in this way. However, on life's journey, many lessons arise due to the grace of other gurus, and the serious student should not reject them. Rather, although the *diksha* guru is one, *shiksha* or instructing gurus may be many. In other words—in addition to the person who gives initiation—the knowledge of other exalted personalities may be accepted, too. In fact, their diverse perspectives can broaden a disciple's view of the Absolute Truth. The *avadhuta* Brahmin is a strong believer in this—so much so that he establishes numerous gurus in the natural world, averring that serious students should learn many lessons from them.

32. **The Supreme Lord said: Having thus instructed King Yadu, the learned Brahmin felt satisfied, and the king offered him all due respect and worship, for he, too, felt satisfied. Not lingering for very long, the Brahmin said goodbye to the king and quickly left the premises.**

33. **O Uddhava, said the Lord, the words of this Brahmin liberated King Yadu, who thereby became free from all material attachment. Although a king, with great opulence, his mind was now steadily fixed on the spiritual platform as a result of all he had heard.**

Chapter 4

The Nature of Self-Centered Acts

1. The Supreme Lord said: Surrendered unto Me, with mind fully absorbed in My service, one should practice the social and occupational system known as Varnashram, without being unduly concerned about personal desire.

Commentary

The *Uddhava Gita* acquaints readers with the ancient Varnashram system of social stratification. Briefly, ancient Indian society—like many ancient cultures—functioned well by categorizing its members according to quality and work. In this regard, Varnashram recognizes (1) Brahmins (intellectuals, teachers, and priests); (2) Kshatriyas (warriors, administrators, and politicians); (3) Vaishyas (merchants and farmers); and (4) Shudras (common workers who help the other factions of society), as well as many subcategories distinguished by subtle nuance. Overall, the overarching four categories were known as *varnas* ("color"), although it was not taken literally, as in "skin color," but rather as in "defining characteristic." It referred to innate talent or disposition—to what "colored" members of society, making them who they are. It defined how they would contribute to their community.

Along these lines, the word *varna* does not literally mean "color," although it is often used in that way. Rather, it is derived from the Sanskrit root *vri*, which means "screen," "veil," "covering," or "external appearance." Thus, the word itself underlines the fact that your *varna* is not "who you are," but it is instead "what you do," how you appear, while encased in a particular body.

Often confused with the caste system, *varnas* originally were assigned according to quality and work, not according to birth. Clearly, vocational aptitude is at the heart of Varnashram Dharma, which was meant to facilitate the proper functioning of society, allowing all members to fit in neatly according to their psychophysical makeup. Krishna is clear about this "quality and work" component in the *Bhagavad Gita*: "I created the four orders of society to allow people to function according to their quality (*guna*) and work (*karma*)" (4.13).

And yet, when confronted with India and its social system, most people still think in terms of birth status. The reason is obvious: Today, in India, each *varna* is divided into a number of *jatis*, of which there are thousands. As opposed to the original Varnashram system, *jati* is in fact usually demarcated according to birth, and India has suffered much as a result of this. People exploit "higher" births and take advantage of others who are of "lower" birth. Not so in the original system as practiced in ancient India. Putting personal desire aside, as Krishna says in this verse of the *Uddhava Gita*, the conscientious spiritual citizen should act according to his skill sets and longstanding inclinations, as ordained by guru and society, and in this way serve the greater good.

An appropriate addendum, perhaps, would be a brief discussion of the four "spiritual orders," for they naturally accompanied the *varna* system. These were known as *ashrams*—hence, "Varn*ashram*." The *ashrams* included (1) Brahmacharis (celibate monk, student life); (2) Grihasthas (married, working in the world); (3) Vanaprasthas (retiring, preparing for renunciation); and (4) Sannyasis (renounced mendicant, preparing for death). Krishna will address Varnashram more thoroughly in Chapters Eleven and Twelve.

2. **One who is advanced in spiritual life can see that conditioned souls, dedicated to sense pleasure, are actually suffering, and that all their endeavors for happiness are, in the ultimate analysis, doomed to failure.**

3. **When a man sleeps, he may see many pleasurable things in his dreams. But these empty promises are merely creations of the mind, without substance. In the same way, people in this world look to temporary objects of gratification as if such things could bring them satisfaction or pleasure. The accoutrements of this world are creations of the Lord's illusory potency—they are limited, deceiving, and have no permanent existence. One who focuses on them, showing that he is a slave of his senses, simply wastes his intelligence.**

4. **If a person truly understands Me as the goal of life, he should give up activities based on mundane sense gratification. Instead, he should perform work that leads to spiritual advancement. Moreover, if one is fully engaged in pursuance of the ultimate truth, he need not accept scriptural injunctions governing fruitive activities.**

Commentary

Charlatans and pseudo-spiritualists have a tendency to abuse such verses, using them to rationalize illicit behavior. When one is a beginner in spiritual life, one must scrupulously follow basic regulative principles and scriptural injunctions. As one makes advancement, he need not consciously bother himself with every last detail, though, in general, he will follow devotional principles as a matter of course. That being said, a seasoned practitioner is more concerned with the essence of a given spiritual injunction, not the details, which can vary according to time, place, and circumstance. Opportunistic devotees, again, take advantage of this fact and ruin their spiritual lives by compromising in the name of pursuing essential truths.

5. **One who has accepted Me as the supreme goal will naturally observe scriptural injunctions and minor regulative duties as well. To practice properly, however, one should surrender to a bona fide spiritual master who has complete knowledge of Me. This teacher will be an inherently peaceful person who, in essence, is My very Self.**

Commentary

True devotees will follow scriptural injunctions and regulative principles, but to understand these teachings properly, one must take guidance from a more experienced practitioner. The spiritual master is thus essential in one's devotional life. Through his own practice, he has become inwardly peaceful, with a strong desire to help others on the path. Because of this, he has become one with Krishna, not ontologically but in terms of essential purpose: Krishna wants to bring all souls to Himself, so that they might experience the pinnacle of love and devotion, and the pure devotee wants this, too. Thus, they are one in purpose.

6. **A good disciple is free from false prestige, always recognizing that God is the ultimate "doer" of all activities. Nor is an accomplished disciple lazy, and he is always eager to work on behalf of the Supreme. Knowing full well that all of his "possessions," including wife, children, home and society, actually belong to the Lord, he is eager to see them engaged in divine service. Such a disciple has feelings of loving camaraderie toward his spiritual master, and he never becomes doubtful or confused. He always works toward advancement in spiritual life, is disinclined toward wasteful words, and is without envy in any situation.**

7. **In this way, he sees that his real self-interest in life is spiritual, and he remains detached from wife, children, home, land, relatives, friends, wealth, and other material assets.**

Commentary

The above two verses describe an ideal disciple. He goes through life knowing that "man proposes and God disposes," meaning that while living beings appear to be doing this or that, Krishna is the ultimate Doer—for nothing happens without His Supreme sanction. A good disciple also knows that everything belongs to God and should be used in His service. While he feels closeness to his teacher, he is always mindful of his master's superior position—for forgetfulness of this fact can bring spiritual ruination. Moreover, the detachment he feels for all material things, including his loved ones, is not to be misunderstood: he regards them highly but sees them as the "property" of the Lord. Therefore, he is detached from a false sense of proprietorship—that "these are mine." Otherwise, he feels great love and compassion for all, wishing them the best in the Lord's service.

8. It is fire that burns and lights up the sky, and this is different from firewood, the substance whose burning provides that illumination. Similarly, the person within the body, the self-effulgent spirit soul, is different from the material body, which is set ablaze by consciousness. In this way, it should be understood that the spirit soul and the body are distinct, possessing diverse characteristics.

9. Just as fire manifests itself with varying intensity, from dormant to weak to brilliant, and so on, depending on what sparks its flame, similarly, the spirit soul enters a material body and displays particular bodily characteristics according to its potency.

10. Both subtle and gross material bodies—composed of mind, intelligence and ego (subtle) and the physical tabernacle (gross), respectively—are created by the material modes (goodness, passion, and ignorance), which expand from the divine energy of the Lord. Material illusion begins when the living entity, who is a spiritual soul, falsely accepts the qualities of both his gross and subtle bodies as being who he really is. Nonetheless, this illusion can be destroyed by real knowledge.

11. Therefore, one should cultivate knowledge and in this way approach the Supreme Godhead, who is situated within the heart of all living beings. By communing with the Lord in this way, one gradually gives up his false vision of the material world as an abiding reality.

12. Using the analogy of fire, the spiritual master is comparable to a lower kindling stick, the disciple to an upper kindling stick, and the instruction given by the guru to a third stick placed in between. Along similar lines, the spiritual knowledge that a guru conveys to his disciple is compared to the fire itself, which arises from the interaction of these three. This "spiritual fire" burns the darkness of ignorance to ashes, allowing great happiness to emerge in the hearts of both guru and disciple.

13. By submissively giving aural reception to an accomplished spiritual master, the sincere disciple develops pure knowledge. In this

way, he casts away the onslaught of material illusion, which arises from the three modes of material nature. In the end, even pure knowledge itself ceases, just as fire eventually goes out when the fuel that started it has been consumed.

Commentary

Knowledge is like a catalyst that brings one to the spiritual platform. In fact, on the path to spiritual perfection, knowledge is indispensable, especially because most living beings have spent lifetimes in illusion. The analogy of fire, therefore, is quite fitting: Knowledge burns away illusion and leaves us in the cool waters of spiritual awareness. Once in these waters, the existence of knowledge, as such, is no longer important. Indeed, at that point, one basks in love of God, with knowledge serving as little more than a pious distraction.

However, until one is swimming in that ocean of spiritual love, it is crucial to cultivate knowledge under the auspices of a bona fide spiritual master. This is accomplished by rendering practical service, hearing from the lips of one who knows, and studying scripture and tradition. Otherwise, for most, spiritual attainment will not arise.

14–16. My precious Uddhava, all that I tell you is true. Even so, there is a class of philosophers who disagree with these conclusions. They argue that living beings should in fact engage in fruitive activities. They further claim that ordinary souls should be the central enjoyers of their work, and that there is no God in control. According to this materialistic philosophy, the world, time, the sacred scriptures, and even the self, are all variegated and long-standing, but existing without a source. On the other hand, they say that ordinary knowledge has a temporary nature, because it arises from the endless permutations that occur in everyday life; for this reason, knowledge itself is always subject to change. Even if you accept such a philosophy, O Uddhava, there will still be perpetual birth, death, old age and disease, since all living entities must accept a material body—and all bodies are subject to the influence of time.

Commentary

The traditional commentators say that Krishna is referring to Mimamsa philosophy, which became popular in India long after the Vedic period came to a close. Its origins can be traced to the great philosopher known as Jaimini Rishi, who lived during the time of the events described in the *Mahabharata*, thousands of years ago.

His primary work, the *Purva Mimamsa Sutras* or *Mimamsa Sutras*, is considered one of the most important ancient Hindu philosophical texts of all time. This book forms the basis of Mimamsa, the earliest of the six orthodox schools (*darshans*) of Indian philosophy.

The text interprets the *Vedas* in an atheistic way and also provides elaborate philosophical explanation for Vedic rituals. It does so, however, in a way that leads to personal liberation, without devotion to a personal God.

In the ultimate analysis, Jaimini's Karma Mimamsa, as his school of thought came to be called, claims that this world is all there is to reality and that it exists eternally. For Jaimini, the cycle of karmic action and reaction is perpetual, with no chance of ultimate liberation or a transcendental realm.

From a truly Vedic point of view, however, Jaimini's philosophy cannot stand. A careful examination of Upanishadic mantras includes descriptions of a higher, spiritual existence. For example, *sad eva saumyedam agra asid ekam evadvitiyam*: "Dear one, the Absolute Truth alone existed prior to this creation, and this is the only truth there is" (*Chandogya Upanishad* 6.2.1). Also, *vijnanam anandam brahma*: "The supreme reality is divine knowledge and bliss, which transcends this material world" (*Brihad-aranyaka Upanishad* 3.9.34). In other words, the theological position of the *Vedas* is clear: There is a God, and material nature is temporary, just as Lord Krishna tells Uddhava here in the *Uddhava Gita*.

17. Even though the mass of people, busily engaged in fruitive activities, desire perpetual happiness, such happiness is not forthcoming. Clearly, they are not independent nor are they in control of their destiny—or they would obtain the happiness they seek. The conclusion should be clear: If one is under the superior control of someone else, how can he expect to be the architect of his own happiness?

18. If one observes the world closely, he will see that even intelligent people sometimes suffer and cannot attain happiness. Conversely, people who are fools sometimes find themselves exceptionally happy, in spite of themselves. Thus, the idea that people become happy through their own expertise is merely an untruth concocted by the needs of the ego.

19. And even if people know the secrets of achieving happiness and of avoiding pain, they still cannot overcome death, which will ultimately exert its power over them.

20. In this world, all mortal are like a person sentenced to death. Moreover, no one wants to die. That said, what possible happiness can one derive from material objects or the "pleasure" they provide?

21. Even the highest forms of material happiness—such as being reborn on heavenly planets, where living beings enjoy a superior form of pleasure—is essentially the same as any other kind of

happiness. No matter how great, it is polluted by jealousy, envy, temporality, and death. The futility of such enjoyment might be brought to light by a comparison: just as it is pointless to raise crops that are already beleaguered by disease, insect plague or drought, similarly, the attempt to attain material happiness, either on earth or on higher planetary systems, is always fruitless because of their inherent obstacles.

22. Indeed, there are difficult Vedic sacrifices that, if performed without any mistake or imperfection, will bring one to higher planets in the next life. But even if executed properly, which is rare, the results are, again, temporary, and will be rendered useless in due course of time. Let Me tell you more about this.

23. When one performs sacrifices for the pleasure of the demigods, as in the ancient Vedic rituals, he can easily be reborn in the heavenly planets in higher material universes. Once there, he enjoys all heavenly pleasures as a result of his previous pious acts.

24. As the result of pious actions while on earth, a person can attain the heavenly planets, at which, it is said, he arrives in a special glowing airplane. Dressed in luxuriant clothes, such a person enjoys the association of beautiful goddesses, as he is entertained by angels who sing his glories.

25. Because of his prior lifetime of sacrifice, a person born on heavenly planets goes on pleasure rides in a wonderful airplane, which is decorated with mellifluous bells, flying wherever he likes. Magnificent women accompany him, and he enjoys godly pleasures. Thoroughly satisfied and at peace, he never considers that he is exhausting the fruits of his piety, and that this will soon make him fall into the mortal world.

26. By enjoying in this way, he is depleting his pious credits, even if he is unaware of it. Once these credits are exhausted, he inevitably descends to a lesser realm, compelled by the forces of time.

27–29. By dint of one's irreligious activities, which are prompted either by bad association or because of failure to control the senses, one inevitably deepens his material desires. In this way, he becomes self-centered, miserly, and always anxious for sexual pleasure. His mind goes to a dark place, where violence and aggression rule, and because he loses sight of Vedic knowledge, he supports the slaughter of innocent animals for the sake of his palate. At worst, he even worships ghosts and spirits, performing hellish activities that are harmful to his own body. In such a degraded state of consciousness, he drags themselves lower and lower into the worst of situations, as if by force. What chance does he have once he begins his journey to the land of death?

30. In the entire cosmos, from heaven to hell, everyone, including the great demigods who live for millions of years, fears Me in My form as time. Even Brahma, who possesses the longest of all life spans, is afraid of Me in that particular feature.

31. People use their material senses to function in the world, whether in a pious way or in a sinful one; the modes of nature allow this to happen. The living being, who is conditioned by the modes and a servant of his senses, experiences the good and bad results of his self-centered actions.

32. All human beings should realize how the modes of material nature work and how they control every move of conditioned entities. Otherwise, without understanding the modes, humans must take birth in different bodily forms and experience the multifarious ways of the material world. Indeed, living beings remain the slaves of fruitive activities because of the modes of nature.

33. All such conditioned souls will always fear Me, the Supreme Lord, because they know, deep down, that I am the one who grants the results of fruitive work, which ultimately lead to pain and suffering. Those who are materialists, who distinguish between goodness, passion and ignorance, thinking material things to be of value, devote themselves to mundane enjoyment. In the end, they are destined for sadness and pain.

34. When the material modes start to do the inevitable, creating havoc in people's lives, they then often turn to Me in various ways, describing Me as omnipotent time, the Supreme Self, Vedic wisdom, the cosmos, one's own inner nature, religious rituals, and so on.

35. Blessed Uddhava said: My sweet Lord, a living entity encased by a material body is conditioned by the modes of nature, and he is subject to the happiness and distress that arise as a result of these modes. It should also be pointed out that the living entity is ultimately beyond these modes—he is a spiritual soul and has nothing to do with his material body. It makes one wonder: How is he ever bound by material nature?

36–37. O infallible Lord, living entities are sometimes described as eternally conditioned, and yet, at other times, they are described as

eternally liberated. I am therefore having difficulty in understanding the truth here. My dear Lord, no one is better than You in answering philosophical questions. Please, then, explain to me the actual truth of the matter, and please describe the symptoms by which one can determine if a living entity is eternally liberated or eternally conditioned. How would each live his life, eat, evacuate, sleep, sit or move through the world?

Commentary

Much Vaishnava ink has been spilled over this question: Are souls in this world eternally conditioned or eternally liberated? From one perspective, the Medieval Bengali text, *Sri Chaitanya-charitamrita*, answers as follows:

> The living entities [*jivas*] are divided into two categories—those that are eternally liberated and those that are eternally conditioned. The former are always awake to their original spiritual position, never submitting to the illusions of the material world. They are eternal associates of Lord Krishna, forever enjoying the transcendental bliss of serving Him in the divine realm. The latter are conditioned souls, who have a tendency to turn away from the Lord's divine service. They are perpetual inhabitants of the material world, always subjected to the material horrors brought about by their many bodily forms. . . . Wandering throughout the universe in this way, such a person may, by good fortune, achieve the association of a pure devotee, whose instructions and spiritual mantras sufficiently silence the witch of material illusion. In this way, the conditioned soul may come into contact with Lord Krishna's service, attaining, once again, his position as the Lord's servant. This is the ultimate liberation. (*Madhya* 210–215)

Vaishnava commentators also say that one's *svarupa*, or spiritual form, is by nature eternally liberated. This holds true for all souls, whether in the spiritual realm or in the world of matter. Were this not the case, attaining liberation would not be possible, as described above, for the soul cannot become what it is not. That being said, once ensconced in a material body, the living being is "considered" eternally conditioned (even if it is ontologically eternally liberated), for his sojourn in the material world goes back to the beginning of time, without any possibility of searching out its origin. This "eternally conditioned state" is reversed when one reaches perfection on the spiritual path, establishing the living being in his original "eternally liberated" condition.

Chapter 5

How to Know Whether One Is Conditioned or Liberated

1. Lord Krishna said: My dear Uddhava, according to how one is affected by the material modes of nature, which are under My control, they are considered conditioned or liberated. It should be known, however, that in reality the soul is beyond such designations, and, furthermore, since I am the Lord of material nature, I, too, am never to be considered liberated or in bondage.

Commentary

In the previous chapter Uddhava asked Krishna exactly how one might distinguish between conditioned and liberated souls. In essence, the Lord replies that the soul is originally transcendental to all such designations, but that because of her tiny nature, she becomes covered by material energy. This covering causes her to become conditioned by the modes of nature: goodness, passion, and ignorance. It is in this artificial state that the soul becomes forgetful of her original nature and acts out according to her deviated identity (bodily covering) in the material world. This has been her plight since the beginning of time. Thus, she is sometimes viewed as eternally conditioned.

Eventually, however, she may come in touch with a pure devotee, receiving his causeless mercy. Once this happens, by the process of Bhakti-yoga, she gradually remembers her constitutional position in relation to Krishna. Increasingly, she cultivates transcendental knowledge, and this frees her from material bondage and forgetfulness.

This knowledge is different from ordinary material knowledge. In the material world, knowledge and ignorance, despite their seeming disparity, are opposite sides of the same coin, both leading to a materialistic concept of life. Therefore, Krishna told Uddhava in the previous chapter that it is foolish to distinguish between the modes—they are all material, whether one enjoys the fruits of goodness or suffers the pangs of ignorance. All material modes lead to conditioning, bringing us further away from our spiritual nature.

Only the touch of a pure devotee, who gives transcendental knowledge, can free one from materialistic life, and only this will situate us in our eternal constitutional position as a lover of the Lord. We are then rightly considered eternally liberated.

2. **I create all material bodies, Krishna continued, and these encase the actual person, covering who they really are. Souls allow themselves to be encased like this under the influence of overwhelming illusion, and so they are unaware of their course of action. Their misconceptions extend into the most subtle of thoughts, bringing them pleasure, lamentation, happiness, distress, and the acceptance of day-to-day reality as ultimate truth. But their bodies and perceptions are all just like a dream, without substance, created in the playground of the mind.**

3. **O Uddhava, knowledge and ignorance are, again, equal, since both are products of My potency. These two qualities are without beginning—one awards liberation and the other material bondage.**

4. **The infinitesimal living entity is My part and parcel—tiny, but totally spiritual. Even though that is the case, due to ignorance she has been suffering with material covering since time began. Nonetheless, through knowledge she can be liberated.**

5. **The original nature of the soul is blissful, but the material covering causes ignorance and unending misery. For this reason, My dear Uddhava, we find opposing characteristics, like happiness and sadness, in the same material body. Both the Supreme Lord, who is eternally free of all material inebriety, and the conditioned soul, reside within the body. I shall now tell you about their respective characteristics.**

Commentary

The great American Vaishnava teacher, Ravindra Svarupa Dasa, once remarked, "Our spirit soars; our molars rot." This sums up the dichotomy of what it is like to be a spiritual soul in a material body. Naturally, such a contradictory state of affairs causes confusion for the entity within. We intuitively know that we are more than just the body; we sense our existence as beings eternal. And yet our everyday experience is one of material limitation, of temporality and demise. It is therefore liberating to encounter true knowledge—either by intuition, in the scriptures, or by the grace of a pure devotee teacher. If any of those three touch our lives in a meaningful way, our spiritual journey begins, and we start to remember something we have long forgotten: That we are originally spiritual, that we are encased in a material body for only a short duration, and that our ultimate home is not here but in the spiritual world.

6. **Consider this: Two birds have nested together in the same tree. They are friends, possessing similar attributes. Still, one of them eats the fruits of the tree, while the other, does not. This second bird does not require the fruits, for He is superior every way.**

Commentary

The analogy of two birds in the same tree (God and the ordinary living entity) is Vedic, originally appearing in the *Shvetashvatara Upanishad*: "There are two birds in one tree. One of them is eating the fruits of the tree, while the other is witnessing his actions. The fruit-eater is the living entity, and the witness is the Lord" (4.6). The idea is this: The living being is enamored of material pleasure and desperately tries to enjoy fruitive activities. But being spiritual by nature, material enjoyment is never quite satisfying. The Lord knows this, and out of love He accompanies us through our material sojourn, waiting for us to come to our senses and to stop our vain attempt at material enjoyment. When we see the futility of our endeavors, when we are ready, He guides us, purifies us, and gives us the association of a pure devotee, who gently takes us the rest of the way.

7. **The bird who does not eat the fruits is comparable to the Supreme Lord, who is all-knowing and perfectly understands who He is and also who the conditioned living entity is—as the latter busily enjoys the fruits of the tree. Totally bewildered by his enjoying propensity, he lacks knowledge of himself and of the Lord, too. His ignorant and self-absorbed nature stops him from seeing things as they are, and his selfishness perpetuates his conditioned existence. Meanwhile, God, the other bird, has perfect knowledge and is eternally liberated.**

8. **Those who are enlightened see themselves as spiritual souls, although living within a material body. They know themselves to be transcendental to the body, just as those who awaken from a dream lose all identification with their dream body. Most people, however, think themselves to be the body, just as those who are dreaming actually believe they are the imaginary body in their mind.**

9. **When a person attains an enlightened state, they eschew material desire and do not consider themselves the performer of bodily activities. Instead, they clearly see that all such activities exist merely because the senses, born of the modes of nature, interact with sense objects, which are also born of the same modes.**

10. **The typically unenlightened person thinks, "I am performing this particular action," but in fact he is not. Confused by a false conception of the self, he is bound by his own body's fruitive**

movements, which are a product of conditioning and carried out by the modes of nature.

11. If one attains true knowledge and is appropriately detached from material life, he may engage his body in lying down, sitting, walking, bathing, seeing, touching, smelling, eating, and so on, just like ordinary living beings, but he is never entangled by such activities. He is almost like an outside witness to all his bodily functions, and he never becomes entangled in them or thinks them to be real.

12–13. Consider the sky, or space: Though it is the resting place of all things, it does not mix with those things, nor is it entangled. In a similar way, the sun has no special relationship with water in which it may be reflected, and the blowing wind is not changed by the innumerable aromas and atmospheres through which it inevitably passes. All of this is meant to teach us something: a self-realized soul, though functioning in the world, is completely detached from his body and the material world around it. He is comparable to a person who has awakened from a dream and can see his real body as distinguished from the imaginary one experienced in his sleeping state. Because of clear vision sharpened by detachment, the enlightened soul slashes to pieces all lesser conceptions of reality. His sharp blades are knowledge of the self and his ability to withdraw his consciousness from the illusions of material life.

14. Real liberation—from both gross and subtle forms of material existence—occurs when one is free from material desire. At that point, one still functions by using the senses, the mind, and the intellect, just like anyone else, but here the "actor" never becomes entangled.

15. In life, we see duality in how people are treated: We notice that people are sometimes attacked violently, either by other people or by creatures. And we also see that people are sometimes offered great respect or worship. If one doesn't become angry when attacked or satisfied when worshiped—such a person is actually advanced in spiritual life.

16. One who is saintly sees everything equally, unaffected by what is normally considered good or bad. For this reason, even though he sees others engaging in both good and bad work, and notices them speaking properly and improperly, he does not praise or criticize them. He remains neutral.

17. A liberated sage never thinks in terms of material good or bad. He is detached and only takes pleasure in self-realization. In this

way, he wanders the earth functioning according to spiritual principles, even if he appears abnormal to outsiders.

18. **Sometimes one becomes expert in reading Vedic literature but makes no endeavor to focus on the Supreme Lord. This is not knowledge proper. In fact, this is comparable to a person who works diligently to take care of a cow that gives no milk. That is to say, the hard work of Vedic study is useless if it doesn't reach the point of meditation on the Lord, which is really its main point.**

Commentary

To be conscious of Krishna—this is where the *Vedas* really hope to point its readers. Krishna, as Lord, is the embodiment of *Vedanta*, a word that means "the ultimate end of knowledge." In the *Bhagavad Gita*, He makes this clear. In His own words: "I am seated in everyone's heart, and from Me come remembrance, knowledge and forgetfulness. By all the *Vedas* I am to be known" (15.15). Therefore, if Vedic study does not lead to Lord Krishna, it becomes meaningless.

A similar phenomenon exists today with yoga: The word itself indicates union with God, but few use it for this purpose. If one practices strenuous *asanas* and *pranayama* but does not attain Krishna or attraction to His holy name, then it is not serving its intended purpose or bringing its practitioners to its stated goal, implicit in the word itself. Here, the same point is made with the *Vedas*: If Vedic study does not lead to God consciousness, it has missed its purpose.

19. **My dear Uddhava, there are certain things that bring only misery: A cow that gives no milk, an unchaste wife, a dysfunctional body, useless progeny, and misused wealth. Similarly, one who studies Vedic literature but is unaware of My glories is also most miserable.**

20. **Enlightened people only read literature that contains descriptions of My activities, which are fundamentally purifying and pleasing to the heart. This literature describes how I create, maintain and annihilate the entire material world. It also describes My incarnations, who manifest many extraordinary and wonderful activities even here on earth. Any text that does not discuss these truths lacks spiritual substance and is unacceptable to the wise.**

Commentary

Here the *Uddhava Gita* defines true transcendental literature, which is always uplifting and purifying. Such texts not only will describe God's function as creator, maintainer, and annihilator of the universe but also will reveal His many esoteric manifestations as an *avatara* ("an incarnation who descends to earth"). This confidential knowledge is offered to the most fortunate souls through the highest scriptural texts and through the teachings of enlightened masters, who witness the Lord's activities in their heart of hearts.

21. As one reaches full knowledge, one should abandon false conceptions of material variety, which cause illusion for the soul. In this way, one can bring his material existence to an end and become firmly established in spiritual reality. In the process, one's mind should be focused on Me—the all-pervading Lord.

22. My dear Uddhava, if you are unable to easily free your mind from material disturbance, thus absorbing it in Me, then perform all your activities as an offering to Me, without trying to enjoy the results.

Commentary

This verse correlates with a section in the *Bhagavad Gita*, Chapter Twelve, Verses 9–12, in which the Lord proposes a gradual process, basically saying, "If you can't do this, then please do that." Here are the pertinent verses from the *Bhagavad Gita*:

> My dear Arjuna, O winner of wealth, if you cannot focus your mind exclusively upon Me, then follow the pious principles of Bhakti-yoga. In this way you will gradually develop a desire to attain Me. If you cannot practice the regulations of Bhakti-yoga, then do your everyday work for Me, because by such work you will eventually know spiritual perfection. Even still, if you are unable to work with your consciousness focused on Me, then try giving up all the fruits of your work in My service. And if you cannot take to this practice, then attempt to cultivate true knowledge. Better than knowledge, however, is meditation, and better than meditation is renunciation of the fruits of action, for by such renunciation you will attain peace of mind.

In other words, Krishna is allowing practitioners to come to Him in a stepwise fashion, taking into account each individual's level of spiritual evolution and their ability to surrender at any given time.

23–24. O Uddhava, know for certain that My activities and qualities are special in every way and, indeed, that they purify the entire cosmos. If one faithfully hears, glorifies, and remembers such transcendental activities, or recreates them through dramatic performance—surrendering fully to Me, performing his religious, bodily and occupational activities for My satisfaction—such a soul certainly comes to Me in the end, attaining unswerving devotional perfection.

25. When one obtains a pure devotional mood by association with My devotees, he always worships Me with a pure heart. Because of this, he very easily attains My abode, which is unveiled by My pure devotees.

Commentary

These verses are important in that they reveal the open secret of the spiritual process elucidated in the *Uddhava Gita*: association with advanced devotees. Of all devotional principles, this association is among the most important. By associating with people who are close to God, one can easily attain the Supreme presence. An analogy might make this more understandable: By befriending and associating with a king's son, one easily gets an audience with a king. By becoming close to one who is dear to the king's heart, one becomes part of the king's inner circle and is commonly granted intimate association. Similarly, if one endears oneself to the Lord's pure devotee, the Lord looks favorably upon such a person and allows him into His inner sanctum.

26–27. Sri Uddhava responded: My dear Lord, many pose as religionists or *yogis*, or even as Your devotees. But I want to know from You: What type of person do *You* consider Your devotee, and what type of spiritual activity do You consider worthy? O universal controller, O Lord of the spiritual world, I consider myself a devotee, without doubt, and I have no other shelter besides You. And yet, with all humility at my command, I still want You to explain to me if I truly *am* a devotee. Again, please define these things for me.

Commentary

These verses are extremely important. It is not that we can define religion in any way we like or that we should consider ourselves religionists or devotees based on sentiment.

Illusion is powerful, and it can even make us think we are devoted to the Supreme when in fact we are not. Therefore, Uddhava wants to know for certain: Is he understanding his own devotion properly? More important, in general, how might one know if one is a true devotee, and does Krishna count him, Uddhava, among these rare souls? Just what do real devotees do? How do they behave, and what are they really all about?

Arjuna asked a similar question in the *Bhagavad Gita* (2.54–72). He wanted to know the symptoms of one who is actually situated in knowledge (*sthita-prajna*). Krishna answers him in summary format, explaining that a self-realized soul is not disturbed in any circumstances; has no material attachments; is equal in happiness and distress; is firmly fixed in knowledge of transcendence; and is in full control of his senses, having the ability to completely focus them on the divine. As we shall see, beginning with Verses 29–32, Krishna will offer a similar answer to Uddhava but with considerable elaboration.

28. My sweet Lord, You are beyond material nature, and, just as the sky remains as it is, no matter what may temporarily pass through it, You are never blemished in any way. Nonetheless, You are controlled by Your devotees' love, and accordingly You accept many different forms, just to accommodate their desires.

29–32. The Supreme Lord gave His considered response: O Uddhava, a true devotee is merciful to all, never injuring others. Even if others show aggression, he will be tolerant and forgiving, with love for all living entities. His inner wisdom comes from truth itself, allowing him to be free from all pride, envy, and jealousy. These qualities, in turn, make him equal in happiness and distress. With this as a backdrop, he spends his time working for others, concerned for their welfare and protection, especially on the spiritual platform. His intelligence is never overtaken by material desires, for his senses are under his control. For this reason, his behavior is always pleasing, never harsh and always exemplary. He is also free from possessiveness, uninterested in ordinary, worldly activities. His eating habits are under control as well, and he therefore always remains peaceful and calm. Such a saintly person thinks about things deeply and accepts Me as his only shelter. Accordingly, he is meticulous during his daily spiritual duties, giving them prime importance, and never allows himself to become subject to superficial considerations, which can agitate the mind. He has conquered the six material qualities—hunger, thirst, lamentation, illusion, old age and death—and is free from all desire for prestige, offering all respect to others. He is adept in helping people revive their spiritual consciousness, and he never cheats anyone by giving them some lesser teaching. Rather, he is a well-meaning friend to all and mercifully tries to give them the highest good. Such a great soul is the most learned of all, knowing the conclusions of various scriptures. He sees these teachings in context, however, and will reject them if they do not accept love for Me as the primary goal of life. He is thus to be considered the best among all living entities.

Commentary

Krishna begins to describe the *sthita-prajna*, the man with true knowledge—the devotee. The sages of India have divided these qualities into a convenient list of twenty-eight, which are explained in English by Hridayananda Goswami in his commentary on this verse. According to Srila Bhaktisiddhanta Sarasvati Thakur (1874–1937), one of the Gaudiya Vaishnava Sampradaya's greatest teachers, the seventeenth quality—taking complete shelter of Krishna—is the most important, giving special meaning to all the others.

33. My devotees may or may not know exactly what I am, who I am, and how I exist, but if they worship Me with unflinching love, then I consider them to be the best of devotees.

Commentary

Krishna is chiefly referring to the *gopis*, the cowherd maidens of Vraja. These paradigmatic female devotees exist eternally with Him in the celestial Vraja and also manifest when He exhibits His earthly pastimes, as He did on this planet 5,000 years ago. Their love for Him was so intense that they "forgot" His supreme position as God and simply loved Him for who He was—focusing on His charming form, melodic flute music, and bewitching personality. His divinity could not be less important to them. They do not know who God is, and they do not care: They just want to have a deep relationship with this enchanting little cowherd boy, known as Krishna.

Indeed, conditioned life, too, begins with a lack of awareness in relation to God; we just do not know who He is. Ironically, after achieving perfection on the spiritual platform, we go back to this lack of awareness—but this time in His divine service rather than in ignorance. In spiritual perfection, we forget who God is so we can enjoy intimacy with Him. It is hard to relish interpersonal exchanges of love if one is always conscious that one's "friend," "nurturer," or "lover" is in fact God. In our perfected state, then, we prefer to think of Him in more intimate terms.

Spirituality begins with concern for morals and ethics, and for obeying God's laws. From this vantage point, God's divinity is extremely important, and one focuses on worshiping Him with awe and reverence. Then, as one's realization increases, a sort of oneness develops, wherein one feels nondifferent from the Lord. This is not only a merger of interests but a deep feeling of sameness, of unity. The danger here, of course, is that one will make too much of this oneness and mistake it for ontological truth. So let it be stated in no uncertain terms: We are never one with the Lord in essence, but only as tiny souls communing with the Supreme soul. If we realize this in full, we are born into a situation in which we can function as His devotees, and His Lordship becomes important once again. But then, something interesting happens—and this is what we see in the example of the *gopis*: We start to love Him for who He is, and His divinity once again recedes into the background. We do not love Him because He's God but, rather, because He's loveable.

So this verse hints at the truth of the *gopis*, who love Him without knowing who He is. Their "unconscious" love will be explored more fully in the next chapter.

This verse might be understood in another way, one that is especially important in a modern context: Practitioners of the world's many religious traditions generally have no specific idea of God's identity, and yet they develop love for Him. They are devotees without knowing details of His Supreme personality, and their love is true all the same. Thus, religionists of any denomination may rightly be considered the greatest of devotees, if indeed they have developed love for God.

To be sure, many of the world's scriptures give a hint of God's greatness, without specific knowledge of His incarnations and manifestations, what to speak of His original form as Sri Krishna. Yet the major religions have produced mystics and devotees with great insight, whose love of God is beyond question. Sri Krishna here affirms their status as Vaishnavas, even though many of the world's religions may not have yet been in existence. The Lord is speaking of a nonsectarian principle, which was subsequently developed by sages in the Vaishnava tradition. Bhaktivinode Thakur (1838–1914), for example, said that when he enters a temple, a mosque, or a church, he does not focus on the differences. Rather, he simply appreciates whether or not his Lord is being nicely worshiped there, according to the standards and customs of the religious tradition in question. This is because all established religions can produce pure devotees—Krishna sees their love, not the particular path that brought them there.

In other words, Krishna considers practitioners of all religions to be His devotees, without qualification, as long as they develop spiritual love. In fact, they may even be counted among the greatest devotees, He says. In this way, the religion of the *Uddhava Gita* is nonsectarian and universal, lauding only the essence of spirituality—love of God—as supreme.

34–41. My dear Uddhava, one can bid adieu to false pride and the need for prestige by engaging in the following devotional activities: Immense purification comes through seeing, touching, worshiping, serving, and offering prayers to My form as the Deity (*archa-murti*) and to My pure devotees. Glorifying My qualities and activities, which are totally spiritual, will evoke that same purifying effect. Thus, one should hear with love and faith the narrations of My glories, constantly meditating on Me and serving My devotees. Realizing oneself as My eternal servant, one should offer to Me whatever one has, giving oneself completely over to Me. Similarly, one should always discuss My "birth" and "activities," relishing them while participating in festivals in My honor, which celebrate My pastimes. With others of similar mind, one should glorify Me on a regular basis by singing, dancing, playing musical instruments and discussing Me with others. One should also observe religious vows as ordained in the scriptures and

according to tradition, and take initiation by the procedures mentioned in the *Vedas*, Tantras, and other sacred texts. My Deity in temples should be respected and one should work hard, in concert with others, to construct and maintain such temples in My honor. Identifying oneself as My humble servant, without question, one should help clean the temple, thinking it to be My home. It is purifying to sweep and dust such places thoroughly, and then to further cleanse them with water and antiseptic agents. Having dried the temple, one should sprinkle scented water and decorate the area with spiritual symbols. In this way, one should consciously act like My servant, without allowing false pride to get in the way. All accoutrements of the temple should be respected as My very self. For example, one should never use lamps that are offered to Me for other purposes simply because one needs lighting here or there, and similarly, one should never offer to Me anything that has first been used by others. The most effective offering is this: Whatever one most desires in this material world, or whatever one considers most dear—it is this very thing that one should offer to Me. Such an offering qualifies one for spiritual advancement.

42. O saintly one, please know that you may worship Me by acknowledging My presence in the following phenomenon: sun, fire, Brahmins, cows, Vaishnavas, sky, wind, water, earth, and all living entities. In other words, I am all-pervading.

43–45. Dearest Uddhava, one can worship Me in the form of the sun by chanting Vedic mantras with deep respect, or as fire by offering sacrificial oblations. One can worship Me through holy Brahmins by dutifully receiving them as guests, even if they arrive unannounced. I can be worshiped through the veneration of cows if one takes care of them properly, with love, offering them grass and other suitable grains and paraphernalia for their pleasure and well-being. Most of all, one may worship Me through the Vaishnavas by befriending them, helping them, and honoring them in all respects. If one is inclined to meditation, I can be found within the inner core of the heart, and within air, too, through an awareness of *prana*, the life air, as chief among elements. I can be worshiped within water by offerings of water itself, along with other elements such as flowers and *tulasi* leaves, the plant which is dearest to Me. One may even worship Me as being nondifferent from the earth, if he learns how to properly chant confidential seed mantras. I may even be found within the

individual living entity, and worshipped that way, by food offerings and other precious substances. I am, after all, the Supersoul—the Supreme spirit within the heart of all living beings—nurturing and loving everyone and everything.

46. **Thus, in all these places of worship—and according to the processes I have described—one should meditate on My transcendentally peaceful form. Know it for certain: Underlying my presence everywhere I am Vishnu, the Supreme Lord, with four arms holding a conchshell, Sudarshan discus, club, and lotus flower. In this way, one should worship Me with fully concentrated attention.**

Commentary

Although the Lord talks about His many manifestations on earth and the multitudinous ways one might see Him in nature, He is clear that He actually pervades everything as Narayana, also known as Vishnu, with four arms carrying the standard symbols of conch, disk, club, and lotus. Vaishnavas know this to be God's ultimate form, an immediate expansion of Krishna, the Supreme Personality of Godhead. In this form, He pervades everyone and everything as Paramatma, the Supersoul, the eternal friend, and confidante of all living beings. Even inanimate objects are given substance through His presence in every atom. Thus, in these verses (34–46), He wants Uddhava to understand a simple truth: His omnipresence, which appears impersonal, is in fact made possible by His personal presence in the form of Vishnu.

47. **All sacrificial performances and pious action is really meant for My satisfaction. One who knows this and who thus worships Me with determined effort will quickly reach the level of pure devotional service. By the superior quality of this service such a worshiper realizes Me in due course.**

48. **My dear Uddhava, it is impossible to escape the clutches of material existence without realizing that I am the ultimate shelter for all that is. Functioning according to this realization is a way of life for saintly liberated souls, who fully engage in My loving service. They relish each other's association and in this way attain liberation and love for Me.**

49. **O beloved of the Yadu dynasty, because you are indeed My servant, well-wisher and friend—My devotee—I shall now speak to you the most supreme form of knowledge. Please listen attentively as I explain these great mysteries to you.**

Commentary

In this concluding verse, Lord Krishna confirms that Uddhava is a devotee of the highest order. And because of this, the Lord will now explain the most confidential knowledge to him, beginning with the next chapter.

In Uddhava's humility, it may be remembered, he had asked Krishna what a devotee actually is—how he might be identified—and if he, Uddhava, should consider himself as one of them. In this chapter, Krishna explained the nature of the true devotees in some detail and concluded by laying Uddhava's doubts to rest: He is without doubt to be counted among the devotees.

Chapter 6

What Lies beyond Renunciation and Knowledge?

1–2. Lord Krishna continued: My dear Uddhava, one can overcome the desire for sense gratification merely by associating with My pure devotees. When one seeks this superior association, it wins My heart, making Me feel a sense of debt that I can never repay. Nothing else is as dear to Me: One may perform Hatha-yoga, become expert in philosophy, practice nonviolence and other principles of piety, sing Vedic hymns, perform penances, renounce the world, execute sacrificial rituals, perform welfare activities, such as digging wells and planting trees, give in charity, commit to difficult vows, worship the demigods, chant esoteric mantras, visit special holy places, or follow regulative principles—but even such glorious activities do not effect Me in the same way.

Commentary

Krishna again explains the open secret of spiritual perfection: association with advanced devotees. Whatever else one might do in an attempt to win His heart, or to make progress on the spiritual path, nothing is as effective as associating and serving those who are dear to Him.

3–6. In every world age (*yuga*), numerous living beings have attained the association of the devotees. In this way, various species, such as the Daityas, Rakshasas, birds, beasts, Gandharvas, angels, Nagas, Siddhas, and so on, as well as more humbly endowed humans, like Vaishyas, Shudras, and others, were able to achieve My supreme abode. Without the association of the devotees, they could not have done it. Even great personalities, such as Prahlad Maharaj, Bali Maharaj, Sugriva, Hanuman, Jambavan, Gajendra, Jatayu, the *gopis* in Vraja and the wives of

the Brahmins who were performing sacrifice—all achieved the Supreme destination through association with pure devotees.

7. **None of the personalities I mention here had performed serious study of the Vedic literature, nor did they worship the great saints of yore. Many of them didn't even execute severe vows or perform prescribed austerities. Simply by associating with Me and My devotees did they achieve the greatest spiritual treasure.**

8. **The inhabitants of Vrindavan (Vraja), including the *gopis*, the cows, immobile beings such as the twin Arjuna trees, as well as bushes and thickets, animals, and even snakes such as Kaliya—all achieved spiritual perfection by their untainted love for Me.**

9. **The following are not enough to achieve the ultimate, which is devotion to My very self: mystic yoga, philosophical speculation, charity, vows, penances, ritualistic sacrifices, teaching of Vedic mantras to others, personal study of the *Vedas*, and the renounced order of life.**

Commentary

The truth of this verse—that *bhakti* cannot be attained by mundane, virtuous activity, that it is completely transcendental—has important implications. Indeed, earlier in the *Bhagavata Purana*, Uddhava himself tells the *gopis* just the opposite of what we find here: "Devotion to Krishna may arise due to one's practice of charity, austerities, *homa, japa,* study, sense control, and other pious works" (10.47.24). So this verse seems to contradict that earlier one.

Some background: Just as the Lord is not dependent on any material or spiritual cause for who He is or what He does, so, too, does *bhakti* (devotion), which is not unlike Him, partake of this independent nature.

Thus, in Vishvanath Chakravarti Thakur's *Madhurya-kadambini* (1.3), a seminal Gaudiya Vaishnava text, we find that *bhakti* is the *svarupa shakti* of Krishna and that she manifests according to her own will. In other words, since she is *sva-prakash*, self-manifest, she appears in one's heart as she likes, paying no heed to external influences or the instigation of outside sources.

How does this affect the verse in question? The scriptures sometimes tell us that prescribed activities (*karma)*—righteous works—performed without personal motives (*nishkama*) can act as a gateway to *bhakti*. As one example, although there are many, look no further than the *Bhagavata* verse cited above.

Such verses must be understood in context. They refer to *bhakti* as it arises from the mode of material goodness, which is more a part of Jnana-yoga—it is *jnana-mishra-bhakti,* or "devotion mixed with a preponderance of knowledge." It is not the higher, fully spiritual dimension of *bhakti* that arises of its own accord. A similar phenomenon exists in relation to Karma-yoga. If in one's service to the Lord he emphasizes a particular kind of work rather than pure devotion, it is *karma-mishra-bhakti*, or "devotion mixed with a penchant for specific action."

In summary, then, *bhakti* certainly can be attained through these indirect methods, and so *Bhagavata* verses like the one found at 10.47.24 are clearly legitimate. But the *Uddhava Gita* is referring to the highest kind of *bhakti,* which leads to *prema*, divine love—it is *bhakti* that is caused by *bhakti*, and nothing more. That being said, all varieties of spiritual devotion are advantageous and tend to lead to the highest kind of *bhakti* in due course.

10. **The residents of Vrindavan, especially the *gopis*, love Me with their entire being, and this is the ultimate perfection. That's why, when My uncle Akrura took Me and My brother Balaram away to the city of Mathura, they suffered untold pangs of separation. Nothing could assuage their pain.**

Commentary

Lord Krishna introduces an important part of Vaishnava theology: the comparative value of union (*sambhoga*) and separation (*vipralambha*) in affairs of the heart. Love for Krishna is sweet when one is united with Him, but this sweetness intensifies when separation arises. We see a hint of this in the material world, when we say, "Absence makes the heart grow fonder." This truth is but a shadow of its higher prototype in the spiritual world, where Krishna's absence brings the love of His intimate devotees to even greater heights. Therefore, He arranges situations wherein He temporarily leaves them, as in the incident mentioned in this verse (Verse 10): Akrura took the Lord out of Vrindavan, causing the residents there, especially the *gopis*, to go mad with loving separation. It is a ploy He uses to increase His devotees' love, and according to the histories related in the sacred books of India, it works.

11. **Dear Uddhava, the many nights I enjoyed with the *gopis* in Vrindavan seemed to pass quickly for them, so much did they love spending time with Me. But when they no longer had My association, as when Akrura brought Me to Mathura, they felt each night an eternity, equal to a day of Brahma (millions of years).**

12. **Great *yogis*, in trance, become totally lost in self-realization, like rivers merging into an ocean. In this state, they are virtually unaware of their names and external forms. Similarly, the *gopis* of Vrindavan, so completely in love with Me, could not think of their own bodies, or of the world around them, or even of what would eventually become of them. Their entire consciousness was simply absorbed in Me.**

Commentary

This comparison of the *gopis* to the greatest of *yogis* is important and fundamental to the teachings of the *Uddhava Gita*. While conventional yoga, with sitting postures, breathing techniques, and so on, is meant to help one gain control of body and mind, so one can then use these physical assets in service to God, eventually developing love for Him, great devotees like the *gopis* already have this love by their constant meditation on the Supreme. Thus, Bhakti-yoga, or the yoga of loving devotion to the Lord, is the topmost yoga system, catapulting practitioners to the perfection of yoga: intimacy with the Supreme.

13. Hundreds of thousands of *gopis*, My greatest devotees, simply saw Me as their alluring lover, oblivious to My divine nature. But despite this lack of knowledge, by intimately associating with Me, they attained the perfection of yoga: union with Me.

Commentary

Krishna is making explicit that which remained only implicit in Chapter Five, Verse 33, namely, that knowledge of Him is simply not required to develop love for Him. He reveals just who He has in mind: the *gopis* of Vraja, the very embodiment of love that transcends knowledge.

Of course, for most of us, knowledge will undoubtedly help, and the great teachers of established Vaishnava lineages recommend, with great clarity, the importance of cultivating spiritual knowledge from the correct sources: the revealed scriptures, one's guru, and saints who are well established in the tradition. That being said, knowledge, when not coming from the proper source, or not dispensed by a qualified guide, can be an obstacle, obscuring one's natural devotion. In the end, whatever contributes to one's love of God should be embraced, and whatever does not should be systematically discarded. For some, knowledge is an advantage, for others—it is merely a distraction.

14–15. Therefore, O Uddhava, declare boldly the uselessness of Vedic mantras and their complex procedures. Shun the positive and negative injunctions of the Vedic literature. Disregard the many "truths" that have been heard in the past and those that are yet to be heard. For, ultimately, there is one truth: Surrender to Me and no one else, for I am the Lord, existing within the heart of all souls. Take shelter of Me with single-minded determination, and, by My grace, become fearless in all circumstances.

Commentary

To be clear: Lord Krishna is not decrying the value of Vedic mantras and of all truths leading up to Him. Rather, He is saying that, *in terms of ultimacy*, these things have little value. In other words, *comparatively speaking*, these spiritual assets are useless, for, in light of surrendering to God, all other attempts at self-realization are ineffectual. Krishna is talking about the essence of spiritual life and how lesser truths and practices fall short.

16. Sri Uddhava responded: O Lord, O master yogic perfections, I have heard Your words carefully, and yet a persistent doubt plagues my heart, causing me great bewilderment.

17. Lord Krishna said: My dear Uddhava, I am the source of life, situated within each person's heart along with life air and spiritual sound. If one concentrates deeply, I can also be perceived within the mind, since I am the inner core of all thinking apparatus, including that of the great demigods. In addition, I assume the form of the *Vedas*, whose sound vibrations are composed of short and long vowels and consonants as well.

Commentary

Lord Krishna, apart from being the Supreme Person, with distinct individual characteristics, is in fact everything. Nonetheless, He is especially present in certain phenomenon in a very particular way. This verse points out three: the heart, the mind, and the *Vedas.*

At first glance, it might appear that Krishna is ignoring Uddhava's doubt, which he mentioned in Verse 15. But the Lord, who knows the hearts of all souls, could understand that Uddhava's query was, in effect, not unlike Arjuna's in the *Bhagavad Gita.* Basically, perfection can be achieved through numerous traditions of knowledge and various yoga systems. And yet Krishna seems to disparage them in favor of merely surrendering unto Him with a heart of devotion. Thus, Uddhava wanted to clarify, like Arjuna: Are these other systems of no value at all? Is devotion to Krishna really the essence of all paths, the highest practice, and the supreme goal? Understanding that these were in fact Uddhava's questions, Krishna proceeded to answer him.

18. By properly rubbing together two sticks of wood, a lighted spark appears. If one adds *ghee* (clarified butter) to such sparks, a full-blown fire easily manifests. In the same way, I appear in the sound vibration of the *Vedas.*

Commentary

As a poetic metaphor, the comparison of kindling wood being set ablaze and Krishna's identity as the sound of the *Vedas* is more profound than it at first seems. The mystical verses of the *Vedas*, after all, mainly describe fire sacrifices used by Brahmins to invoke the divine. These are a series of mantras that are properly recited only when accompanied by sacrificial fire, which can be ignited only by qualified priests. If everything is in place—in just the right way—the light of the Vedic hymns will burn brightly. Lord Krishna is drawing on these facts and their associated imagery in this verse (Verse 18).

19. I have a material form found in nature: All of the working senses (the organ of speech, the hands, the legs, the genitals and the anus) and the knowledge-acquiring senses (the nose, tongue, eyes, skin and ears) are part of this form. So, too, are the subtle dimensions of mind, intelligence, consciousness and each individual's false sense of self. In addition, I am the subtlest of elements, such as *pradhana* (undifferentiated material substance) and the interaction of the three modes of material nature.

20. A single element, soil, can produce so many trees, bushes, vegetables, and so on, just so long as the appropriate seeds are placed in an accommodating field. Similarly, the Supreme Person, who is the life of all that lives, is one, but He appears in an unlimited number of forms by endlessly extending His multifarious potencies. He originally exists beyond the material creation. Nonetheless, by employing the energies of the three modes of material nature, He manifests the cosmic manifestation, which appears variegated and diverse.

21. Just as stitched cloth is composed of crosshatched threads, so, too, is the entire universe expanded in this way, through the all-encompassing potency of the Supreme Lord. Within this realm, all materially infected souls have been reincarnating since time began, with bodies that are like great trees in the soil of material existence. Just as a tree first blossoms and then produces fruit, one's material body comes into existence and then perpetuates itself through extended activities.

22–23. This tree of material existence consists of two seeds, hundreds of roots, and three lower and five upper trunks. It brings forth five flavors, sporting eleven branches and a nest made by two birds. Moreover, the tree is covered by three varieties of bark; it gives two fruits and extends up to the sun. Those desirous for material enjoyment and dedicated to ordinary family life enjoy one of the tree's fruits, and swanlike, spiritual people, who are renounced, enjoy the other fruit. If one learns properly from one's teacher, one understands this tree to be a manifestation of God's potency—which is one, even though it appears in many forms. Those who know this truth actually understand the meaning of the *Vedas*.

Commentary

The traditional commentators tell us that the "two seeds" of this tree are sinful and pious activities, while the "hundreds of roots" are the countless material desires that we all have, keeping us bound to material existence. The "three lower trunks" are the three modes of nature—goodness, passion, and ignorance, which condition us in various ways—and the "five upper" consist of the gross material elements: earth, water, fire, air, and ether.

The five "flavors" produced by this tree, write the commentators, consist of sound, form, touch, taste, and aroma, and the "eleven branches" are the five working senses, the five knowledge-acquiring senses, and the mind. The "two birds" in the same nest are the Supreme Lord and the ordinary living being—you and I and everyone else—and the "three types of bark" are bile, mucus, and air, the substance of our material bodies. The "two fruits" are happiness and distress, our constant companions during our material sojourn.

24. O Uddhava, utilizing your mature intellect, you should practice unmotivated devotional yoga (*bhakti*) by attentively seeing to the needs of the spiritual master, and with the razor sharp axe of transcendental knowledge you should slice to pieces the subtle material covering that engulfs your soul. And when you fully realize Me, the Supreme Person, you should abandon that axe of knowledge in favor of love.

Commentary

Krishna is putting a cap on His answer to Uddhava's doubt. He affirms that devotional love is the culmination of all spiritual pursuits. Numerous aids help us reach this point, like the cultivation of knowledge, but in the end, it is love of God, facilitated by association with His pure devotees, that grants the highest perfection.

Chapter 7

The Swan Incarnation (Hamsa Avatara) and the Sons of Brahma

1. The Supreme Lord said: The three modes of material nature, i.e., goodness, passion and ignorance, only affect the material intelligence, not the soul. The jurisdiction of these modes is thus limited to the material world. The secret of breaking free of the modes is herein revealed: By becoming a good person, one can conquer the modes of passion and ignorance. This serves as a gateway to higher reality, for by cultivating "transcendental goodness," which is superior to ordinary material goodness, one may break free of the modes altogether.

Commentary

Lord Krishna herein reveals the secret of self-realization. Usually, the material world conditions us to passion and ignorance. That is to say, we have selfish desires, which virtually compel us to act (passion), and a resignation mechanism, which leads us into sloth and darkness when we do not get what we want (ignorance). But if we, through discipline, cultivate awareness and proper action, revolutionizing our consciousness, we will cause a change that leads us toward light and knowledge (goodness). Once situated in this latter mind-set, we have an opportunity to engage in spiritual life proper, thus transcending the material modes of nature, complete with their concomitant conditioning and illusion.

One can, of course, pursue spiritual life while still in passion and ignorance, but it is much more difficult, and one is likely to fall from the path. Gradual evolution through material goodness is recommended, even as one pursues spiritual life simultaneously.

In this verse, an interesting distinction is made between "goodness" (*sattva*) and "transcendental goodness" (*vishuddha sattva*). Generally, the line between the two is blurred, with people often confusing one with the other. For example, morals and ethics are often thought of as spiritual; and mundane, sectarian religion is seen as transcendental truth. But the *Uddhava Gita* teaches something different. It tells us that no human-centered laws—however altruistic or pious they may be—can take us beyond the material world; no religion that has an origin in time or is beleaguered by material concerns can reach the Ultimate Destination. Real spiritual life centers on love of God, completely transcending the material world. Actions or dispositions that enhance such love are indicative of "transcendental goodness," as opposed to all seemingly wholesome derivatives, which have material betterment as their focus—this is merely material goodness.

2. **If living beings, through proper action, situate themselves in the mode of goodness, then religious principles have ample opportunity to arise.**

3. **Following such religious principles, when aided by goodness, causes the influence of passion and ignorance to subside in due course. As this happens, irreligion loses its appeal.**

4. **There are different standards of religious scriptures, each in their own way explaining how to use the things of this world in God's service. Particularly important are the following: (1) water, (2) one's association with one's children or (3) with people in general, (4) particular places in which one lives or worships, (5) time, (6) activities, (7) birth, (8) meditation, (9) chanting of mantras, and (10) purifying rituals.**

Commentary

Scriptures in the mode of goodness tend to help people achieve goodness—and then transcendence—more effectively than scriptures that pander to the senses. Make no mistake: such scriptures do exist. In fact, sacred texts serve to elevate people in a stepwise fashion—some even taking them from the ground up, catering to those whose lives are consumed by passion and ignorance. Other sacred texts are more advanced, assuming a certain level of spiritual maturity and enabling practitioners to make more rapid progress.

The ten items in Verse 4 are described in all religious scriptures, and exactly how these respective texts deal with these factors determines whether they are in goodness, passion, or ignorance.

5. **The wizened sages who have insights into Vedic knowledge have looked deeply into the ten items I just described. After due consideration, they endorse those that reflect the mode of goodness, disparage those in the mode of ignorance, and are nonchalant about those in the mode of passion.**

6. **Limited by ignorance of the spirit soul and an illusory identification with the material body, which is instigated by the three modes of**

nature, one must gradually elevate oneself to the mode of goodness. By functioning within this mode, one becomes more accustomed to religious principles. And by practically applying these principles, transcendental knowledge is awakened.

7. **Ironically, a bamboo forest can destroy itself: Sometimes the wind will by happenstance rub two stalks together, causing friction and eventually a blazing fire that burns the entire forest to the ground. Once burned down, calmness ensues. Similarly, the material modes of nature generate all material bodies. And yet, one can use these same bodies to cultivate higher knowledge. In the end, such knowledge can destroy the influence of the modes, which generated these bodies in the first place. Thus, like the fire, the problem of bodily existence is pacified by the body's own actions in destroying the source of their material entanglement.**

8. **[These words prompted Uddhava to ask a question:] My dear Krishna, we see that, in general, human beings know—at least deep down—that material life leads to discomfort and sadness. Still, they try to enjoy material life, flying in the face of everything they know to be true. My dear Lord, how can one in knowledge act in such a way, ignorant, like a dog, an ass or a goat?**

9–10. **The Supreme Lord answered: My dear Uddhava, it all begins when one falsely identifies with the material body and mind. As a result of such false conceptions of the self, material passion, the cause of all man's suffering, overtakes the mind, which is originally governed by goodness. Now contaminated by passion, the mind becomes absorbed in schemes for pleasure and material advancement. This is how a foolish person is gradually afflicted with lust, which in turn leads to ignorant action.**

11. **In this way, if one does not control their senses, they become indentured servants to them, and thus become bewildered by strong waves of passion. Such a person becomes more and more engrossed in material activities, as if by force, even though the results will be less than desirable.**

Commentary

This verse—and the entire section for that matter—brings to mind the *Bhagavad Gita*, beginning with Arjuna's question:

> O Krishna, by what is one impelled to sinful acts, even unwillingly, as if engaged by force? [3.36] The Supreme Lord answered: It is lust only, O Arjuna, which forces living beings to act. It is born of contact with the material mode of passion and later transformed into wrath—it is the

most intense enemy of this world. [3.37] As smoke covers fire, dust covers a mirror, or as the womb covers an embryo, lust similarly covers the spirit soul, in varying degrees. [3.38] Thus, even people who are wise become covered by lust, man's eternal enemy, which is never satisfied and which burns like an endless fire. [3.39] The senses, the mind and the intelligence are where this lust hides itself. These are the bodily contrivances used by lust to cover man's real knowledge, bewildering him lifetime after lifetime. [3.40] Therefore, O Arjuna, immediately curb this great symbol of sin—lust—by regulating the senses, thus becoming the victor over this destroyer of knowledge and self-realization. [3.41] The body's senses are superior to dull matter; the mind is higher still; intelligence rises beyond the mind; and the actual person—the soul—is even higher than the intelligence. [3.42] In this way, knowing yourself to be transcendental to the material body, O Arjuna, steady your mind with focused spiritual intelligence. Utilizing that facility—with strength borne of spiritual perception—you can conquer the insatiable enemy known as lust. [3.43] (3.36–43)

12. Even if a learned person allows his intelligence to be bewildered by the modes of passion and ignorance, he should systematically try to bring his mind under control once again. By clearly observing how the modes of nature have contaminated his ability to reason and act properly, he can overcome them.

13. One who is wise tends to be attentive and conscientious, and this will help in overcoming the modes. Never succumbing to laziness or a morose disposition, such a person can master all yogic procedures, including breathing (*pranayama*) and sitting postures (*asana*). Most importantly, a person of good character should practice fixing the mind on Me throughout the day—at dawn, noon and sunset—gradually becoming completely absorbed in Me.

14. True yoga, as taught by My greatest devotees, headed by Sanaka Kumara, may be understood as follows: One must withdraw the mind from all other objects, and in due course directly and completely absorb it in Me.

Commentary

Interestingly, in Krishna's day, as now, there were both proper and improper conceptions of yoga. Therefore, He instructs Uddhava that one should actually learn yoga from His devotees. Only then will one understand it in perspective. Breathing exercises, sitting postures, and even meditation were meant for one thing alone—to gain mastery over the senses, which were then meant for focus on the Supreme Lord. Here, Krishna confirms what yoga really is: to have the mind completely absorbed in Him.

15. Sri Uddhava said: My dear Krishna, You mention Sanaka Kumara—at what time and in what way did You instruct the science of yoga to the Kumara brothers? I would love to know about these things.

Commentary

Lord Krishna is referring to the initial sons of Brahma, the first created being, who was deputed by the Lord Himself to manifest the material world. Brahma requested his first four offspring, the Kumaras—Sanaka, Sanandana, Sanat-Kumara, and Sanat-Sujata, who emanated from his mind—to beget children, to populate the cosmos. But they refused, preferring to remain forever celibate in the form of five-year-old boys.

Uddhava may be asking this question to underline the fact that Krishna is speaking about Himself in a supernatural way, for the interaction with Sanaka Kumara predated His discussion with Uddhava by many centuries. It is not unlike Arjuna's question in the *Bhagavad Gita* (4.1), which begins with Krishna explaining His relationship with Vivasvan, the sun-god: "The Supreme Lord said: I instructed this eternal teaching of yoga to the sun-god, Vivasvan, and Vivasvan instructed it to Manu, the father of mankind, and Manu in turn instructed it to Ikshvaku." This obviously refers to an ancient revelation, at the dawn of time, and to the fact that the teachings were gradually passed down in a secret lineage. This prompts Arjuna to ask (4.4), "The sun-god Vivasvan is senior to You by birth. He existed before You. How am I to understand that in ancient times You instructed this science to him?" This is what Uddhava, too, is asking here: How could Krishna, who exists in Uddhava's generation, have instructed Sanaka in a previous era?

In the *Bhagavad Gita*, Krishna uses Arjuna's question as an opportunity to explain the eternality of the soul, reincarnation, and the difference between God and ordinary living beings (4.5): "You and I, O Arjuna, have gone through many, many births—but I, as God, can remember all of them. You, however, cannot, O conqueror of the enemy!" In the *Uddhava Gita*, Krishna does not immediately express these same ideas but rather just moves on with the discussion. Still, in due course, He eventually brings out the same truths for Uddhava, teaching him about the nature of the soul and ultimate reality.

16. The Supreme Lord said: My interaction with them was long ago, when the mentally generated offspring of Brahma, i.e., the young sages led by Sanaka, inquired from their father about the ultimate purpose of life and the supreme goal of yoga. Let me tell you what they said.

17. The young sages inquired of Lord Brahma: O Lord, most people are attracted to material sense objects, whose subtle form, i.e., the desire for these objects, engulf the mind. This is a problem for those who desire liberation: How does one rise beyond sense gratification if the desire for it is so deeply embedded in the mind?

18. The Supreme Lord said: My dear Uddhava, Brahma himself, who is born directly from the body of Vishnu and who is the creator of the material world, thought deeply about his sons' query. Interestingly, Brahma's intelligence was affected by his own activities of cosmic creation, and so he could not actually answer their question.

19. Lord Brahma desperately wanted to know the answer, so he could accommodate the Kumaras. Accordingly, with nowhere else to turn, he fixed his mind on Me, the Supreme Lord. At that time, I became visible to Lord Brahma in My form as a great swan (the Hamsa Avatara).

Commentary

The *Uddhava Gita* asserts that Krishna appeared as a great swan (*hamsa*) before Lord Brahma, just to assuage the latter's inability to answer his sons' question. His difficulty came from his own involvement with the modes of nature, which were bewildering him. The desire to create the material world, like any other desire for creation, is borne of passion, which clouds the mind, and so Brahma was temporarily distracted. He needed to be lifted out of his preoccupation with creation by focusing on transcendence.

In this sense, the swan, in addition to being a manifestation of the Lord, provides a beautiful metaphor as well: According to the traditional literature of India, the particular talent of the swan is that it can separate milk from water. In a similar way, Krishna sought to extract Brahma's pure consciousness from its immersion in the modes of material nature—to situate him in his original, clear state of being, without material contamination.

20. Seeing Me in this strange yet beautiful form, the sages, with Lord Brahma leading them, came forward, worshiping My sacred feet. With this, they asked Me, "Who are You?"

21. My dear Uddhava, these sages were eager to understand the ultimate truth of yoga, and they inquired from Me accordingly. Now please listen carefully as I explain to you what I said to them.

22. My dear sages, you have asked Me to identify Myself. But what do *you* believe about My essential nature? Do you think Me an ordinary soul and that there is no ultimate difference between us?

If all souls are ultimately one, and individuality is an illusion, as some people think, then we must wonder if your question even makes sense. Consider this: What is the ultimate resting place of all that is—is your original home the same as mine?

Commentary

In the next few verses, Lord Krishna unveils an effective technique in answering questions. Often, the guru will not answer directly but rather show the disciple, through a series of related questions and commentary, various ways a particular subject might be viewed, allowing the disciple to come to the proper conclusion by himself.

Krishna articulates Mayavadi philosophy, in which practitioners think themselves one with God, disavowing any individuality or separate existence. Certainly, this is a valid spiritual perspective, even if it has its limitations. Krishna wants the sages to deeply think about this and to realize how it falls short. He also wants them to contemplate their ultimate destination, as well as His, for in so doing they will realize that they, in the end, must submit to Him—*He* does not have to submit to *them*. This question of ultimate destination also clarifies the subject of individuality, showing that Krishna is, indeed, an individual—the Supreme Individual. And that the many sages who stand before Him are individuals as well—subservient beings who are meant to serve Him.

23. Then again, in asking Me "Who are You?" you may be referring to the material body. If so, then I must inform you that all material bodies are made of five elements—earth, water, fire, air, and ether. Thus, a more appropriate question would have been this: "Who are you five?" And if you think that all material bodies are really one, being constituted of the same elements, then your question is still a bit strange: Why distinguish one body from another? I must say, it appears that in asking My identity, you are uttering foolish verbiage, without any real meaning or purpose.

Commentary

Here, again, Krishna is suggesting lesser conceptions of the self that might have some meaning on a certain level but that have no value in terms of ultimate reality. He is testing the sages, hoping to bring them further by thinking deeply about their initial question.

The bodily conception of life is clearly shunned by all classes of transcendentalists, since living beings most certainly have an existence beyond the body. Thus, Krishna is almost poking fun at the sages by presenting this as a possibility. Yet He wants to be clear and to ensure that the sages before Him know for certain that neither He nor they are made of material elements. Thus, in the next verse, He begins to answer them more directly.

24. Whatever is perceived by the mind or the senses—know that to be Me in some form, for there is nothing that stands outside of Me. A simple analysis of the facts will reveal this quite clearly.

25. My dear progeny, the mind of the conditioned soul naturally focuses on material sense objects. And yet both mind and objects are merely external coverings of the spirit soul, the actual person, who is part and parcel of Me.

26. A person who realizes his essential oneness with Me also understands that the material mind is absorbed in sense objects because of nonstop sense gratification. He further understands that all attachment to material objects can be overcome by controlling the mind. In other words, if he truly understands who I am, he gives up his false attachment to both the material mind and its objects.

27. There are three functions of the intelligence—waking, sleeping, and deep sleep—and each is caused by the modes of material nature. The true person within the body is not subject to these three states and is a witness to them. He is therefore different from the material body.

28. Still, the spirit soul is trapped by his own creation: material intelligence, which keeps him bound by constantly engaging him within the precincts of the modes of nature. Where do I stand in all this? I am the fourth stage of consciousness, beyond wakefulness, dreaming, and deep sleep. Thus, when one becomes absorbed in Me, he naturally gives up the bondage of material life. Indeed, at that time, one automatically renounces material sense objects and the mind itself as a matter of course.

Commentary

Krishna answers the initial question the sages asked of Lord Brahma. To refresh the readers' memory: There is a relationship between sense objects and the mind, which keeps conditioned souls engulfed in a world of illusion, fueled by material desire. Because of this, the sages asked, "How will those souls who desire to obtain liberation ever achieve their goal? How can they overcome this complicated network of illusion and thereby conquer the mind?" This verse explains the answer: By becoming absorbed in Krishna, one automatically eschews material consciousness. And with this same act of absorption, the mind is controlled, too, transforming all desires into spiritual hankering.

Krishna also answers the question "Who are You?" Brahma and the sages asked Him this when He appeared before them as a great swan (Hamsa Avatara). Whether as a swan, as Vishnu, or in His original form as Krishna, the Lord is always the ultimate spiritual personality, hinted at when He identifies His existence as "the fourth dimension," that is, beyond all things knowable and unknowable, totally transcendental. Because He is the ultimate resting place, or God, absorption in Him is the ultimate goal of life, and this is His message not only to Brahma and the sages standing before Him, but to all of us.

29. The false conception of the self, which all conditioned living entities are subject to, is the basis of all bondage, foisting upon people the exact opposite of what they initially desire. Because of this truth, one who is wise will relinquish the constant pushing to enjoy material life and instead become focused on the Lord, who is beyond the permutations of material consciousness.

30. Abiding by My instructions, one's mind should be focused on Me. If one does not do this, valuing other things in life, then one is still in illusion, even if nominally adhering to a particular spiritual path. They are still dreaming due to incomplete knowledge, imagining that they have awakened when in fact they are still asleep.

Commentary

Krishna refers to a common phenomenon in the material world: People adhere to a particular religious path, either because of inclination or because they are born into it, but they do not develop a true sense of spirituality. This usually occurs because they miss the essence of religion and, instead, become absorbed in superficial rituals and external customs. Thus, even while claiming adherence and perhaps even practicing to some degree, they miss the central core of all religion: to develop love of God.

The test is one's focus in life. If one is still addicted to material sense gratification and the normal concerns of the material world, then one's love of God is obviously still dormant. This means that one is not practicing their religion properly and thus missing the essence. Such a person would do well to take instruction from one who already has love for God (*guru*) and thereby develop this same love in his own life.

31. People often conceive of themselves as having no relation to the Supreme Lord, but this is simply illusion, creating a sense of separation from the Absolute Truth. In the same way that a person who is dreaming might imagine themselves in many different situations, performing numerous activities, those who view themselves as separate from God erroneously identify with each situation in which they find themselves, falsely interacting with this world, hoping for both enjoyment and future rewards.

32. While awake, living beings utilize their senses to enjoy the temporary pleasures of the material body and mind. While dreaming, they make similar attempts, but only within the mind. Finally, in deep, dreamless sleep, all endeavors fall to the wayside and only darkness prevails. By contemplating these truths about wakefulness, dreaming and deep sleep, living entities can understand their existence beyond these three stages of consciousness. In this way, they may become masters of their senses.

33. Through the influence of My illusory potency, these three states of the mind, totally material, are seen as real, existing as part of My essential nature. But know for certain that this is untrue, and that you are the soul within the body—you have nothing to do with matter. Making full use of this knowledge, which is like a sharp sword, cut to pieces the false conceptions of the self that pervade the world. Such knowledge can be acquired through logical reflection and through the instructions of sages and sacred texts. All of you—Lord Brahma and the assembled sages—having already attained this knowledge should worship Me, who is situated within the heart.

34. The material world is a particular kind of illusion generated by the mind. All objects in this world have a temporary nature, existing for some time and then disappearing in due course. They can be compared to the streaking red line created by a whirling stick of fire. Not so for the spirit soul proper, who, by nature, exists in an unchanging state of pure consciousness. Be that as it may, in this world the soul appears in many different forms and stages of existence, as if partaking of the illusions of the material world. When engulfed in this endlessly changing state of affairs, the modes of nature take over, dividing the soul's consciousness into normal wakefulness, dreaming, and dreamless sleep. However, these varieties of perception are actually an illusion, dreamlike in their own right, ephemeral and temporary.

35. If one truly understands the temporary and illusory nature of all things material, and thus learns to see reality in a clear way, he will naturally overcome all material desires. In this way, he will experience the happiness of the soul, renouncing all material talk and action. That being said, at times one naturally has to interact with the material world, but, even in such a case, a wise person will always remember that it is not ultimate reality and, eventually, must be renounced. If one manages to keep this understanding throughout one's life, one will not again fall into illusion.

36. Just as an intoxicated person is often unaware of the condition of his shirt or coat, or, for that matter, even if he's wearing them, a perfectly realized soul, who knows his eternal identity, might not notice the specific actions of his temporary body. For example, he might not know whether it is sitting or standing or whatever. Indeed, if by the will of God such a person's bodily existence comes to an end or he obtains a new body, he might not even notice, just as a drunken man could care less about his clothing.

37. Because of karma, or the natural reactions that come from one's work, the material body moves forward according to its destiny, engaging its senses and vital air from life to life. A self-realized soul, however, who is awakened to the absolute truth and the perfection of yoga, will never again take shelter of the material body and its endlessly mutable manifestations. Rather, such a person knows that his material vehicle is just like a body conceived in a dream.

38. My dear Brahmins, in essence, I have just explained the truth of Sankhya to you—this is the philosophical system by which one learns to distinguish between matter from spirit. I have also explained here the essence of yoga, by which one unites in spirit with the Supreme. Please understand that I am God Himself, the Lord of Sacrifice, and that My only reason for appearing before you is to explain your religious duties.

Commentary

Krishna, in the form of Hamsa Avatara, sums up His teaching to Brahma and the sages: He has explained the difference between matter and spirit (Sankhya) and how one might unite with Him (yoga) through higher realization and practice. He also reveals the fact that He is God, specifically, "the Lord of Sacrifice." This, for His immediate audience, is a clear identification with Vishnu, who in the *Vedas* is referred to by this term (*yajno vai vishnuh*), because all Vedic sacrifice, in the end, is directed to Him.

39. O best of the Brahmins, you should know that I am both the source and the conclusion of yoga, analytic philosophy, virtuous action, religious principles, power, beauty, fame and self-control.

40. I am the source and resting place of all truly spiritual qualities, such as being beyond the modes of nature, detached, the benefactor of all, the most dear, the Lord in the heart, equally stationed everywhere, and free from material interest. Qualities such as these, when free from any material taint, are desirable and wholly spiritual.

41. [Lord Krishna then spoke to Uddhava, having completed His retelling of the Hamsa Avatara story:] My dear devotee, in this way, all of the doubts of the sages, who were led by Sanaka, were vanquished. Worshiping Me with hearts full of devotion, they sang My glories with beautiful hymns.

42. Thus, the greatest of sages properly worshiped Me, glorifying My various activities with song and dance. And as Lord Brahma and the rest of them looked on, I returned to My supreme abode.

Commentary

The final two verses of this chapter hint at the prescribed method of self-realization for the current age: *kirtan*, call-and-response singing in glorification of God, usually accompanied with dance and celebratory clapping of hands, or simple instrumentation. Devotees from the time of the *Uddhava Gita* onward, to the present day, engage in such *kirtan* as their preferred means of communing with the Lord.

Chapter 8

Lord Krishna's Explanation of Yoga: An Introduction

1. **Sri Uddhava said: Great teachers of the Vedic literature promote diverse practices for advancing in spiritual life. Which of these, my Lord, would you say is most important, or are they all equal?**

Commentary

In this chapter, Lord Krishna will introduce His discussion of the yoga system, which will neatly lead into the next chapter, where He delineates the various virtues and drawbacks of these practices. Ultimately, of course, He lauds Bhakti-yoga, loving service unto Him, as supreme. The *Bhagavad Gita* offers the final word in this regard: "Of all *yogis*, he who thinks of Me with great faith, worshiping Me in a mood of loving service, is most intimately united with Me in yoga and is the highest of all" (6.47).

2. **Uddhava continued: My dear Lord, I appreciate all that You have taught me thus far, especially the process of uncompromised devotional service, whereby a devotee rises beyond the vicissitudes of material life. By such practice, he is able to focus his mind on You without distraction.**
3. **The Supreme Lord said: The original spiritual sound vibrations of the *Vedas* were lost when the world was previously annihilated. For this reason, when creation took place yet again, I repeated the Vedic knowledge to Brahma, the first created being, because I am nondifferent from the religious principles that are taught in these Vedic texts.**

Commentary

Lord Krishna here reveals several standard Vaishnava concepts: (1) The *Vedas* are completely spiritual; (2) the creation and destruction of the material cosmos comes and goes in cyclical fashion, like the seasons or the days of the week; (3) each time, when creation begins anew, He repeats Vedic knowledge to Brahma, the first created being; and (4) the process of Vedic revelation is important to Krishna because He "is" the knowledge contained therein.

4. After I revealed the Vedic vibration to Lord Brahma, he repeated it to his eldest son, Manu, who then passed it on to the seven great sages led by Bhrigu Muni.

5–7. These forefathers and other sons of Brahma led to the appearance of numerous offspring and descendants, who assumed various forms, such as demigods, demons, human beings, Guhyakas, Siddhas, Gandharvas, Vidyadharas, Charanas, Kindevas, Kinnaras, Nagas, Kimpurushas, and others. Untold numbers of species, with different natures and desires, came about due to the three modes of material nature. It is for this reason—because of the diversity in the universe—that there are any number of Vedic rituals, mantras, and pious results.

Commentary

As the *Srimad Bhagavatam* tells us, "Different people are of different mentalities. Therefore, one should not praise them or blaspheme them, but rather should only desire their welfare, praying that they eventually agree to move forward toward the Supersoul, the Lord in the Heart" (7.13.42). This is the mood of the true devotee. He or she is nonjudgmental and, recognizing the diversity of living beings, considering their background and tastes, wishes them well in their journey, hoping they soon move toward God.

That God, too, feels this way is implicit in the fact that many religious paths exist in the world today. In other words, God recognizes that many different kinds of people have diverse characteristics—with varying needs and inclinations due to conditioning—and therefore He puts in place numerous methods of self-realization, or processes of religion, so that there is a method for everyone to make gradual advancement toward the ultimate goal of life. He states this more directly in the next verse.

8. Accordingly, because there are different kinds of human beings, with equally differing natures and inclinations, there are numerous spiritual paths for them to pursue. These processes of religion are all conveyed through tradition, custom, and sacred lineages. Meanwhile, other teachers preach ideas that counter the authorized conclusions of the scriptures, supporting non-theistic perspectives.

Commentary

We learn that there is an authorized process for receiving transcendental knowledge, whatever the tradition. In the Sanskrit to this verse, the important word *parampara* is introduced. It refers to "sacred lineage" or "disciplic succession." Traditionally, Vedic knowledge, in particular, is passed down from teacher to disciple, and the inner truths of the teaching are conveyed in this way. The importance of this concept cannot be stressed enough. A mere "reading" or even "studying" of Vedic texts will not suffice: One must hear the vibration from a self-realized soul, who is a living example of the truth—such a teacher or someone who has heard this same truth from a teacher himself, whose teacher also received the knowledge in the same way, ad infinitum. Only in this way will Vedic knowledge proper enter the heart of an aspiring practitioner.

Krishna emphasizes this point in the *Bhagavad Gita*: "The science of the soul is received through a lineage of disciplic succession, and the saintly kings understood it in that way" (4.2). It is therefore recommended that one take initiation from a self-realized soul, who represents one of the well known authorized lineages coming down from time immemorial. The *Bhagavatam* further tells us:

> Any person who wants to be truly happy must search out a legitimate spiritual teacher and take shelter of him by initiation. The qualification of such a guru is that he has realized the conclusions of the scriptures by deliberation and is able to convince others of these conclusions. Such great personalities, who have taken shelter of the Lord, leaving aside all material considerations, should be understood to be bona fide spiritual masters. (11.3.21)

9. O dear Uddhava, most people are bewildered by My illusory energy and, because of this, they try to explain various truths in their own way.

Commentary

The term *maya-mohita* in the original Sanskrit indicates that the varieties of expression mentioned in this verse do not refer to authorized variations in spiritual knowledge—this instead refers more to the defective explanations of nonpractitioners, who feel they know something about spiritual life when in fact they do not. Thus, in addition to the varieties of spiritual paths that are legitimate, Krishna warns that most ideas about spirituality are highly speculative, at best, and, in the end, are usually untenable.

The great nineteenth-century Vaishnava teacher Bhaktivinode Thakur summarizes five kinds of pseudo-religion in his theological work, *Sri Chaitanya Shikshamrita*: outright atheism (*nashtikyavada*); skepticism (*sandehavada*); seeing matter as all that is (*jadavada*); the doctrine of no soul (*anatmavada*); and the idea that God exists but has no form (*nirvisheshavada*) (1.1). All five forms of pseudo-religion are elaborated on in numerous Indic texts.

10. Some teachers try to convey the idea that one can achieve perfection through ordinary piety. Others say that it is attained through popularity, sensual indulgence, truthfulness, self-control, being equal to all, selfishness, political activism, opulence, renunciation, eating properly, sacrifice, penance, charity, vows, dutiful acts or strict discipline. Each of these ideas has its supporters.

11. But know this to be the truth, O Uddhava: All that I have just mentioned only award temporary results, which are material. In fact, the meager and even miserable assets obtained from them are based on ignorance. And so, even while people are in the midst of these various kinds of work and actions, they are filled with distress.

Commentary

One might wonder how popularity or opulence, to cite but two examples, could in fact be harbingers of distress. Krishna is speaking of a subtle truth, one that might not be directly perceivable at first. But those who analyze material nature and the causes for misery know that unless one is engaged in God's loving service, all activity ends in pain. We merely need to look at the lives of most popular movie stars and the richest people in the world—are they generally happy? "Money can't buy me love," as the Beatles famously sang. Krishna indicates that all such material pleasures and even attempts at religious austerity will yield only fleeting rewards, leading to misery and frustration, and that unless one has love for God, distress necessarily will ensue in due course.

12. But devotees who focus their consciousness on My transcendental form, renouncing their material desires, experience a happiness that goes far beyond any kind of sense gratification.

13. There are those who do not desire anything in this material world, having achieved peace by controlling their senses. This is a person whose consciousness does not vary in diverse conditions and whose mind is wholly peaceful. These are My devotees—the only people who know true happiness.

14. These pure souls, who have concentrated their consciousness on Me, do not desire to be like Brahma or Indra, nor do they aspire to some leadership position on Earth—they desire no sovereign position anywhere, nor do they want the perfections of the eightfold yoga system. Indeed, they do not even aspire after

liberation from birth and death. Such a person desires to attain Me and nothing else.

15. **My dear Uddhava, being My devotee, you are dearest to Me, more than Lord Brahma, Lord Shiva, Lord Sankarshan, the goddess of fortune, or even My own self.**

16. **The entire universe is purified with the dust emanating from My devotees' sacred feet. For this reason, I always try to follow in their footsteps, for they are free from all desires that do not lead to My service; they are absorbed in thinking of My pastimes; and they are characterized by peacefulness, lack of enmity, and a harmonious disposition.**

Commentary

The mutual love between Krishna and His pure devotees is described in many Sanskrit texts. The *Srimad Bhagavatam* offers numerous examples, such as this one: "The pure devotee can be found within the core of My heart, and I am always in his. Such devotees know nothing beyond Me, and I know nothing but them" (9.4.68).

Moreover, Krishna hints in Verse 16 about His appearance as Chaitanya Mahaprabhu (1486–1534), who, according to the Gaudiya Vaishnava tradition, is God Himself in the guise of His own devotee. Briefly, Krishna wanted to taste the love and devotion His devotees feel for Him. He does so, it is said, by appearing as Sri Chaitanya. Consequently, He "follows in His devotees' footsteps," as indicated in this latter verse.

17. **Those who do not desire personal gratification, whose minds are always taking shelter of Me, who are peaceful, without misconceptions of the self and merciful to all living entities—and who are not opportunistic when it comes to personal enjoyment—these devotees relish a happiness that cannot be known or achieved in the material world.**

18. **My dear Uddhava, even if My devotee is not fully in control of his senses, and is burdened by material desires, he will not be defeated by sense gratification. This is because his faith in Me is without question.**

19. **In the same way that fire can burn firewood into ashes, devotion directed toward Me totally destroys the sins committed by My devotees.**

Commentary

One might question why devotees would act sinfully at all. The plain fact is that humans are fallible—they tend to falter and revert back to old habits. In general, of course, devotees do *not* act sinfully, but temporary aberrations can certainly occur. In such a case, they are to be forgiven, especially if they are remorseful and determined to once again rise to their normal level of devotion. As Krishna says in the *Bhagavad Gita* (9.30): "If one's tendency is to engage in devotional service (Bhakti-yoga), then he can be excused for any and all indiscretions—even if they are most reprehensible—because in general he acts in a saintly way."

20. My dear Uddhava, nothing brings Me under its sway like the loving devotion of My devotees. Not mystic yoga, Sankhya philosophy, pious work, Vedic study, austerity, or renunciation.

21. And so only by such faithful devotional service can one attain Me, the Supreme Lord. Indeed, My devotees have a natural love for Me, and they know Me as the goal of life. By engaging in pure service, as they do, even those of low birth and bad habits can purify themselves in due course.

22. Standard religious activities, even when performed with honesty and mercy, and the difficult pursuit of knowledge, obtained with great penance, are insufficient to completely purify one's consciousness. The necessary ingredient is devotion for Me.

23. If one's heart truly melts in My loving service, would one not naturally experience ecstatic symptoms, like the hair of one's body standing on end? Indeed, the heart *must* melt—or how will tears of love flow from the eyes? Without crying due to spiritual happiness, one's service to the Lord will necessarily be lacking in various ways. And without this highest kind of service, the consciousness will never be purified.

24. A devotee whose heart melts in this way will sometimes find that his speech falters as he chokes up; he cries continually and sometimes laughs, too, inexplicably. He shouts loudly and then dances with wild abandon—such a devotee, who loves Me dearly, purifies the entire universe by his mere existence.

Commentary

The prior two verses refer to eight verifiable symptoms (*ashta-sattvika-bhava*) that are said to occur, involuntarily, in the bodies of those who experience ecstatic love of God. These symptoms include the state of being stunned, perspiration, standing of the bodily hairs on end, faltering of the voice, trembling, fading of the body's color, tears, and devastation. They are described or listed variously by diverse authors, but the main point is this: The tradition teaches that spiritual life is a science, and one's love of God, according to Gaudiya Vaishnavas, can be gauged by how intensely these symptoms occur in the practitioner's body. Naturally, similar symptoms arise for nonspiritual reasons as well, but one properly trained in spiritual science can distinguish these signs from their material counterparts.

25. When gold is placed in fire it loses its impurities, returning to its pure and brilliant state. In the same way, the spirit soul, when he places himself in the fire of Bhakti-yoga, becomes purified of all contamination, even that caused by previous works. As a result, he inevitably regains his original life as My servant in the spiritual world.

26. With proper medicinal ointment, one can help a diseased eye recover its power to see. In the same way, any living being who thoroughly takes the medicine of hearing and chanting My glories will cleanse himself of material contamination and be able to see Me once again in My original spiritual form.

Commentary

This verse hearkens to the ancient text *Sri Brahma-samhita*, in which Lord Brahma, the creator of the universe, sings, "I worship Govinda (Krishna), the primeval Lord, who is Shyamasundara, the beautiful flute-player with inconceivable attributes, whom the pure devotees see in their heart of hearts—they see Him with the eye of devotion tinged with the salve of love" (5.38). This "salve of love" is often described as "a medicinal ointment," used to correct a sincere disciple's vision. With its proper application, pure devotees see the Supreme Lord in their hearts—whether as Vishnu (Narayana) or in His original form as Krishna.

Vaishnava texts tell us that not everything is seen with the eyes—though great devotees also see Him standing in front of them. Primarily, devotees tend to "see" Him within, because their hearts are saturated with devotion. In fact, when the devotion of the fledgling devotee reaches the stage known as Bhava-bhakti, wherein one's steadiness in practice reaches a point of spontaneous attraction, the inner eye becomes tinged with the salve of love, enabling him to see the Lord face to face.

27. One whose mind is focused on the objects of sense gratification will necessarily become entangled in the senses. But if one instead consistently remembers Me, then I will be His primary absorption.

28. For this reason, one should abandon all material ways of being, which are as ephemeral as a dream, and should instead completely absorb one's mind in Me. By such absorption, one becomes thoroughly purified.

29. Being conscious of the individual self within the body, one should give up association with women and those who frequently associate with women. Sitting without concern in a solitary place, one should focus the mind on Me with unswerving determination.

Commentary

The *Uddhava Gita* does not intend to put forward a sexist doctrine. Rather, since the text originally was directed to a primarily male, celibate audience, the idea of women as temptresses and as people who distract male renunciants from pursuing spiritual life is understandable. In the broadest context, however, this verse is indicating that those who are trying to be conscious of themselves as spirit-soul, beyond the body, would do well to avoid the association of the opposite sex. For women, this could refer easily to men.

Additionally, Patanjali lists *brahmacharya*, or celibacy, as being among his five *yamas* ("restraints"), which are essential for one seeking to reach perfection in yoga.

Krishna is, in fact, speaking about how to properly practice yoga, which necessitates a steady mind and no distractions. Sexual indulgence is considered among the highest pleasures in the material world. Therefore, the *Uddhava Gita*, like other religious texts, tries to dissuade practitioners from falling into this ultimate trap, which easily can sidetrack the greatest of *yogis*.

30. Of all the varieties of suffering and bondage that come from attachment, the worst is that which arises from attachment to women or close association with others who are attached to women.

Commentary

Again, one must be cautious when associating with the opposite sex. The pull of lust is intense, making a living being—even a pious living being—forgetful of the need for virtue and other progressive values in life. Therefore, the scriptures repeatedly warn us to be on guard, aware that deep attachment to pleasure naturally arises when in proximity to those who stimulate our sexual desires.

The *Bhagavad Gita* offers a similar caution, "O Arjuna, it is lust only, which is born of contact with the material modes of passion and later transformed into wrath, that is the most intense, disturbing enemy of this world" (3.37). Krishna repeats that same message in Verse 30.

According to Patanjali, the root cause of distress (*klesha*)—and a chief impediment to the practice of yoga—is ignorance (*avidya*), which he defines as misidentifying that which is temporary and impure with that which is eternal and wholesome. In other words, the primary manifestation of ignorance, says Patanjali, is in identifying the body with the self. Because most Indic texts are clear that sexual pleasure binds one to the bodily conception of life, preoccupation with sex is discouraged for those who want to advance in yoga.

31. Sri Uddhava said: My dear lotus-eyed Krishna, through what means should those who desire liberation meditate upon You? What kind of meditation should it be? And upon which of Your holy forms should they meditate? Kindly answer these questions.

Commentary

One may wonder why a liberated soul such as Uddhava is asking about meditation, because, as Krishna's surrendered servant, he well knows how to meditate on Krishna in the best and most effective ways. The commentators clearly state that Uddhava asks these questions for others, so that those who are not surrendered will learn how to begin meditation and gradually evolve to more advanced levels. This also is implicit in Krishna's forthcoming answer, which is directed to ordinary *yogis*.

32–33. The Supreme Lord said: One should sit on a level seat that is not too high or too low, but just right. He should keep his body straight and erect, like a board, yet comfortable, placing his two hands easily on his lap. The eyes should be focused on the tip of the nose, where the pathways of breathing should be purified by the mechanical exercises of *puraka* (inhalation), *kumbhaka* (retention of breath) and *rechaka* (exhalation). After this, it should be done in reverse (*rechaka, kumbhaka, puraka*). Having fully controlled the senses, one can thus enact the practice of *pranayama* in a step-by-step fashion.

Commentary

It is clear from this verse, and from the ones that follow, that Krishna is explaining meditation from the ground up, so that even a fledgling *yogi* can understand how to meditate on Him.

Indeed, even Patanjali, contrary to popular belief, focused more on techniques of meditation than on physical exercises. His main purpose, of course, was to help people learn how to focus their minds in various ways, ultimately to attain the Supreme. And to this end, he popularized techniques of breathing and sitting and meditating, using technical terms such as those mentioned above (*rechaka, kumbhaka, puraka*). But the end result for Patanjali, and for any system of yoga, is linking with God.

34. The *yogi* should move the life air upward, like a lotus stalk, until it reaches the heart, where the sacred syllable OM vibrates like a bell. He should continue in this way up through the inner core of the body, where the sound of OM is joined with that of *anusvara*, its last letter.

Commentary

Anusvara refers to the nasal vibration that is commonly pronounced after one chants the fifteen Sanskrit vowels. By combining OM with this sound—a sound that naturally occurs at the end of the mantra itself—one moves forward in the process of mystic yoga. Again, it is clear that the technical information is meant to gradually take *yogis*, whose practice was popular in Krishna's time as Raja-yoga, to the topmost level of meditation, which is to focus on His divine form.

35. Focused on the sound of OM, one should carefully practice *pranayama* techniques ten times during each sunrise, noon and sunset. In this way, after one month one will have learned how to control the life air in the body.

Commentary

Patanjali, too, in *Yoga-sutras* (1.27 and 1.28), recommends the chanting of OM to attain the perfection of yoga. Although there are numerous ways to understand this mantra, in its ultimate sense, it is seen as the sound representation of Krishna, as mentioned in the *Bhagavad Gita* (9.17) and later in the *Uddhava Gita*, too (10.12).

36–42. With eyes half closed and focused on the tip of the nose with great attention, one should meditate on the lotus of the heart. Comprised of eight petals, the flower is situated on an effulgent lotus stalk. One should meditate on the sun, moon and fire, too, imagining them in sequential order within the colorful whorl of that lotus flower. Next, My transcendental form should be seen within the fire, and one should focus on it as the highest prize of all meditative endeavors. Envision that form as perfectly proportioned—as well as gentle and full of good cheer. It has four gorgeously long arms, a charming, aristocratic neck, a large forehead, a pure smile and glowing, shark-shaped earrings suspended from two perfectly symmetrical ears. That spiritual form, who is My very self, is the color of a dark rain cloud, which is especially beautiful when contrasted with My golden-yellowish silk *dhoti*. One will also see the images of Shrivatsa (a curl of white hair) and the goddess of fortune, which are like beauty marks, on My chest. In this form, I am holding a conch, disc, club, lotus flower and garland of forest flowers. My two soft lotus feet are decorated with ankle bells and bracelets, exhibiting a precious gem along with a richly illuminated crown. My upper hips sport a golden

belt, while My arms are decorated with a variety of valuable jewelry. All of the limbs of My beautiful form naturally seize the viewer's heart, and My face is characterized by My merciful glance. In this way, while restraining the senses from the sense objects, one should be sober and self-controlled, using his intelligence to undeviatingly focus his mind upon My transcendental limbs. In this way, he should meditate upon My most delicate spiritual form.

Commentary

This, ultimately, is Krishna's response to Uddhavaji, who, in Verse 31, asked about which of the Lord's forms he should meditate on. The answer, especially for the aspiring *yogi*, is Vishnu, particularly Kshirodakashayi Vishnu, the four-armed form of God who appears in the heart of every soul and within every atom as well. This form is mentioned throughout the Vedic literature.

43. **When one is fully immersed, he should pull his consciousness back from viewing the limbs of My transcendental body. At that time, he should meditate only on My wonderful, smiling face.**

44. **As one becomes firmly fixed in meditation on My face, one should withdraw his consciousness, so it can be focused on the sky. Then, renouncing such meditation, one should become established in who I really am and give up the process of meditation altogether.**

45. **In this way, one who has perfected his meditation should see Me within his own soul, and he should see all individual souls within Me, for I am the Supreme. In this way, such an expert transcendentalist sees individual souls truly united with the Supreme Soul, just as one can see the sun's rays as being indisputably united with the sun.**

46. **Thus, when a *yogi* controls his mind by such divinely focused meditation, his illusory interests, as well as his identification with material phenomena and knowledge, is fundamentally destroyed.**

Commentary

The entire yogic enterprise is meant to free one from all illusion. Thus freed, one transcends the usual bodily concept of life. After this, one is eligible for understanding who one really is. This begins with an awareness of oneself as an eternal spirit soul, but gradually evolves into an understanding of one's original identity in relationship to Krishna. This, then, is the culmination of self-realization.

Chapter 9

The Limitations of Yogic Perfection

1. **The Supreme Lord said: My dear Uddhava, if one masters his senses, he will achieve the fruits of mystic yoga. These perfections are awarded to one who has controlled his mind, mastered the breathing process, and concentrated his mind on Me.**

Commentary

Krishna refers to the ultimate rewards of yoga practice—the "perfections" (*siddhis*) or powers that one develops as a result of performing massive austerities. By controlling the mind, mastering *pranayama* and other yoga techniques, and learning how to meditate on Krishna, one develops certain powers that aid in one's service to the Divine. Such powers are almost invariably abused, however, and, as a result, the candidate for spiritual perfection inevitably falls from the path. This all is explained in this chapter. Furthermore, if one does not learn to focus one's mind on Krishna, attaining union with God, all the benefits of yoga will be rendered useless, for they are then not serving their intended purpose. Such "yoga" will not bring happiness, spiritual awareness, or liberation.

2. **Sri Uddhava said: My dear infallible Lord, how does one attain mystic perfection, and what is such perfection really like? Are there a specific number of mystic powers that accompany yogic perfection? I would like to know, and, indeed, You are the person to tell me, since You are the ultimate resting place of all mysticism.**

3. **Sri Krishna replied: The traditional teachers of yoga have described eighteen types of mystic perfection and meditation. Of these, eight are primary, since they focus on Me, and ten are secondary, stemming from the material mode of goodness.**

4–5. **To begin, there are three mystic perfections that involve the transformation of one's own body. They are (1) the ability to** become smaller than the smallest; (2) to become greater than the greatest; and (3) lighter than the lightest. Then, moving down the list, the remaining perfections include (4) being able to acquire whatever you want; (5) the ability to experience any worldly enjoyment, either in this world or in the next; (6) a potency that allows you to manipulate various aspects of illusion; (7) a similar energy facilitating manipulation of material elements, freeing the aspiring ***yogi*** from the constraints of the modes of nature; and finally (8) the ability to obtain anything from any material planet, from the lowest to the highest. My dear Uddhava, these are the eight primary perfections, naturally blissful and unsurpassed within the world of matter.

6–7. There are also ten secondary perfections, but these relate to the modes of nature: (1) The power to become free from hunger and thirst and other bodily demands; (2) the ability to see and (3) hear things at great distances; (4) transporting yourself to distant places at the speed of the mind; (5) taking on any form you desire; (6) usurping other people's bodies; (7) choosing your time of death; (8) the ability to perceive the exchanges between the demigods and the *apsaras* (celestial girls from higher planets); (9) to accomplish whatever you set out to do; and (10) to have your determined efforts fulfilled without difficulty.

8–9. There are five other perfections: (1) The ability to know past, present and future; (2) tolerance of heat, cold and other dualities of material existence; (3) reading the minds of others; (4) counteracting the influence of fire, sun, water, poison, and other material elements; and (5) remaining undefeated by any and all opponents. I am briefly listing these here according to their essential characteristics. But you should also know how these mystic perfections arise as a result of specific types of meditation, and you should be aware of the particular processes involved.

10. If you worship Me in My atomic form, as I exist within the heart of all subtle elements, focusing on that aspect of Me without distraction, you can attain the first of these perfections, i.e., you can become smaller than the smallest.

Commentary

Interestingly, by meditating on Krishna in His Supersoul (*Paramatma*) feature, as He exists in the hearts of all souls and in the central portion of every atom, one can become smaller than the smallest. The irony is that this is precisely what Krishna is in that particular form—He is so small that He enters into all.

In essence, then, the mystic perfections are merely a form of transcendental mimicry, in which *yogis* can get a taste of Krishna's mystic potency.

11. **There are those who think of Me as the essence of everything they see, meditating upon Me as the Supreme Soul of material existence. Such *yogis* achieve a mystic perfection by which they can embody similar greatness. By absorbing their minds in the material elements, such as sky, air, fire, and so on, they can take on the greatness of each of these.**

Commentary

In the next group of verses, Lord Krishna briefly will refer to highly technical processes of meditation. These will include almost incomprehensible procedures that involve material elements, both gross and subtle, meant for very serious *yogis*. For example, meditating on Krishna through the element of sky or making one's vision and the sun become nondifferent—these are esoteric procedures that are only briefly mentioned, as we shall see. The meaning behind them are anything but clear. In addition, the rare few adepts who can perfect these processes will develop dangerous powers, making them imitation lords with a facsimile of divinity. Krishna mentions these yogic tactics to make a point, which will become clear as the chapter comes to a close.

12. **All things are pervaded by Me, for I am the very essence of all material substances. By focusing on Me in this form, the *yogi* may achieve the third primary perfection, through which he may realize the subtle truths of time.**

13. **If one focuses on Me as the essence of his own material identity, at the height of the mode of goodness, he is awarded the power of mystic acquisition, conquering the senses of all living beings. He achieves this perfection because of his expertise in absorbing his mind in Me.**

14. **In my indwelling form as the Paramatma, I am the source of even the subtle form of material existence, which gives birth to fruitive activities. One who concentrates on this form, in this specific way, can realize whatever one desires, and this is yet another mystic perfection.**

15. **Then again, one whose consciousness is focused on Me as Paramatma, specifically as the original instigator of the external energy consisting of the three modes, will be able to control all other conditioned souls, down to the movements of their material bodies and the manipulation of their bodily designations.**

16. If a *yogi* focuses on My form as Narayana, with all potencies, as the fourth factor of existence, he will embody My essential nature, thus displaying the mystic perfection that allows him to subjugate everyone and everything.

17. And for those *yogis* who concentrate on Me as the impersonal Brahman—the supreme pervading force of the universe—the greatest happiness is theirs, and all their desires are inevitably fulfilled.

18. Those who focus on Me as the support of religious principles, the embodiment of purity, and the Lord of the spiritual realm, will be granted an existence of purity, freed from the six kinds of material pains, i.e., hunger, thirst, decay, death, anxiety, and illusion.

19. Those purified souls who concentrate on the supernormal sound vibrations emanating from Me through the element of sky can thereby perceive within this same sky all the words of ordinary beings, wherever they may be.

20. If one's ability to see becomes one with the sun planet, which then becomes nondifferent from one's eyes, one can eventually see anything, at any distance. This is because such a *yogi* has become expert in meditating on Me, who is in essence both sun and vision.

21. By absorbing one's mind in Me, making use of the wind, one can obtain the mystic perfection of harmony between body and mind, so that one's body works in perfect conjunction with one's mental faculties.

22. Certain *yogis*, who are expert at focusing their mind in a particular way, can assume any form they desire, making it appear with the power of their mind. A miracle such as this is only possible because these *yogis* have learned to concentrate on My inconceivable mystic potency, by which I, too, assume innumerable forms.

23. When a perfect *yogi* desires to enter another person's body, he should visualize himself in that particular form. With the power of his developed concentration, he can then abandon his own material body and enter the one he is focusing on—all through the medium of air, in the same way that a bee flies from one flower to situate himself on another.

24. There are *yogis*, too, who know the art of blocking the anus with the heel of the foot, thus lifting the soul from the heart to the chest. From here, the soul goes to the neck and finally to the head. The wise *yogi*, establishing himself within the *brahma-randhra*

(the ***chakra*** at the very top of the skull), leaves his material body and journeys to his next destination.

25. There are other ***yogis*** who want the pleasures found only in the celestial gardens of higher planets. To get there, they meditate on the most profound level of goodness, which is the core of My being. If they do so to perfection, women from heavenly planets will approach them in divine flying machines, ready to take them there.

26. All ***yogis*** must have faith in Me, absorbing their minds in who I am, knowing that My purpose should always be fulfilled. If they do so, they will always achieve their own purpose, too, simply by the nature of their chosen path.

27. Because they have perfected their meditation on Me, they acquire a nature similar to My own, for I am the supreme controller of all that is. The desires of such true ***yogis***, like Mine, can never be thwarted in any way.

28. One who is expert in yoga has purified his existence through devotion to Me. Because of his focus, he is adept in meditation, with knowledge of past, present and future. Indeed, he can see his own births and deaths and those of others.

29. Fire, sun, water, poison, and other phenomena cannot injure the accomplished ***yogi***, just as aquatics cannot be harmed by any amount of water. This is because the consciousness of a true mystic is fundamentally peaceful, with a total absorption in My essential nature that protects him from any potential calamity.

30. Because My devotees meditate on My various forms, manifestations of Myself who carry various weapons and who are decorated with holy marks, such as flags, ornamental umbrellas, and elaborate fans, they become unconquerable.

31. Those wise devotees who worship Me through yoga and meditation can eventually develop the mystic perfections that I mentioned here.

32. Indeed, the wise have no doubt conquered their senses, controlled their breath, and stilled their mind. They are self-controlled and always absorbed in meditation on Me. With this as a basis, how can they ***not*** develop mystic perfections?

33. But know this: Those who are well-versed in the science of yoga proclaim that these mystic perfections are actually impediments—a mere waste of time for one who actually wants the goal of yoga. It is this ultimate goal that one achieves directly from Me.

Commentary

In many ways, this latter verse is the most important in Krishna's entire discussion of yoga in the *Uddhava Gita*. Although the Lord entertains the significance of the yoga process and the mystic perfections one might thereby achieve, His ultimate conclusion is that it is simply a series of impediments (*antarayan*) and a waste of time (*kala-kshapana-hetavaha*). This also is mentioned in Patanjali's *Yoga-sutras* (3.37), in which the mystic powers are even referred to as "obstacles" (*upasargah*).

Naturally, when asked by Uddhava how one might meditate on Him, in terms of both the form to be meditated on and the process by which one might focus one's attention, the Lord addresses Raja-yoga, the system of meditation so popular in His day. He briefly outlines the process and the mystic perfections one might develop through proper practice. But then He delivers the real point: It ultimately is a side issue, a distraction from yoga's real purpose, which is to link with God.

For three verses before this (Verses 30–32), Krishna hints at these truths by referring to His devotees, their meditation on His forms, and how they develop mystic powers, almost as a by-product, through the process of being His devotee. In Verse 33, however, he says it directly, and in the next verse he highlights it even further.

34. The same mystic opulence that can be acquired through good birth, the taking of medicinal herbs, austerities and the intonation of mantras can be had by devotional service (Bhakti-yoga) directed to Me. Know this for certain, O Uddhava, the actual perfection of yoga cannot be attained by any other means.

Commentary

A similar verse is found in Patanjali's *Yoga-sutras* (4.1), wherein the mystic perfections also are said to arise due to good birth, herbs, mantras, and austerity. Patanjali adds *samadhi* to this list, which is the perfected state of yogic achievement. Interestingly, he does not reveal, at least in *Yoga-sutra* 4.1, exactly what he means by *samadhi*, and because the word is defined variously throughout his text and elsewhere, the reader is subject to unclear conclusions. Not so for those who study the *Uddhava Gita*. The added factor, as expressed in Verse 34 of the *Uddhava Gita*, is *yoga-gatim*—the actual perfection of yoga, which is devotion to God. This is the ultimate form of *samadhi*, by which one actually achieves the perfection of yoga.

35. My dear Uddhava, I am the cause, the reservoir, and the controller of all mystic perfections, whether they be generated through the yoga system, the cultivation of knowledge, from acting in a pure way, or coming from a community of spiritual teachers.

Commentary

Patanjali's *Yoga-sutras* (2.45) also tell us that, of all the *yamas* ("restraints") and *niyamas* ("observances"), it is only submission to God (*ishvara-pranidhanat*) that affords *samadhi*, or spiritual perfection.

36. In the same way that all material elements can be found both inside and outside all material bodies, I am the same both within and without—there is nothing other than Me. I can be found within everything as the Soul of souls (Paramatma), as well as outside of everything as the spiritual dimension of existence.

Chapter 10

The Qualities of the Lord

1. **Sri Uddhava said: My dear Lord, You are timeless, without beginning or end—the Supreme Spirit, with no limitations. You are the source of life and everyone's protector; You are the creation and dissolution of everything.**

Commentary

Uddhava begins this chapter by glorifying the Lord's unique characteristics. Krishna will soon continue on this theme, enlightening Uddhava further by elaborating on His own outstanding qualities.

2. **My dear Lord, most people, due to a lack of virtue, cannot understand that You are in fact the essence of everything. But those who are wise, who actually know Vedic conclusions, worship You in truth.**

3. **Please tell me more about the different forms in which the great souls worship You with devotion (*bhaktya*), and also about the perfections they achieve by doing so.**

Commentary

Krishna had previously revealed to Uddhava those aspects of Himself that are cherished by mystic *yogis*. He revealed secret information about the powers such *yogis* could develop as a result of their practice. But the Lord also had said that the essence of yoga was devotion to Him, which again is hinted at in this verse with the word *bhaktya*, and that most people who pursue conventional yoga, with its concomitant mystical *siddhis*, are simply missing the point. Therefore, Uddhava wants to know more details about Krishna's internal nature—who He actually is and what His opulence really looks like. These are truths that go beyond yoga as understood by most people. In the end, yoga is a process whose culmination is found in the realm of *bhakti*, devotion to Krishna, the most complete yogic path.

4. Dearest Lord, O supreme entity who sustains everyone, even though You are the indwelling spirit in the hearts of all living entities, they cannot perceive Your presence. And yet, even in the midst of their blindness, You are witnessing their many activities.

5. O omnipotent Lord, please let me hear of Your limitless energies, which are manifest everywhere—on the earth, in heaven, and even in hell. My respects go out to You in innumerable ways, for You are the shelter of everyone and everything.

6. The Supreme Lord said: Your questions are worthy, just like Arjuna's. When he and I were on the Battlefield of Kurukshetra, he asked Me questions similar to your own.

7. On that Battlefield, Arjuna had concluded that killing his relatives would be reprehensible and irreligious, instigated by little more than his desire for sovereignty. For this reason, he declined to fight, thinking, "How can I murder my relatives? I would surely destroy them in battle." Arjuna's considerations were thus noble but mundane.

8. Because of this, I used logical arguments to enlighten him, that most potent of men. In the course of these arguments, just prior to the battle, he asked questions in the same way that you do.

9. O Uddhava, I dwell within the hearts of all, and I am therefore a natural friend to everyone, as well as being God Almighty. In essence, I am one with all living beings, since I am their creator, maintainer and destroyer.

Commentary

Krishna used similar words to describe Himself when talking to Arjuna in the *Bhagavad Gita*. He identifies Himself as "the self" (*aham atma*) of all souls. Therefore, one might mistakenly think that each individual is not unlike Krishna or is in some way Krishna Himself.

However, it should be clear from alternate verses that Krishna, while existing as the inner reality of each soul, is also distinct from all individuals—He is both their very essence and an individual who stands outside of them. The philosophy He ultimately articulates is that of *achintya-bhedabheda-tattva*, which is the inconceivable oneness and difference between God and the living entity. To overemphasize only the oneness is the great mistake of modern-day spirituality.

This will be explained more directly as the *Uddhava Gita* moves on, just as it was made clear in the *Bhagavad Gita*, too, when Krishna told His dear devotee that all beings are eternally individuals (2.12). Although we may be one with God in an abstract, metaphysical sense, we are ontologically separate—we are one in loving embrace but not in substance. We are unique individuals, and for this reason the devotee can develop love and devotion for the Supreme—for God is fully Other. Such love and devotion would be impossible if all living entities were in fact the same. Love requires difference.

10. **Those who seek spiritual life are ultimately searching for Me, and I am the unstoppable flow of time as well. I am the harmony found in the modes of material nature, and also the good qualities that distinguish the pious.**

Commentary

For the next thirty verses or so, Krishna will describe how He can be seen in nature and in various phenomena as well as the foremost entities both on this planet and on others. This is similar to His revelation in the *Bhagavad Gita*, Chapters Seven, Nine, and Ten. Basically, He describes Himself as the best in every general category—He is the beginning and the end and everything in between. God is all.

11. **I am the best among things with attributes, and in that topmost category I am the total material creation. I am the spirit soul, which is the subtlest of things, and I am the mind, which is most unconquerable.**

12. **When considering the *Vedas*, think of Me as their original teacher, Lord Brahma; and in the realm of mantras, I am the sacred OMKARA, which consists of three syllables. Among letters I am the first in any alphabet, and among sacred meters know Me as the Gayatri mantra.**

13. **Among beings from higher planets, I am Indra, and among Vasus consider Me to be Agni, the god of fire. If you search among the sons of Aditi, you will find that I am Vishnu (Vamanadeva), and among the class of beings known as Rudras I am the one with the blue throat: Lord Shiva.**

14. **Of Brahmins I am Bhrigu Muni, and of history's saintly kings I am Manu. If you consider the saintly people who are godly, I am Naradaji, and amongst cows I am the famous Kamadhenu.**

15. **Of perfected souls I am Lord Kapila, and among birds, Garuda. Among those who originally propagated human forms, I am Daksha, and as a primary ancestor I am Aryama.**

16. **O Uddhava, among the *daityas* arising from Diti's womb, I am Prahlad Maharaj, the boy saint who is known as "lord of demons." I am also the moon, which benefits all stars and herbs,**

and among the kinds of beings called Yakshas and Rakshasas, I am Kuvera, widely famous as the lord of wealth.

17. I am Airavata, the regal elephant, and Varuna—king of aquatics and lord of the seas. No one or nothing can heat and illuminate this world like Me, for I am the sun, and among human beings I am the king.

18. I am Uchchaihshrava, the best of horses, and among metals I am naturally gold. If you consider Me amongst those who mete out ultimate punishment, think of Me as Yamaraj, lord of death. Among serpents I am Vasuki, who churned the ocean of milk at the dawn of creation.

19. O sinless one, among many-hooded snakes I am Anantadev, also known as Sesha, and among vicious animals with sharp teeth consider Me the lion. In the *ashram* system please identify Me with the fourth stage of life, *sannyasa*, or the culmination of renunciation; and when considering the *varna* social system, see me as the Brahmin.

20. Holy places with rivers that flow know perfection in the Ganges, of which I am nondifferent. Meanwhile, among major bodies of water I am the ocean. If I am to be thought of as a weapon, consider Me the bow, and of those who use such weapons I am Lord Shiva.

21. The best of dwelling places is Mount Sumeru—consider it to be Me—and among impenetrable places, I am none other than the Himalayas. Among trees I am the *ashvatthah*, and among plants I am those that bring forth barley and other life-giving grains.

22. Among known Vedic priests I am Vasishtha Muni, and among those who have deep spiritual knowledge I am Brihaspati. Note, too, the great military commanders: Among them I am Kartikeya. And among those who know the progressive values of life, I am Lord Brahma.

23. To see Me among sacrifices, look to those of the *Vedas*, and among urgent vows, see Me as nonaggression (*avihimsanam*). Among purifying substances, I am the wind, fire, the sun, water, and sound vibration.

24. In the yoga system, I am the final stage, *samadhi*, in which the soul reaches perfection. If one desires victory, in any field, I am that necessary counsel that gets one through. Among processes of well thought-out calculation, I am the science of the self,

enabling one to distinguish between spirit and matter. And among those who debate philosophy, I am the ability to see things in many ways.

25. In the category of women, I am Shatarupa, but among men I am Svayambhuva Manu, her husband. Consider Me Narayana among the sages and Sanat-kumara among celibate students.

26. Among religious duties see me as renunciation, and as for those concepts that allow the heart to be peaceful, I am awareness of the eternal soul. I am the great secrets found in speech and silence, and among beautiful couples I am Lord Brahma [who is here referred to as "a couple" because he brought forth the original beautiful couple, Shatarupa and Svayambhuva Manu, mentioned in the previous verse].

27. There are repetitive cycles of time, and among those I am the year. Similarly, I manifest as spring as well. Among months I am Margashirsha [November–December, an auspicious time of year], and among astrological houses I am the much-desired Abhijit.

28. Among ultimate time cycles, the best age is Satya-yuga, the age of truth, with which I can easily be identified, and among well-known sages I am Devala and Asita. Clearly, I am the divider or editor of the *Vedas*, Krishna Dvaipayana Vyasa, and among noted scholars I am Shukracharya, the knower of the self.

29. Among those who are called Bhagavan I am Vasudeva, or Krishna [the son of Vasudeva], while, you, Uddhava, represent Me among the devotees. In the world of Kimpurushas, I am Hanuman, and among the Vidyadharas I am Sudarshana.

Commentary

The honor of being singled out by Krishna, especially when He is enunciating a sacred list wherein He identifies Himself as first and foremost in all categories, should not go unnoticed. Uddhava is thus the superlative Vaishnava, whom Krishna regards even before Himself as far as devotees go. The "best" devotee is mentioned elsewhere in scripture as Srimati Radharani, Lord Shiva, and few others. Clearly, Uddhava is the member of a very exclusive group, and Krishna is making it clear in this verse.

30. Among magnificent jewels consider Me to be the ruby, and among beautiful ornaments I am the lotus cup. In the realm of fine grass see Me as the sacred *kusha*, used by *yogis* on which to sit as they meditate, and of sacrificial offerings I am *ghee* [clarified butter] and other ingredients that come from the cow.

31. Of those who want to get ahead in life, I am desirable wealth, and among all cheaters I go by the name of gambling. I am the forgiveness of compassionate souls and the many virtues of those who value goodness.

32. I am both bodily and mental strength among those who are powerful, and I am the righteous actions of those who know best. These knowledgeable souls worship Me in nine different forms, though I am the original—Krishna, son of Vasudeva.

Commentary

The Lord appears in numerous incarnations and manifestations. The traditional list of nine mentioned here is one among many: Vasudeva, Sankarshana, Pradyumna, Aniruddha, Narayana, Hayagriva, Varaha, Nrisimha, and Brahma (who is sometimes an ordinary living entity and other times the Lord Himself). Significantly, in this verse, Krishna identifies Himself as the source of all incarnations and manifestations of God with the words *adi-murti* ("primary form").

33. Among the angelic-like Gandharvas I am Vishvavasu, and among the heavenly Apsaras I am Purvachitti. I am the calm, unmoving nature of mountains and the pure-smelling aroma of the earth.

34. The sweet taste of water is My essence, and among things that shine brightly I am the sun. Indeed, the effulgence of luminous objects in the sky, such as the sun, moon, and stars, are My very self, and I am that spiritual sound vibration that moves through the sky.

35. Though there are many who are dedicated to the ways of the Brahmins, I may be identified with Bali, the son of Virochana. Among heroes, please know that I am Arjuna. And in the end, I am the embodiment of all creation, maintenance, and annihilation.

36. I am nondifferent from the five working senses, consisting of the legs, speech, rectum, hands and sex organs, and I can also be identified with the five knowledge-acquiring senses—touch, sight, taste, hearing and smell. In addition, I am the miracle by which each sense object is perceived by the senses.

37. Again, I am form, taste, smell, touch and sound as well as the false conception of the self stemming from the body; I am the subtle basis of all material elements; earth, water, fire, air and sky; the living person within the body; material nature; the modes of goodness, passion and ignorance; and I am the Supreme Lord Himself. In fact, I am all of these elements, along

with the knowledge of exactly what they are and how they function.

38. Because I am the Supreme Lord, I am the source and resting place of all living entities, as well as that of the modes of nature and of the aggregate of material elements. In essence, I am the soul of all, with everything depending upon Me for its existence.

39. While it might be possible to count all the atoms in the universe, My many qualities cannot be counted, for they are infinite.

40. While the following qualities might indeed be wonderful, they are but a fraction of My splendor: power, beauty, fame, wealth, humility, renunciation, pleasure, fortune, strength, tolerance, or realized knowledge.

41. And so now you have heard, in summary, about My mystic opulence, which includes special aspects of My material creation. These are all perceived variously, according to the nature of each individual's mind, with particular circumstances dictating how they are to be defined in each case.

Commentary

The traditional commentators have thoroughly analyzed the Lord's catalogue of qualities as expressed in this chapter, and have divided them into two distinct categories: The first (1) focuses on His spiritual forms, their incarnations, and manifestations; and the other (2) highlights the best aspects of material creation.

The spiritual forms of the Lord come to living beings through revelation, through scripture and the mercy of saintly people. But the material dimensions of the Lord's opulence are dependent on correct perception, and therefore Krishna says that proper understanding depends "on each individual's mind." If one learns how to perceive creation, one can then see Krishna's presence and benefit from it. Otherwise, one remains spiritually blind. The *Uddhava Gita* helps people open their eyes to God's glory, both by the examples Krishna gives in this chapter and by others too numerous to mention.

42. In summary, living beings seeking perfection must control what they say, conquer their minds, manipulate the breath within their bodies, master the senses, and, through properly directed intelligence, bring their course of action under control. If they do this properly, they will never again lose their spiritual direction.

43. A spiritual seeker who does not gain mastery over what he says and how he uses his mental faculties will eventually see that his previous commitment—his vows, austerities, and his ability to

give to others—drips away, just like water from a clay pot that is not thoroughly baked.

44. By surrendering to Me while properly utilizing speech, mind, and the subtle airs within the body, one can develop spiritual devotion (*bhakti*) and fulfill life's purpose.

Commentary

It is here highlighted that spiritual devotion for Krishna is the ultimate goal of life, and that one can achieve this by properly utilizing one's body, mind, and words in His service.

Chapter 11

The Varnashram System

1–2. Sri Uddhava said: My dear Lord, You have already briefly described Varnashram, the social-spiritual system delineated in the Vedic literature, and how both the faithful and those who are not given to religious practices might use this system to execute the principles of Bhakti-yoga. O Lord with the lotus eyes, now please elaborate on how one might use this system in one's personal life, thus achieving devotion for You.

Commentary

Uddhava is referring to casual references to Varnashram in Chapters Four, Seven, and elsewhere in the *Uddhava Gita*. Now Lord Krishna will discuss the topic at length. The idea of *varna*, or social stratification, goes back to the *Rig Veda*, thousands of years prior, and Krishna had explained the system to Arjuna in the *Bhagavad Gita*, mentioning that such social divisions were created by the Lord Himself (4.13), thus claiming for the system divine status. As a creation of the Lord, it occurs naturally in every culture of the world, in some form, to some degree. All societies have intellectual authorities or priests (Brahmins), administrators or warriors (Kshatriyas), mercantile people and farmers (Vaishyas), and a class of workers who are best suited to help the rest (Shudras). In addition, there are natural stages of life wherein one pursues spirituality up until the time of death. Taken as a whole, and in the most general sense, this is Varnashram.

3–4. O mighty-armed Lord, I remember You told me that, in Your form as Lord Hamsa, You conveyed the idea of religious duties to Brahma, the first created being, knowing that such duties are the source of real happiness. But O Madhava (Krishna), those conversations transpired long ago and will soon fade into memory.

5–6. My dear infallible Lord, You are the real creator and protector of religious principles. You know this subject, and all subjects, better than anyone else. I therefore beseech You, my dear Lord, now that You are leaving the earth, please make this knowledge clear.

7. As the supreme knower of all religious truths, who is better positioned to describe to me the actual duties of human beings, and how we might properly execute the path of devotion to You?

8. In this way, Sri Uddhava, king among great souls, asked the Lord a series of questions. In response, Lord Hari (Krishna) articulated the truth of religious principles for the benefit of all souls, both conditioned and liberated.

9. The Supreme Lord said: O Uddhava, because you faithfully ask about eternal religious principles, which are for the ultimate good of everyone, I will explain all that you need to know, and this knowledge will benefit both ordinary human beings and those fortunate enough to be followers of the Varnashram system.

10. In first world age, at the dawn of the millennium, there was only one social class known as *hamsa*, or swanlike souls, and all humans partook of the same godly characteristics. In that age, people were virtually perfect devotees from birth, prompting the learned to refer to this time as Krita-yuga—the age of perfect harmony and spiritual awareness.

Commentary

Commonly known as Satya-yuga, "the Age of Truth," or "the Golden Age," this was a time, millions of years ago, when the Varnashram system was simply not needed. Everyone was naturally pious and functioned according to his or her propensity, always mindful of the greater good of society. Needs were few and people lived long (some texts say that 100,000 years was the average life span), prosperous and focused on God.

This state of affairs, however, would change with Treta-yuga, the next world age, and after one more verse to elaborate on Krita-yuga, Krishna will explain how life devolved as the ages wore on.

11. In Krita-yuga, the sacred syllable OM was the expressed sound of the *Veda*, prior to its division into four separate books. I was the focus of all mental activities, and whatever people did was done as an offering unto Me. At that time, too, I appeared as a four-legged bull, representing religiosity. In this way, those who existed in Krita-yuga, who adored austerity and thrived in a sinless state, knew Me as Lord Hamsa.

Commentary

The bull of *dharma*, or religious duty, is a recurring image in the *Srimad Bhagavata Purana*, particularly in Book One, Chapter Seventeen. As a symbol for spiritual values, the bull stood on all four legs during the Krita-yuga. Later, in the Treta-yuga, however, it would stand only on three, and then on two in the Dvapara Age. Now, in the degraded age of Kali, it stands on one leg. These legs represent austerity, cleanliness, mercy, and truthfulness, respectively, with this latter quality being the only one that remains, and that in compromised fashion.

12. **As time moved on, O greatest among My devotees, Treta-yuga established itself, with Vedic knowledge arising from the very core of My being. Initially, it manifested in three divisions: the *Rig, Sama* and *Yajur Vedas.* From this knowledge, the threefold divisions of sacrifice appeared.**

Commentary

As commonly understood, the one *Veda* was divided into four—but three of these texts, the ones mentioned above, were specifically related to the performance of sacrifice (*yajna*). The fourth is the *Atharva Veda*, a collection of spells, incantations, stories, predictions, and hymns.

13. **At that time, My universal form brought forth the natural social orders: the Brahmins appeared from My face, the Kshatriyas came from My arms, the Vaishyas from My thighs, and the Shudras from My feet. These social divisions can be understood by an individual's activities and aptitudes.**

14. **This same universal form was responsible for creating the ashram divisions of spiritual life: The practices for married couples (Grihasthas) arose from My loins even as the celibate students (Brahmacharis) manifested from My heart. The retired forest-dwellers (Vanaprasthas) came from My chest, and those in the renounced order of life (Sannyasis) emerged from My head.**

15. **Although living beings are endowed with what might be called inferior and superior natures, often manifesting from the time of their birth, what matters are their various talents and inherent natures, for it is these that dictate how they fit into the social divisions of the Varnashram system.**

16. **People who are true Brahmins will manifest these qualities: equal-mindedness, self-control, austerity, cleanliness, peacefulness, tolerance, simplicity, a devotional mood toward Me, mercy, and truthfulness.**

17. Kshatriyas will embody these characteristics: dynamism, physical strength, determination, heroism, tolerance, magnanimity, a pronounced work ethic, consistency, dedication to Brahmins, and powerful leadership.

18. People who are Vaishyas will have faith in tradition, steadiness in giving to charity, freedom from hypocrisy, a tendency to serve Brahmins, and a desire to consistently earn money.

19. Shudras want to serve those who are qualified, including Brahmins and higher beings. They have an inclination for serving cows, too, and they work hard to sustain themselves. Shudras are satisfied with minimal income and live a simple life.

20. But those who insist on functioning outside the Varnashram system are unclean and given to dishonesty, thievery, faithlessness, senseless quarrel, lust, anger and endless desire.

Commentary

The modern world is characterized by these qualities. It might be argued that one need not adhere to Varnashram per se to overcome these lesser traits. But the *Uddhava Gita* teaches that a peaceful mind comes from engaging in divine service according to one's propensity, and that this is, essentially, what is meant by Varnashram. Furthermore, unless one learns how to become so engaged under a qualified teacher (*guru*), it is likely that the less savory qualities mentioned here will rise to the surface more and more, despite the best of intentions. Indeed, unless one's mind is peaceful due to proper engagement in the Lord's service, fully utilizing one's innate, God-given talents and inclinations, havoc invariably will ensue, with the world eventually being overrun by demoniac forces.

21. And all who want to contribute to society must work toward developing these very general principles of piety: nonaggression, truthfulness, honesty, concern for others, and an avoidance of lust, anger and greed.

22. The three higher classes of society (Brahmins, Kshatriyas, and Vaishyas) are said to have achieved "second birth" because they engage in certain "purifying ceremonies," including Gayatri initiation, whereby they are awarded a sacred thread. For some time, such twice-born devotees will reside in their teacher's dwelling, and, in a disciplined way, study the Vedic literature.

23. Traditionally, Brahmacharis will wear deerskin clothes and a straw belt. They often have matted hair, and they carry a walking stick and a waterpot. You can often see them with rosary beads

for chanting and a sacred thread adorning their bodies. They carry their own *kusha* grass in hand, so they need not accept an opulent sitting place from those who want to serve them. In addition, a true Brahmachari is not concerned about the whiteness of his teeth or the quality of his clothes.

Commentary

The image evoked is that of Brahmacharis from days of old. In essence, the principle is that a Brahmachari is focused on chanting and living simply, not necessarily on having matted hair or deerskin clothes. The reference to his not being concerned about white teeth comes from the Sanskrit phrase *adhauta-dad-vasa*, which means that he does not want an alluring smile or nice-fitting garments for the sake of attracting women. The basic principle of celibate student life, then, is simplicity, dedication to God, and avoidance of sexual interaction. All other specifics are meant to facilitate these three things. Otherwise, the minutiae of Varnashram are unnecessary.

24. For Brahmacharis, silence is always a virtue. Accordingly, they should avoid uttering unnecessary sounds while bathing, eating, during Vedic sacrifices, while chanting on rosary, or going to the bathroom. Furthermore, Brahmacharis should not cut their nails or hair—this refers even to the hair under their arms or in pubic areas.

Commentary

Again, this is the traditional model for Brahmacharis living in the forest, usually at the hermitage of their teachers. The essential teaching is that silence is golden, and that a true spiritual practitioner is conscious of all sounds that come out of his mouth—if they facilitate his spiritual life, they are to be embraced, and, if not, they should be avoided. This is the general rule in Bhakti-yoga.

According to the Medieval Vaishnava theologian, Srila Rupa Gosvami, there are six impediments in the performance of *bhakti*, and he lists them all in his work *Upadeshamrita* (Verse Two). Among these he mentions *niyamagraha*, which refers to "following rules and regulations for their own sake, without understanding." Readers of the *Uddhava Gita* are advised to be on guard against such shallow adherence as well. Both, being overattached to rules and regulations or, conversely, neglecting them, are harmful in spiritual practice. One needs to find balance, which comes from good sense and the advice of the sages. The other five impediments to *bhakti* are "to eat too much, or to collect too many material sense objects"; "overendeavor"; "idle talk"; "association with worldly-minded people"; and "ardent yearning or greed for material things."

In Verse 24, Krishna explains the standard approach to Brahmachari life, but He is open to any method that might work. He is not attached to a particular way of doing things. The references to unkempt nails and hair are, again, attempts to ward off the opposite sex. Today, other means might be employed with better results.

In fact, the *Bhagavata* is clear that such teachings should be adjusted according to the needs of each individual, taking into consideration both time and circumstance. In this regard, the *Bhagavata* offers two references, in particular. The first one can be found in sage Narada's instruction to Dhruva Maharaj, in which he mentions the importance of religious duty but specifies that such duties should be executed "while considering time (*kala*), place (*desha*), and attendant conveniences and inconveniences" (4.8.54). The second instance comes from the mouth of Grandsire Bhishmadev, who is one of the most respected religious authorities in the *Bhagavata* (1.9.9): It is said that he welcomed and addressed numerous spiritual masters in a particular holy place—and that he did so according to specific circumstances. He is the expert in adjusting truth according to time and place (*vibhaga-vit*), says the text.

The tradition considers this significant, and the commentators make much of it. The plain fact is this: Spiritual knowledge loses its life if it is not adjusted according to the needs of people in the real world. If it remains an abstraction or a mere principle, it is virtually useless. Only when practically applied, according to time and circumstance, does it have meaning. The same is true regarding the principles of Varnashram—such principles must be adapted according to the wisdom of contemporary spiritualists and the guru, who knows his disciple's psychophysical makeup. Otherwise, Varnashram is relegated to archaic theory, without purpose or effectiveness.

25. A true Brahmachari, attempting a life of celibacy, will never voluntarily ejaculate. If, by chance, his semen spills of its own accord, he should quickly cleanse himself with water, initiate breathing exercises (*pranayama*) for purification, and chant the Gayatri mantra.

26. The Brahmachari, pure and determined, should worship Agni (the fire-god), the sun, the *acharya*, cows, Brahmins, his guru, venerable respect-worthy individuals and higher beings. Observing silence and yet quietly chanting the appropriate mantras, he should perform such worship both when the sun rises and when it sets.

27. The spiritual master and I are one—never disrespect him in any way. Don't envy him, mistaking him as someone ordinary. Know this for certain: he is the sum total of all the demigods.

Commentary

Although Krishna appears to have gone off on a tangent here, He is making clear the importance of the guru in spiritual life, particularly in the life of a Brahmachari. In the next five verses, the Lord will connect the spiritual master's importance to the everyday activities of a celibate student. But this introductory verse is more general, showing how fundamentally significant the bona fide teacher is.

This should be understood in terms of Varnashram as well: All the specific information about Varnashram given in this chapter and in Chapter 12 can be adapted and revised by a bona fide guru, as indicated earlier. Therefore, while the specifics, as revealed by Lord Krishna, certainly had a place in ancient India, it is expected that they will be updated and made relevant by one's teacher, whose primary duty is to express the ancient teachings of the *Vedas* in a contemporary way.

Thus, it becomes clear how fundamentally important it is to have a genuine spiritual master. In fact, if the Brahmachari is negligent in all other forms of worship, as described above, and focuses on worshiping the guru alone—he can still achieve perfection. Therefore, this important verse is meant to underline the unique position of the spiritual master, the *acharya*, who is virtually the center of the disciple's life.

28. **A Brahmachari should beg edibles and other things from local people and offer them to his teacher. Being self-controlled, he should accept nothing for himself, except that which his spiritual master gives to him.**

29. **A humble servant of the spiritual master, the true Brahmachari always walks behind his teacher, showing respect. If the master decides to sleep, the disciple should lie down next to him, when invited. And when the teacher wakes up—there waits the good Brahmachari, ready to massage his master's feet and offer other, similar services. As the teacher sits in his chosen seat, the good disciple waits nearby, showing reverence and waiting for his order.**

30. **In this way, the good disciple should remain busy in his teacher's ashram until his education is complete. While there, he should avoid any form of material sense gratification and should observe strict celibacy.**

31. **Most Brahmacharis seek to attain Maharloka or Brahmaloka—higher planets—after death. If they have any hope of achieving these goals, they must surrender to their spiritual master and be consistent in their vow of celibacy. With this determined state of mind, they must pursue their higher scriptural studies.**

Commentary

The traditional Brahmachari, who follows the *Vedas*, is not necessarily a Vaishnava, that is, he may not be attempting to reach the ultimate goal of life. There are many lesser goals, and the *Vedas* generally direct their votaries in that direction. Most Vedic texts, in fact, hope to elevate people gradually, first by recommending practices that help them rise beyond passion and ignorance, and then by substituting these with other practices that bring them into goodness. These steps sometimes require several lives, and in the process, practitioners may take birth on various heavenly planets as a result of their austerities. Ultimately, however, the *Uddhava Gita*, like the *Bhagavad Gita*, does not encourage this. Rather, it recommends focusing on Krishna, God, and developing a loving relationship with Him by chanting His holy names. If one does this, while following Varnashram, one can immediately be promoted to Krishna's supreme kingdom, which is far beyond both Maharloka and Brahmaloka.

32. Having thus reached the platform of true knowledge by faithfully serving the spiritual master, a Brahmachari is released from all sins, thus overcoming the dualities of material existence. In this purified state, he worships Me as the Indwelling God, noting that I appear everywhere—in fire, in the guru, in one's own heart, and in that of all living beings.

33. Brahmacharis, Vanaprasthas, and Sannyasis—those in ashrams that do not partake of married life—must scrupulously avoid women. Not only should they avoid overt sexual behavior, but they should not glance at, touch, talk to, joke with, or otherwise interact with the opposite sex. In addition, they should avoid all living beings who show signs of sexual appetite, whether human, bird, or beast.

34–35. Here are more general principles to be followed by all members of society: cleanliness, purification rites, bathing, obligatory religious duties at sunrise, mid-day, and sunset, formal worship, pilgrimage, chanting softly on beads, avoiding forbidden things, and remembering that I am present in the hearts of all living entities.

36. When Brahmins commit to the ultimate vow, which is the vow of celibacy, they become effulgent like fire. This allows them to burn away at the tendency to perform material activities. Rising beyond mundane interests in this way, he becomes My devotee.

37. As for Brahmacharis, when they complete their spiritual education they may want to marry in due course. At that time, they should offer something valuable to their teacher, groom themselves properly, and, with the permission of their master, plan for their future.

38. Reacquainting himself with his family home, the Brahmachari should approach householder life with a desire to purify his consciousness. Thinking in this way, if he is serious, he should enter

the forest to perform austerities. Gradually, if he is an advanced Brahmin, he should become a Sannyasi, living according to the rules of the renounced order. It is important to gradually progress from one *ashram* to another, always behaving according to religious principles.

39. **If one wants his marriage to work, he should find a wife whose interests and inclinations are similar to his (*varna*), someone who has a good reputation and is younger in age. Sometimes, a person accepts several wives, but, if he does, the marriage should take place well after the first one, with each sequential wife possessing fewer and fewer of his characteristics.**

Commentary

In Vedic culture it was not uncommon for a man to marry more than one woman. However, this was not encouraged. Even in this verse, we see a subtle attempt to veer Brahmacharis away from marrying more than once: First of all, the person is encouraged to take some time to think about his decision. Secondly, each progressive marriage finds him wedded to a woman who he is less inclined to be with. Traditionally, he was obliged to find a woman from a lower caste, someone with whom he had less in common. This did not, of course, dissuade every man from multiple marriages, but it did give one reason to pause.

40. **Religious sacrifices, study of sacred texts, and giving in charity must indeed be performed by all twice-born men, i.e., Brahmins, Kshatriyas, and Vaishyas. But, amongst these, only Brahmins may accept charity, teach scriptural texts, and perform the actual sacrifices mentioned in the *Vedas*.**

41. **However, if a Brahmin thinks that accepting charity from others will cause him to lose his sense of austerity, inculcating a desire for fame, he should instead embrace the two other occupations of his status, i.e., teaching Vedic knowledge and performing religious sacrifices. And if he fears that even these two activities might sway him from the spiritual path, he should then create a livelihood by collecting rejected grains, without compromising his principles.**

Commentary

Krishna is showing the importance of preserving Brahminical integrity. There are standard duties that a Brahmin must perform. However, if they compromise his position as a spiritual leader, he should reject those activities and adopt others. At no time should he do anything that tempts him or caters to his lower desires. Society depends on him to be spiritually strong, for when Brahmins are compromised, as has often been the case in contemporary India, the whole society goes to hell.

42. **Generally, Brahmins do not have bodies that are appropriate for material sense gratification. Instead, they are better suited to austerities for spiritual advancement. In fact, if a Brahmin chooses this latter path, he knows, he will enjoy unlimited happiness in his next life.**

43. **The Brahminical householder (Grihastha) should gather rejected grains for religious sacrifices, and then he should perform those sacrifices. Purified of material desire, he should be compassionate and empathetic to everyone, always abiding by religious principles and fully absorbed in Me. By observing such practices, even at home, a Brahmin who is unattached to worldly pleasure can easily achieve lasting peace.**

44. **I show special mercy—like a ship that comes to rescue a drowning man—to those dear souls who give aid to twice-born sages. And, make no mistake—the latter, like ordinary people, do sometimes experience suffering.**

45. **A true king, like a protective father, will tend to the needs of his citizens even while he takes care of himself. This is reminiscent of large male elephant, who protects all the smaller elephants in his charge while defending himself at the same time.**

Commentary

Lord Krishna, with Verse 44, concluded his analysis of Brahmins and begins His assessment of Kshatriyas who, in Vedic culture, were associated with the kingly class of men.

46. **One who is a proper king has in mind not only his own welfare but also that of his citizens. As an empowered servant of God, he has the ability to remove sinfulness from his kingdom and, if he does so, he will experience the pleasure of Lord Indra, flying in airplanes that glisten like the sun.**

47. **When Brahmins can't function according to their essential nature, they suffer greatly. If this persists, they may act like Vaishyas, even if they are disinclined to the life of a merchant. If even this proves ineffective, such a person may function as a Kshatriya, engaging himself as an administrative officer. Under no circumstances, however, should he become like a dog, working hard for a lesser master.**

Commentary

Lord Krishna, in His compassion, recognizes that people sometimes experience difficulties even when properly engaged according to Varnashram. Using the example of a distraught Brahmin, He says that such a person might try to function as a Vaishya. Why does He immediately refer to the mercantile class, without even considering that a Brahmin might first choose to be a Kshatriya, which usually is considered higher than a Vaishya? The reason is simple: Brahmins are averse to violence of any kind, and Kshatriyas must necessarily employ combative tactics as part of their profession. That being said, if the life of a Vaishya is inappropriate for the fallen Brahmin, he may choose to act as a Kshatriya, if all else fails. But under no circumstances should he act as a Shudra. This is what Krishna means when He says that they should "not be like dogs working for a lesser master." Again, He is trying to preserve the integrity of Brahminical culture.

48. **So too must a king avoid working as a Shudra at all costs. Indeed, he may, if necessary, function as a Vaishya; earn a livelihood by hunting; or may take the role of a Brahmin.**

49. **Now, a Vaishya, if he needs to, can work as a Shudra, and a Shudra, without proper engagement, can make baskets or straw mats—simple jobs to keep himself busy. Be that as it may, anyone who has taken on a secondary, inferior status because of less-than-desirable circumstances should return to their rightful work when the troubled time is over.**

50. **People who are married (Grihastha) should regularly worship higher beings, sages, the forefathers, and all humans, seeing them as manifestations of Me, in the following way: The sages can be appeased by Vedic study; the forefathers by chanting the mantra *svadha*; the demigods appreciate the chanting *svaha* and all related incantations; all humans should be offered a share of one's meals, and they should be given donations of grains and water. In this way, one should serve all living beings.**

51. **Grihasthas should support their household with funds that come naturally, without much endeavor, or from making an honest living. Although it should never be a burden, one's life should also have room for religious sacrifices and other spiritual duties.**

52. **If there are numerous family members who are dependent on a hard working Grihastha, he should avoid being overly attached to them. In addition, he should not let their dependence go to his head—thinking that they cannot survive without him. If he is wise, he will note that all happiness—before, now, and in the future—is limited and temporary.**

Commentary

This is not to say that a Grihastha should avoid responsibility or be negligent when it comes to those who depend on him. Rather, he should indeed do his duty, but he should also keep perspective about his part in the household. After all, God is the ultimate provider, and the head of family is merely playing a role on God's behalf. He is a servant, and he would do well to keep this in mind, not allowing his preeminent position among his family members to get the better of him. If he remains humble and serves the family in a realistic way, all members benefit and become happy, including him. In fact, all happiness comes from the Lord—it is never really dependent on our material situation, although sometimes it may seem like it is.

The family belongs to God. This is the realization that this verse is meant to evoke. Therefore, Krishna tells Uddhava that a Grihastha should not be attached to his family. He is not referring to natural loving interrelation, or the warm, nurturing feelings that one naturally has for family members. He is referring to the false sense of proprietorship so common among fathers, especially—the false notion that "the family is mine." In essence, Krishna is saying,

> No, don't be attached. Your family actually belongs to Me and they should be engaged in My service. You were born into this body and they were born into theirs. But none of you are actually your bodies. You are spirit souls, part of Me, and your proper engagement is as part of My family.

This is clarified in Verse 53.

53. The relationship between family members—wife, children, relatives, and friends—is comparable to the passing meeting of travelers. Your relationship with them disintegrates in due course. This is especially true once you change your body, the mere act of which will distance you from all your cherished associates. It is similar to possessions cherished in one's dream—upon awaking where are those cherished objects?

54. Because he is conscious of these metaphysical truths, a truly liberated soul will stay at home with the disposition of a guest, without the illusions of proprietorship or inflated sense of self. Accordingly, he remains aloof, without getting unnecessarily entangled in family life.

55. If a person properly worships Me through his family duties, he can remain at home or perform his duties from a holy place. In fact, if he has qualified offspring, he can even take to the renounced order of life.

56. Alternatively, a Grihastha can become attached to his home while entertaining base desires and thus ruining his life. He can exploit his money, wife, and children, womanize to his heart's content, and fall into the foolish illusion, so common in household life, wherein one thinks, "Everything is mine and I am the Lord."

57. "Everyone depends on me," thinks the deluded Grihastha, "my sick, elderly parents, my wife with our newborn baby in her arms, and my other young children, too—they all need me desperately. Without me they will all suffer—I am their only hope. I am the center of everything and nothing can go on without me."

58. Victimized by this illusion, the average Grihastha is deeply attached and never satisfied. Absorbed in familial relations and the sense enjoyment they can bring him, he eventually dies and enters the dark mode of ignorance.

Commentary

These are the three options for a sincere householder: (1) He can remain at home and do his duties from there, with family; (2) he can retire to "the forest," that is, go to holy places and perform his same duties in semirenunciation; or (3) he can take Sannyasa and renounce the world altogether. The main requirement is properly worshipping the Lord, whatever one's station in life.

Chapter 12

Varnashram Continued

1. **The Supreme Lord said: When one becomes a Vanaprastha, which is the third order of life, he should peacefully retire to the forest, either leaving his wife behind in the company of her grown sons or bringing her with him.**

Commentary

Krishna previously explained the *varnas* and Brahmachari life, to some degree, in Chapter Eleven. He now discusses the two higher *ashrams* in some detail—Vanaprastha and Sannyasa. He will briefly address how perfected devotees behave and think. Such persons exist at the pinnacle of the Varnashram system. Indeed, unless one becomes an accomplished devotee, there is no meaning to Varnashram and its procedures and methods become a mere distraction from the ultimate goal of life.

2. **Having made this decision, he should live on simple foods, such as pure bulbs, roots and fruits that grow in his immediate area of the forest. Dressing in ways appropriate for his environment, he should cover himself with tree bark, grass, leaves, or animal skins.**

Commentary

The *Uddhava Gita* outlines what traditional Vanaprastha looks like. In the simple agrarian culture of Vedic times, going off to the forest to live a life of renunciation was quite common. In the modern era, however, certain adaptations may be necessary for most who want to follow this path.

The basic principle is to live simply and to direct one's life toward renunciation. This will prepare one not only for Sannyasa but also for the ultimate stage of renunciation—death—which is when each and every one of us must give up everything we hold near and dear. The entire Varnashram system is meant to prepare us for this ultimate fact of life, which is inescapable and, for most of us, traumatic.

In its essence, then, Varnashram is a scientific procedure for gradually extricating oneself from materialistic life, thus allowing the living being to develop his relationship with the Lord and to face death gracefully.

3. One living in this way should not be concerned about being kempt, either in terms of the hair on his head, body or face, or in regard to the length of his nails. He should evacuate at regular intervals and should not pay close attention to dental hygiene. He should take his obligatory tripartite bath in local rivers and sleep peacefully on the ground.

Commentary

Again, the point is that he is not interested in physical comforts and is preparing for ultimate renunciation. He also is not interested in attracting the opposite sex, and for this reason, he deemphasizes bodily grooming and the various accoutrements of a comfortable life.

4. In this way, a Vanaprastha performs austerities throughout the year: during the hottest summer days and also during the rainy season, when he is obliged to stay outdoors, subjecting himself to severe rainstorms. In the unbearable winter, too, he should remain submerged in water up to his neck.

Commentary

The Vedic system recommends severe penances for those who want to renounce their prior life of sense gratification. The *Vedas* outline a path of gradual elevation through the modes of nature, and practitioners who strive for the heavenly planets, as promoted in the *Vedas*, will attain their goal only by situating themselves in the mode of goodness—which arises due to austerities such as those mentioned in this verse.

The Vaishnava is not interested in such gradual elevation. By worshiping the Lord with love and devotion, one can bypass much of this grueling practice. That being said, the essence, of course, must still be enacted. That is, one must renounce the bodily concept of life and live simply, as recommended here. But such renunciation and simple living need not manifest as extremely as indicated in the verse under discussion (Verse 4).

As the *Uddhava Gita* goes on, it becomes clear that chanting the holy name and observing certain basic regulative principles will yield the same results. This is, after all, Kali-yuga, and because it is a difficult age, wherein people are disqualified in so many ways, the Lord, in His compassion, minimizes requirements for spiritual life and compensates for our lack of spiritual depth.

5. The Vanaprastha may cook foods, such as grains, or eat fruits ripened by time. He may prepare his edibles with mortar and stone or grind it with his teeth.

6. He should go out and personally beg whatever he needs to keep body and soul together, ever mindful of time, place and his ability

to do so. However, he should not consider the future when he collects materials for his sustenance.

Commentary

In traditional Vedic culture, one who practices renunciation, whether Brahmachari, Vanaprastha, or Sannyasi, is advised to be concerned only about his immediate welfare, never planning for future needs or keeping surplus. This is how he cultivates dependence on the Lord, having full faith that he will be provided for. It instills a sense of detachment: "If God wants me to have what I need, He will provide it. If not, then perhaps it is my time to leave this bodily frame and return to Him."

7. **The Vanaprastha should perform religious sacrifices appropriate to the season, making use of rice and other grains found in the forest. But he should never offer Me animal sacrifices, even though such sacrifices are mentioned in the *Vedas*.**

Commentary

The *Vedas* recommend certain animal sacrifices for those seeking elevation to heavenly planets. These outmoded sacrifices were meant for previous ages but are still performed by an unscrupulous Brahmin caste. Nonetheless, Krishna is clear that he never accepts such sacrifices, especially by Vanaprastha and Sannyasis, who are preparing for ultimate renunciation. For such souls, nearing the end of their material sojourn, only vegetarian offerings are recommended, and in this way they can achieve the Supreme destination.

8. **He should regularly enact the standard religious rituals, which he would already be familiar with from his life as a Grihastha. These include the *agnihotra, darsha, chaturmasya*, and *paurnamasa* sacrifices—recommended for Vanaprasthas by all Vedic experts.**
9. **Having undergone untold penances and leading a hard life, the Vanaprastha eventually becomes rail thin and somewhat sickly. But because he worshiped Me and lived a life of dedication, he travels after death to the planet of Maharloka and eventually comes to Me.**

Commentary

Vedic sacrifices lead to heavenly planets, of which Maharloka is quite desirable. Once there, living beings lead pious lives and focus on the essence of spirituality: hearing and chanting the glories of the Lord. Through such hearing and chanting they may perfect the process they began on earth and return to Krishna's Supreme abode.

10. There are those who undertake these difficult austerities simply to achieve sense gratification, which is insignificant when compared to the pleasures of an advanced spiritualist. Those who look for such lesser goals must be considered the greatest of fools.

11. Sometimes old age renders the well-meaning Vanaprastha feeble, and his frail body is no longer able to perform the necessary religious sacrifices. In such a case, he should visualize the sacrificial fire as existing within his own heart by meditation. With this image, focusing on Me, he should enter into the fire and voluntarily accept death.

12. The pious Vanaprastha may eventually realize that even life on Brahmaloka, the highest heavenly planet, is in fact miserable. With this understanding, he can develop complete detachment from all sense gratification. Only with such a state of mind may he move on to the next *ashram*, Sannyasa, the renounced order of life.

13. Having abandoned all one's property and living one's life solely for Me—following the scriptures—one is ready to merge the external fire sacrifice with one's heart. In this way, with a mind full of detachment, one can become a Sannyasi.

Commentary

With this verse, Lord Krishna moves the discussion to that of Sannyasis.

14. Higher beings from the heavenly planets, noting that the Vanaprastha is taking Sannyasa, feel a surge of envy. "Who is this person who is so endearing themselves to the Lord?" With this idea as their focus, the envious demigods test the fledgling Sannyasi by appearing before him as his former wife, as other women, or as various sensual attractions. If he is fortunate, the new renunciant is able to ignore these temptations.

15. Generally, a Sannyasi merely wears *kaupins*, a cloth belt that covers his genitals. However, he may tie other simple garments around his waist and hips as well, but only if he deems it necessary. He should always carry his staff of renunciation (*danda*) and waterpot (*patrabhyam*).

16. If he is truly saintly, he will look carefully at the ground when he walks, trying to avoid the unnecessary killing of living creatures, such as insects, who might be harmed underfoot. Similarly, to avoid harming microscopic entities, he will filter his drinking

water through a portion of his cloth, and his words will not harm, either, for they will possess the purity of truth. With all his actions, in fact, he endeavors to be pure.

17. Be aware, O Uddhava: One is not a Sannyasi merely because he carries bamboo rods (*danda*). Only if he is expert at avoiding useless speech, abandoning activities of sense gratification, and controlling the life air within can he truly be considered a renunciant.

Commentary

Mayavadi Sannyasis usually carry a single staff (*danda*), representing their belief that they have become one with God. Vaishnava Sannyasis, on the other hand, carry a *tridanda*, a combination of three sticks into one carrying staff, which symbolizes their total surrender of mind, body, and words to the Lord.

Krishna confirms the importance of this internal commitment by mentioning them in relation to what Sannyasa really is. Speech must be controlled by chanting and only by talking about spiritual subjects; the body should be controlled by engagement in Krishna's service, not in sense gratification; and controlling the life airs is a yogic way of expressing the need to control the mind. A true Sannyasi has mastered his senses in these three ways.

18. The true renunciant survives by begging, and he may do so by approaching any home occupied by people within the four orders of life. Only avoiding those homes where the degraded and untouchable live, he should proceed with his service, not considering, "Oh, I will get a good meal here and a less opulent one there." Rather, he should just live simply and focus on God.

19. Traveling far from urban areas, one should gather the food he acquired from begging and find a reservoir of water in a secluded place. Then, having cleansed oneself thoroughly, one should willingly distribute the food to others who are nearby, and while doing so he should not utter a word. After this, he can consume whatever remains, without leaving anything over for a future meal.

20. Completely renounced and without any material attachment, the Sannyasi's senses are fully controlled. He is enthusiastic in life and satisfied due to realization of the Supreme Lord. Such a saintly person generally travels alone, seeing everyone equally. Most of all, he is steady in his spiritual practices.

21. Deeply contemplative in a solitary dwelling, his purified mind is constantly absorbed in thinking about Me. He also focuses on the self, realizing that he and I are one.

Commentary

A Sannyasi, by nature, has deep realizations about God, about how he is both the same as and different from all things divine. The Sannyasi knows that he, like all living beings, is one with God in quality but not in quantity. Like drops of water in comparison to the ocean, the living entity partakes of the same spiritual nature as the Lord. God is great, however, and we are small. As the *Uddhava Gita* progresses, it becomes clear that our oneness with God is only one side of the story—the difference between us exists, too, and it is glaring. It is the basis of *bhakti*, or loving devotion to Krishna. This is so because sameness precludes love; difference fosters relationship. It takes two to interrelate. This is the realization of the Vaishnava.

22. By carefully studying the nature of things, an enlightened person can understand why people are trapped in materialistic life and how they ultimately achieve liberation. Such bondage, he knows, comes about because one misuses his senses for selfish enjoyment. These same senses, when properly guided and controlled, will lead to liberation.

23. Consequently, a wise person will master the six senses, which include the mind, by absorbing them in Me, thus experiencing spiritual bliss within his heart of hearts. In this way, he lives without material sense gratification and experiences unending happiness.

24. Although he is inclined to places steeped in goodness, such as those with flowing rivers, forests, and the peaceful solitude of mountainous areas, he will also venture into cities or towns for begging purposes, asking worldly people to help him.

Commentary

The Sannyasi often goes into larger, populated areas, where numerous people work regular jobs, for the sake of *bhikshu-artham*, "begging alms." He, however, is not merely asking for a handout without giving something in return. No. A true Sannyasi gives much more than he takes. Indeed, in exchange for the simple foods or other necessities of life that might be given to him by a successful householder, he shares his considerable wisdom and learning, affording all fortunate souls who come into contact with him a chance to pursue spiritual life. This is the real reason that Sannyasis travel to hellish cities and towns.

25. Vanaprasthas and other renounced mendicants should not shy away from taking charity from others. The very act of accepting things on God's behalf is purifying and allows one to quickly advance in spiritual life.

26. The temporary things of this world should never be confused with ultimate reality. Knowing this, one should refrain from endeavors for material progress, both in this life and the next.

27. **Even in terms of logic, one can see that the material universe and one's own body, composed of mind, speech, and subtle airs—although related to the Lord—are ultimately products of Maya, the Lord's illusory energy. Armed with this knowledge, one should abandon his faith in these things and see them for what they are.**

28. **If one is truly dedicated to the cultivation of knowledge, and is thus detached from material world, or if he is My devotee, who doesn't even want liberation, he becomes disinterested in duties based on external rituals or customs. Indeed, his spiritual interests lay far beyond mere rules and regulations.**

Commentary

This verse and others that follow now describe the topmost devotees, who are mindful of the rules and regulations of scripture but who do not let them rule their lives. Rather, such devotees function according to a higher love. They are naturally absorbed in love of God, observing scriptural rules when they are particularly meaningful. Otherwise, they allow such rules to fall to the wayside in favor of their natural devotion.

Generally, the scriptures guide neophytes so they can gradually make advancement—with the rules and regulations working for the mass of people but not for everyone. Or working for some people at one point in their lives but then becoming a mere distraction at some other point. Again, one should be mindful of the *niyamagraha* principle—attachment to rules and regulations without deep understanding, or neglecting them for the same reason. Expert devotees and spiritual mentors therefore are needed to help one assess just where one stands in relation scriptural mandates.

A short note on the comment that Krishna's devotees are not interested in liberation: This is the distinguishing quality of advanced Vaishnavas. Although other spiritual practitioners are looking for relief from material miseries or promotion to higher planetary systems (both are considered forms of liberation), the devotee wants only service to Krishna, whether Krishna treats him roughly by His embrace or makes him broken hearted by not appearing before him. True love wants nothing in return, and, for the devotee, or one practicing Bhakti-yoga, this includes liberation.

That being said, devotees do, of course, want ultimate liberation—that is, relishing with Krishna a life of love in the spiritual world, where they serve Him in one of several intimate relationships forevermore.

29. **In many ways, the greatest of devotees, although vastly learned, is like a child, unconcerned about honor and dishonor. He enjoys life in a simple way, and although he knows what he's doing, he sometimes behaves as if he doesn't. Although he has great knowledge, he sometimes speaks like a fool; and while learned in Vedic texts, he can easily appear like he never read a book in his life.**

30. Such a great soul never engages in the fruitive rituals mentioned in the *Vedas*, nor does he become an offender, acting or speaking in opposition to spiritual principles. In addition, he never partakes of mundane arguments or becomes a skeptic.

31. One who sees things as they are never lets others frighten or disturb him, nor does he frighten or disturb other beings. He is tolerant of insults and never says harsh words to others. Indeed, there is no animosity found in him, for he has shrugged off all animalistic tendencies that arise due to identification with the body.

32. In the same way that the moon is reflected in innumerable bodies of water, the Supreme Lord, although one, is found within the hearts of all. And this is also true: Every material body, which is many, is made up of God's energy, which is one.

Commentary

This verse is related to the preceding one: If we are all of one substance, embodying that same one Supreme Lord, who is situated in our hearts, why should we entertain enmity or bickering in any form? This is why the realized soul has no animosity for others, or why he has no harsh words for the people around him—he recognizes his spiritual bonding with all that is. We are all brothers and sisters under God's fatherhood.

33. A self-realized soul is even-minded: He is not angry when denied his preferred foodstuffs, nor does he rejoice when offered the foods he likes. Being steady in either case, he understands that God is in control and takes solace in that.

34. His main reason for getting sufficient food is to maintain proper health. For he knows: When the senses, mind, and subtle airs within the body function as they should, one has better facility to focus on spiritual truth. And this, of course, leads to liberation.

35. One who is wise will accept whatever food, clothing or other necessities come by the will of God, without considering if they are of good or bad quality.

36. In the same way that I, the Supreme Lord, play My role as God according to My own free will, those with true spiritual knowledge will naturally keep themselves clean and follow the regulative duties of spiritual life, not because it's mandatory but because they want to.

37. Such a spiritually gifted soul sees Me in everything, without lines of demarcation, for his realized knowledge has destroyed all

shreds of illusion. Even if, due to the nature of his body or mind, he seems to fall back into the world of misperception, in the end, when death comes, he will enjoy qualities not unlike Mine.

38. If one desires spiritual attainment but is unaware of how I might be realized, he should approach a bona fide spiritual master and in this way learn the truth. The main thing is that he must be detached from sense gratification, knowing that it leads to misery. With this as a basis, he has a chance for self-realization.

39. If a devotee continues with great faith to render personal service to his spiritual master, who in essence is nondifferent from Me, he will soon clearly realize the truths of spiritual perfection.

40–41. There are certain things no Sannyasi should ever do, and if he does do them he is to be considered a deviated practitioner, without hope for redemption in this life or in the next: (1) Lose control over the six forms of illusion [lust, anger, greed, material excitement, pride in the body, and compromised awareness]; (2) utilize intelligence for materialistic purposes; (3) minimize the importance of knowledge and detachment; (4) become a Sannyasi just to make a living; (5) deny the presence of higher angelic beings or the Supreme Lord, especially as they exist within himself; and (6) to again become infected by material misconceptions.

42. Sannyasis should focus on equal-mindedness and nonaggression; Vanaprasthas on austerity and the distinction between the body and the self. The central charge for Grihasthas is to be compassionate to all living beings and to perform religious sacrifices; while Brahmacharis should render menial service to the spiritual master.

43. A Grihastha should practice celibacy, though he can, of course, engage in sex at the appropriate times of the month, when his wife might easily get pregnant. He should also practice austerity, cleanliness of mind and body, simple satisfaction, and friendship toward all living beings. And like all others, of course, regardless of his social or status-of-life considerations, he should worship Me.

44. The fruits of worshiping Me according to prescribed duty (Varnashram) are obvious: If you have no other object of worship, and if you remain always conscious of Me, especially as I exist in the hearts of all living entities, you will, in the end, develop your pure devotion (***bhaktim***) for Me.

Commentary

The ultimate goal of Varnashram is mentioned in Verse 44, and it is extremely important: It should lead to devotional service to Krishna. This means that all of the specific duties Krishna mentions throughout these chapters on Varnashram are meant to evoke a particular result. To whatever degree this result is being achieved, the system should be embraced. And to the degree that it is not, it can be discarded. Varnashram is a method, not a goal. The goal is love for Krishna. Such love pleases the Lord greatly, and pleasing Krishna is the underlying purpose of Varnashram.

This conclusion is repeated throughout the *Bhagavata Purana*, as summarized in Verse 1.2.13: "O best among the twice-born, it should be understood that the highest perfection one can achieve by discharging one's occupational duties according to Varnashram is to please Hari, the Personality of Godhead (*hari-toshanam*)." Thus, it is clear that if the pleasure of the Lord is not the outcome of one's involvement in the social system expressed here, the entire enterprise is a waste of time, with practitioners never realizing its intended fruits.

45. O Uddhava, as the ultimate cause of everything, I am the Supreme Lord. I create and destroy all universes, for I am the Absolute Truth. And I promise you this: One who worships Me with unswerving devotional service will come to Me in the end.

46. Make no mistake, one who has purified his existence through Varnashram, who fully understands Me as God, and who is learned in both the scriptures and in realized knowledge, will achieve Me in the near future.

47. Those who accept spiritual principles according to standard religious traditions will naturally embrace Varnashram. But their practice of the system must be dedicated to Me in loving service, for only this will grant them ultimate perfection.

Commentary

Krishna repeats the real goal of Varnashram: If it doesn't lead to His loving service (*bhakti*), it is not realizing its intended purpose.

One may wonder why this explanation appears so late in the text. In fact, this is not the first time Krishna explains things indirectly, without getting right to the point. His method in various parts of the *Uddhava Gita* is clearly roundabout. For example, in Chapter Eight, Verse 31, Uddhava asks the Lord how one should meditate on Him. Krishna answers not by saying, "Just look at Me—here I am, standing right in front of you." Instead, He describes the system of Raja-yoga, and only after elaborating at some length, does He explain that one should meditate on His four-armed Vishnu form, as He appears in the heart of all souls and in the core of every atom.

Or, to cite another example, in Chapter 11 (Verse 7, to be exact), when Uddhava asks about religious truth, duty, and the best way to practice devotion, Krishna neglects to directly mention the science of Bhakti-yoga, which is the most immediate and effective way of serving Him. Rather, He explains Varnashram at some length, continuing on to this chapter and the verses immediately preceding this one. Why does He do this?

There are two reasons for Krishna's indirect method, as proffered by the great teachers of the Vaishnava tradition: (1) "The Time-Appropriate Factor." Krishna was speaking to Uddhava in historical context. The people of His day were deeply involved in both Raja-yoga and Varnashram, and so He deigned to explain ultimate truths to His devotee in a way that would be meaningful to His contemporaries. This leads to the second explanation: (2) "The Everybody Motif." The commentators of both the *Bhagavad Gita* and the *Uddhava Gita* tell us that Krishna revealed the truths of these texts not just for His immediate interlocutors—Arjuna and Uddhava, respectively—but for everyone. That being the case, it makes sense that He would explain the details of traditional systems of knowledge, such as yoga and Varnashram, for these would be useful to one and all. And then, after all is said and done, He reveals the truths of *bhakti*, which is clear from the last chapter of the entire *Uddhava Gita*, which is indeed called "Bhakti-yoga."

48. O saintly one, because you have asked, I have explained to you how My devotee, by engaging in his individual prescribed duty, can become reestablished in consciousness of Me—which everyone should invariably do, for I am Supreme.

Commentary

The great Vaishnava teachers throughout history have endorsed Varnashram as a "scientific" method for attaining the Supreme, meaning that if one follows its procedures and practices, under the directions of a bona fide spiritual master, one undoubtedly will attain love for God. That being said, it also should be clear that the specifics of Varnashram must be adapted, with wisdom, according to time, place, and circumstance. Thus, a bona fide guru is essential for the proper functioning of the system.

Srila A. C. Bhaktivedanta Swami Prabhupada (1896–1977), arguably the foremost Vaishnava guru of the modern era, made clear the importance of adaptation and change in his now famous talks with Russian Indologist Professor Kotofsky. When the professor asked him if he intended to introduce the ancient Varnashram system in contemporary society, the Swami told him that he did not, but rather that he was simply interested in taking the best of the original idea. This mood of contemporary awareness and selective application are necessary if the Varnashram system is to prove useful in the modern age.

Chapter 13

Perfect Spiritual Knowledge

1. **The Supreme Lord said: A truly knowledgeable person, well-versed in the scriptures and far beyond the tendency to misinterpret them, will naturally understand the illusory nature of the material universe. Such a person should bequeath to Me all previous knowledge as well as the methods by which he attained it.**

Commentary

Krishna is basically saying that the cultivation of knowledge eventually will lead to Him, but, He is also saying that, once having attained that knowledge, one should surrender to His lotus feet, understanding that very act to be the essence of all wisdom. In other words, knowledge can take you only so far. And when you realize that Krishna is everything, you should relinquish previous methods in favor of His service, cultivating further knowledge, not for its own sake, but for service to Krishna.

2. **If one truly has knowledge, I become his sole focus and Lord. He then realizes that I am the reason he exists, his means for achieving the ultimate goal of life, and the absolute end of all knowledge. In fact, he comes to see Me as his only purpose for being, knowing well that I am the cause of his happiness and his freedom from pain.**

3. **Those special souls who have thoroughly achieved perfection through philosophical acumen and practically applied knowledge recognize My lotus feet to be the supreme goal of transcendence. Such a person is most dear to Me, and by his perfect knowledge we both abide in unending happiness.**

Commentary

The Sanskrit words *padam sreshtham* ("My lotus feet are the supreme goal") are significant in Verse 3. First of all, readers should know that Krishna's feet are celebrated throughout the Puranas and the Epics as being "lotus-like." The reasons for this are numerous. Primarily, His feet are compared to a lotus because, even though the lotus might grow on a muddy lake, its stem rises above the mud, allowing it to blossom in the clean air, free from the contaminating filth just below the surface. Similarly, Krishna's feet symbolize His ability to appear among us and yet still transcend the modes of nature, untouched by the contaminants of the material world. His feet are also compared to lotuses because they are indescribably soft, like the petals of the flower in question.

Most important, perhaps, this verse flies in the face of Mayavadi commentators, who sometimes argue that it is not the person Krishna to whom we should surrender but rather to the unborn within each of us, or perhaps to some impersonal void or an abstract Godhead without substance or form. Mention of Krishna's feet should lay all such interpretations to rest. He has feet, He has a transcendental form, and He has love—all traits that can be found in a personal Godhead, but *not* in some nebulous, otherworldly abstraction.

4. **Although performing penance, visiting sacred places, softly chanting on beads, giving in charity, and performing other pious works is no doubt laudable, such activities cannot compare to even a small amount of genuine spiritual knowledge.**

5. **That's why I say to you, O Uddhava: The cultivation of knowledge is valuable in understanding who you really are. Still, having attained some modicum of clear realization in this way, you should worship Me with great devotion.**

Commentary

Krishna is praising the cultivation of knowledge as a step toward self-realization. But He also is saying that when one becomes aware of His preeminent position, as the Lord of all and as existing both inside and outside of everything, one would do well to abandon previous methods and to surrender to Him with a heart of devotion. Thus, Bhakti-yoga is the ultimate path recommended by Krishna, even after giving so many instructions with respect to Varnashram, yoga, and so forth.

6. **The sages of bygone years, through performance of Vedic sacrifice, became knowledgeable and even enlightened. They worshiped Me within themselves and as the essence of their religious rituals. In this way, they achieved the ultimate goal.**

7. **O Uddhava, the three modes of material nature are what the material body and mind are composed of. They enter into your sense of being and remain there for some time, but they are actually an illusion, and you can know this is so because they have**

only temporary existence as part of you—they are not who you really are. Indeed, the body goes through various transformations, from birth to death, revealing that it has no relation to your eternal self. The phases of bodily existence began at a particular time, and they will end at a particular time as well. Thus, the body exists merely at the present moment but has no substance in terms of ultimate reality.

Commentary

Krishna is showing, in terms of logic, how the self is different than the body. He had explained this truth at length to Arjuna in the *Bhagavad Gita* and now does so again to Uddhava in various parts of this text. Clearly, this is an important teaching for Him, since He repeats it so often. Indeed, spiritual life begins with an awareness of the self as different from the body. If one does not have at least a glimmer of this realization, it becomes difficult to progress on any spiritual path.

8. **Sri Uddhava said: Please—O Lord of the universe!—explain to me how one can cultivate detachment from material things and thus gain direct perception of higher reality. I want to know all related spiritual truths, as revealed by the great philosophers from days gone by. I know for a fact that this knowledge, which even spiritually advanced souls are always seeking, involves loving devotion unto You.**

Commentary

Uddhava expresses his realization that by cultivating genuine detachment from material things one can acquire spiritual realization, thus directly perceiving the kinds of truths Krishna is talking about, beginning with the realization that the body is not the self. He further confirms that this knowledge culminates in Bhakti-yoga, or loving devotion toward the Lord.

9. **Since living beings are naturally tormented, O Lord, by the terrors associated with birth and death, which are exacerbated by the threefold miseries of material existence, their only real shelter is Your two lotus feet, which can be compared to an umbrella that showers nectar.**

Commentary

The threefold miseries of material existence are (1) those caused by one's own body and mind; (2) those caused by other people (or creatures); and (3) those caused by natural calamities, and so on. Uddhava is clear: Our bleak sojourn in this world is punctuated by moments of relief, but even these are ultimately few and far between as the death of loved ones, and eventually our own death, brings to an end any semblance of happiness the material world has to offer.

Illusion keeps us hoping for it nonetheless, whispering in our ears, "Oh, you know it's not so bad." But the reality of material existence is harsh, and it subsides only when one takes shelter of Krishna, whose soothing lotus feet defeat all material miseries, for they are the harbinger of real happiness.

The image of an umbrella that drips nectar may be difficult to understand. Envision a rainy day as you walk out into the street with your large umbrella. It is a terrible downpour, but your handy collapsible canopy, as it were, protects you from the heavy shower. Still, you notice on each edge of your umbrella small raindrops dripping down, creating a stream of water on all sides. This is the image the analogy in Verse 9 is meant to evoke, with the added fact that, because it is Krishna's feet we are talking about, the dripping comes from sweet nectar, not mere water. The analogy is illuminating, for love of Krishna is like the most wonderful, refreshing rainfall, bringing life to all sincere souls.

10. The serpent known as time has bitten me, O almighty Lord, and so I pray for Your mercy, that You may uplift me, a hopeless soul, who has fallen into the darkness of material existence. Despite this pitiable state of affairs, or perhaps because of it, I passionately hanker after all forms of happiness. Please rescue me, my Lord, by pouring down the nectar of Your knowledge, which leads to liberation.

Commentary

Uddhava humbly depicts himself as a typical conditioned soul as a way of expressing their plight. Their situation is not pretty. They are victims of time, which kills them in due course. Because of intense misery, they relentlessly seek all forms of sense pleasure, which always remains just a few feet away, beckoning, like a donkey with a carrot dangling in front of its head.

In India, to get donkeys to do their work, farmers often tie a stick with a carrot over the animal's nose. As it moves forward to get the carrot, the stick makes the carrot move in commensurate fashion, while the donkey, as a result, carries the heavy load the farmer attaches to its back. In a similar way, human beings carry the burden of sense gratification on their backs, thinking that with every step their ideal situation will arise, and that the carrot will be theirs for the taking. Such an ideal situation never takes place in the material world.

Rather, through knowledge, one becomes liberated from material existence, and this is the beginning of true happiness. Then, through surrender to God, one can perfect one's existence and know the carrot of freedom, wherein one no longer works hard like a donkey but instead revels in pastimes of love with the Lord in the spiritual realm.

11. The Supreme Lord said: This reminds Me of a conversation that took place years ago—King Yudhishthira, who is without enemies, inquired in a similar vein from Grandfather Bhishma, one of the greatest spiritual leaders of all time, as we all carefully listened.

Commentary

This verse refers to the story in the *Mahabharata*, when Bhishma was lying on a bed of arrows, preparing to die. All the remaining participants in the Kurukshetra war gathered around to hear his profound words of wisdom. The philosophy that ushered forth from his lips at that time is preserved not only in the Epic but also elsewhere in the *Bhagavata Purana* and in other Puranas as well.

12. Toward the end of the great Battle of Kurukshetra, King Yudhishthira was overcome by the massive toll the war had taken on his family and loved ones. Thus, he carefully listened to Bhishma's many words on spiritual truth, and when it was over, he asked a question of his own: about the path of final release, liberation, or *moksha*.

13. Listen closely as I reveal to you the same divine knowledge we heard that day from Sri Bhishma, for it leads to detachment, self-realization, and devotional love.

14. I support this knowledge fully, for by understanding it properly, an aspiring spiritualist learns to see in all living beings the combination of nine, eleven, five, and three elements. Moreover, they learn to see the ultimate "one element" within those twenty-eight.

Commentary

The initial nine elements are the sum total of all material components (*mahat-tattva*), material nature itself, the living being, the false conception of identifying with the body, and the five objects of sense perception: sound, form, touch, taste, and aroma. The next eleven elements are the five active senses: voice, hands, legs, rectum, and genitalia; the five feed-in senses: the ears, eyes, nostrils, tongue, and the tactile sense; and the mind, which is central for the activation of these senses. The next five are the five gross elements: earth, water, fire, air, and ether; and the final three are the modes of nature: goodness, passion, and ignorance. All material bodies are made up of these components. The one in the center of it all is Paramatma, the Lord in the heart, who gives life to all that lives.

15. As if clearly seeing these twenty-eight material elements is not enough, there comes a time when one can see the essence of all existence—the ultimate truth that lay beyond these elements. Such a

person sees the ultimate cause itself, which is the Supreme Godhead. When one is able to do this, he has achieved self-realization.

16. **Origin, maintenance, and destruction are the basic phases of all things material. The one thing that consistently accompanies all these material phases from one creation to another, remaining aloof and constant when all material phases have come and gone, is the one eternal truth.**

Commentary

The Vedic literature assigns deities to these phases: Brahma for creation, or origin, Vishnu for maintenance, and Shiva for destruction. These are manifestations of the Supreme, meant for specific aspects of material life. Because maintenance is ultimately the nature of spirit (it is eternal, always subsisting), Vishnu is the essence of the Godhead, and proper worship culminates in surrendering to Him.

The one eternal truth mentioned in Verse 16, of course, is God, who manifests variously as described above. All living beings, in fact, are part and parcel of God, tiny sparks of this one truth, whose best interest lay in becoming reunited with Him (*yoga*) through love and devotion.

17. **There are four ways by which one can understand the temporary, insignificant nature of the material world—direct experience, traditional wisdom, logical argument, and Vedic knowledge. By applying any of these methods, one can become detached from the duality of mundane life.**

18. **Anyone who is genuinely thoughtful can see the temporary nature of all things material and that misery must then necessarily reign even on the highest of heavenly planets. Just consider: If all that you've seen in your life is temporary, the rest of the material universe must also have a beginning and an end.**

19. **O sinless one, because you have deep affection for Me, I have already explained to you the secrets of Bhakti-yoga. But because it is so important, I will again explain this topmost process of God-realization for you.**

20–24. **Hear from Me the actual principles of Bhakti-yoga, the mere knowing of which begins one on the path of developing love for Me: Firm faith in hearing about My exploits, call-and-response chanting of My name and fame, determined attachment to My ceremonial worship, glorifying Me with beautiful hymns, deep respect for those who serve Me, using one's body for bowing down to Me, performing opulent** worship of My devotees, seeing Me in all living beings, offering one's everyday activities to My service, poetically using words to describe My characteristics, offering one's thoughts to Me, neglect of one's material desires, giving up wealth if it can't be used in My service, avoiding material sense gratification and its so-called pleasures, and performing all religious activities, like giving in charity and performing austerities with the purpose of achieving Me. These are the activities of My devotees.

25. If one's consciousness is peaceful, a quality that is always enhanced by the mode of goodness, it is easy to focus on the Supreme Lord. In that state of mind, one achieves religiosity, knowledge, detachment, and power.

26. However, if one's consciousness is absorbed in the material body and its extensions, like home, family, and other, similar objects of sense gratification, he will spend all his time chasing shadows—material pleasures that ultimately cause him pain. Thus, when one's consciousness is overtaken by the mode of passion, he finds himself addicted to temporary things, and these lead him to irreligion, ignorance, attachment, and a generally dissatisfied state of being.

27. For religious principles to be legitimate, they must lead to ***bhakti***, or devotional service. Similarly, real knowledge must reveal My presence in all things. Know this, too: Real detachment is complete indifference to material sense gratification, and real opulence consists of yogic powers, such as ***anima-siddhi***, in which one can make oneself smaller than an atom.

28–32. Sri Uddhava said: Please, O Krishna, O chastiser of the enemy, tell me of the ***yamas*** and the ***niyamas***, the ethical obligations, things to be avoided and things to be embraced. Also, my Lord, what exactly is mental equilibrium, self-control, tolerance and steadfastness—and how do these impact one's spiritual practices? How would You define charity, austerity, and heroism, and how are we to understand reality and truth? What is renunciation, and what is true wealth? What is it we should want in life, what is sacrifice, and what can one expect from religious practice? O Krishna, My beautiful Lord with gorgeous hair, how is one to understand true strength, opulence, and profit? What are real education, humility, and beauty? How do we define happiness and sadness? Who is learned, and who not? Which is the right way to go, and which the wrong, and what are heaven and

hell? What is a true friend, and how do we determine if a place is really our natural dwelling—our real home? Who is rich and who is poor? Who is well off, and who is not? O Lord of the devotees, I am curious about all these things and so much more.

Commentary

Devotees are deep thinkers. They wonder about things that most people take for granted: Is someone poor merely because he has no money, or rich because he can purchase whatever he likes? Is formal education a sign of knowledge, and can a dropout actually be wise? Does a smiling face mean one is happy, and does a frown necessarily imply sadness? Does religious ritual bring one closer to God, or is a pure, simple heart more in line with what the Lord actually wants from us? Such questions are endless and thought-provoking. Uddhava, as a deeply contemplative person, places such questions before Krishna, the Lord, for only He can answer them in an absolute way, without hedging or compromise.

33–35. The Supreme Lord said: Non-aggression, truthfulness, not coveting or stealing the property of others, detachment, humility, freedom from possessiveness, trust in religious principles, celibacy, quietude, steadiness, forgiveness and fearlessness are twelve very important religious principles. Internal cleanliness, external cleanliness, chanting the holy names of the Lord, austerity, sacrifice, faith, hospitality, worship of Me, pilgrimage, functioning and desiring only for spiritual purposes, satisfaction, and service to the spiritual master are twelve prescribed duties. These twenty-four, taken together, bestow numerous benedictions upon those fortunate individuals who consciously adhere to them.

Commentary

Traditional yoga offers the world, among other things, its famous *yama-niyama* ("restraints-observances") list, which is not all that different from the catalog of qualities Krishna enunciates. In most Indic texts, this list, with some variation, is described as the first two of Raja-yoga's eight limbs—representing the fundamental ethical codes of Hinduism and the foundation for all spiritual progress. The list appears in numerous scriptures, including Patanjali's *Yoga-sutras*, the *Shandilya Upanishad, Hatha Yoga Pradipika*, the *Tirumantiram* of Tirumular, and so on. All the above texts list ten *yamas* and ten *niyamas*, with the exception of Patanjali's *sutras*, which lists only five of each. Here, Krishna lists twenty-four as a partial answer to Uddhava's question. He will elaborate in upcoming verses.

36–39. If you want to know what mental equilibrium is, it is simply this: absorbing the intelligence in Me. Complete discipline of the senses is self-control. Tolerance requires patiently enduring the inevitable reverses of material existence, and steadfastness only manifests when one masters the tongue and genitals. The greatest charity consists of giving up all aggression toward others, and if you want to practice real austerity, renounce any shred of lust that remains in your heart. Real heroism is when one conquers his unfortunate tendency to enjoy material life, and reality means seeing Me everywhere and in everything. Truthfulness is not merely saying what we know to be true but also expressing that truth in a pleasing way, for this is what our sages have taught us. Cleanliness means being detached from material enjoyment, whereas renunciation can be found in the Sannyasis who live according to the rules of their ashram. Real wealth for human beings is religiosity, though few people know this, and I, the Supreme Lord, am at the heart of real sacrifice. One is achieving the real fruits of religion if they are developing devotion to the spiritual master, and real strength comes from the *pranayama* system of breath control.

Commentary

Krishna is succinctly answering all of Uddhava's questions. He is giving the essence of each answer, leaving elaboration in the hands of each individual's guru. As one studies this text under a qualified spiritual master, Krishna's responses are fleshed out so that the entire theology of Vaishnavism can be easily understood and presented as an inspirational system of knowledge.

40–45. Actual opulence, in its fullness, only manifests in Me, since I am the Supreme Lord—much is known about My essential six (strength, beauty, wealth, fame, knowledge, and renunciation). The ultimate goal in life is devotional service to Me, and actual education consists of eradicating the false conception of the self—the misperceived notion that the living entity is in fact the material body. Real modesty arises when one is disgusted with impious behavior, and beauty is actually not something visual but good qualities, such as detachment. Real happiness only comes to those who can transcend the dualities of happiness and distress, and misery arises when one is addicted to finding sex partners. A wise man is one who knows how to become free from material bondage, whereas a person who is unwise identifies with his

material body and mind. Where should one want to go in life? Any path that leads to Me. What path should one not take? The path that leads to sense gratification, for such a path causes bewilderment in one's consciousness. Actual heaven manifests when there is a predominance of the mode of goodness, whereas hell rises to the fore when ignorance predominates. Who is everyone's truest friend? I am, of course, for I accompany each living entity wherever he goes. And one's real home, I have to tell you, is the human body. My dearest Uddhava, one who has good qualities is actually a rich person, and one who has few, being dissatisfied in life, is actually poor. A person who cannot control his senses is the person who is not well off, whereas one who is not attached to sense gratification has everything in life. Indeed, sense gratification transforms a person into a slave—a slave of the senses. In this way, O Uddhava, I offer you summary answers in regard to your inquiries. But understand this: there is no need for Me to go into more detail, nor is it even desirable, for to overanalyze these dualities of good and evil is itself a sort of evil. The best course of action is to transcend such dualities and simply surrender unto Me with a pure heart steeped in devotion.

Commentary

Some of Krishna's answers might be surprising, especially for those trained in Vaishnava thought. For example, in response to Uddhava's question about what constitutes a person's true home, Krishna tells us that it is the body. Clearly, in the ultimate analysis, the body is not our real home—it is temporary and, if a "home" at all, it is one from which we will soon be evicted. Vaishnava theology, and that of the *Bhagavata Purana* more generally, teaches that our original home exists in the spiritual world, in Krishna's Supreme kingdom far beyond material existence. So why, then, would Krishna tell Uddhava that the material body is to be considered his home?

The answer to this conundrum involves Krishna's overall strategy, and it can be perceived throughout the *Uddhava Gita*. The Lord tends not to give ultimate answers to any of Uddhava's questions, not immediately at least. Rather, He adopts a stepwise method, so that even fledgling spiritualists can absorb and benefit from His instructions and then move on to more advanced levels of spiritual perfection.

For example, when asked how He is to be visualized, as already described, Krishna launches into an elaborate explanation of yoga and how the *yogi* comes to see Him in his heart of hearts. Or when asked about how to worship Him, He explains Varnashram and the sociopolitical system of ancient India. These are not direct answers. Krishna simply could have described His supreme form, standing right there in front of Uddhava, or the process of Bhakti-yoga, which is the most direct method of attaining His grace. To be sure, these truths come out as the *Uddhava Gita* goes along, both in verses peppered throughout the text and in its culminating chapter on devotional mysticism. But Krishna is clever in how He reveals these truths, with a plan to bring all levels of spiritual seekers to the ultimate path of Bhakti-yoga.

One might think of the body as one's "ultimate home" in the initial stages of spiritual life, just to become comfortable with the idea that one is not the body but rather a spiritual soul inhabiting the body. In due course, however, when one's existence as spirit is thoroughly assimilated, the developing practitioner should learn to see his ultimate home as Krishna's kingdom in the spiritual world.

Chapter 14

Loving Devotion Surpasses Karma-yoga and Jnana-yoga

1. Sri Uddhava said: O lotus-eyed Lord, You are the Supreme Godhead, and I never doubt Your words. But all religious scriptures speak in terms of positive and negative injunctions, and by observing the good and bad qualities of a given action, we ordinary souls are able to understand Your desires.

Commentary

Uddhava continues the conversation that began in the final verse of Chapter Thirteen. Krishna had told him that he should not overanalyze the distinctions between good and evil and instead should just surrender unto Him. Uddhava obviously found this interesting and wanted Krishna to elaborate. After all, Uddhava reasoned, all religious injunctions are based on good and bad, advising votaries to embrace good acts and reject bad ones.

2. Vedic texts are clear that material nature is full of variety: Superior and inferior natures, for example, make Varnashram work, even when there are mixed marriages and the offspring is unpredictable. In this way, righteous and sinful modes of living are inescapable components in our everyday lives. Indeed, the *Vedas* themselves refer to heaven and hell, which are post-death destinations based on pious or impious behavior.

Commentary

Uddhava continues his argument, hoping to instigate a lengthy response. He wants Krishna to clearly explain devotional surrender, and how it is transcendental to all good and bad action. He realizes that Krishna's words can be confusing: If scriptures and other religious authorities speak in terms of good and bad, how is it that the Lord is now saying that good and bad are opposite sides of the same coin, and that transcendence has nothing to do with them, for they are merely dualities in the material world.

A brief explanation: Matter is engulfed in duality—good and bad—but spirit is beyond both. True spirit involves service to Krishna, and nothing more. Whereas good and bad (pious and impious) are merely relative terms, applying to the world of three dimensions, Krishna's service is transcendental to this world. Distinguishing between good and bad acts in fact will help one reach a certain level of material goodness, and therefore they are recommended in the scriptures. But when one graduates to the platform of advanced goodness, he must move beyond the dualities of this world and become engaged in Krishna's fully spiritual service. This is the main point of this verse.

Additionally, Krishna's minimization of the dualities of existence, particularly that of right and wrong, or good and bad, should not be misunderstood or taken out of context. The fledgling spiritualist, especially, should consider it mandatory, in fact, to follow scriptural teachings and the moral and ethical codes found therein. Such adherence allows one to reach the level of goodness. Why is this important? Because goodness promotes honesty and integrity. When one surrenders to Krishna and deemphasizes the rules and regulations of scripture, it becomes easy to feign advancement on the spiritual path, exploiting one's status in the community of devotees and the assets that come with spiritual seniority. Thus, if passion or ignorance predominate in a given devotee's life, it is not uncommon that impious behavior will again rise to the fore, causing compromise and the ruination of spiritual progress.

3. **If one doesn't acknowledge distinctions between righteous behavior and sin, Uddhava continued, how can he understand Your instructions as revealed in scriptural texts? These sacred writings suggest that one act in a pious way, avoiding sin at all costs. Indeed, these authorized scriptures must be respected, for they lead to liberation.**

4. **My Lord, the scriptures help us understand realities beyond our sense perception—whether general esoteric subjects, liberation, or the attainment of heaven. Therefore, all progressive beings naturally consult Vedic texts, for here they will find Your own laws, which comprise the highest truths and the most profound revelations.**

Commentary

Uddhava glorifies the Vedic scriptures to bolster his case: The sacred texts of India, which, it is often argued, are more comprehensive than other religious scriptures, convey truth in terms of good and bad, pious and impious. Surely, then, there must be validity to seeing reality in this way. These are Uddhava's basic arguments, which he puts forward in an attempt to get Krishna to elaborate. He sums up with the following verse.

5. That there is a distinction between good qualities and bad ones is clear from the scriptures, which You endorse—these truths do not arise of their own accord. Indeed, You are the source of this knowledge, and yet You are now saying something else. This will undoubtedly cause confusion.

6. The Supreme Lord said: It is My desire that human beings achieve perfection. I have therefore given them three paths of spirituality—the path of knowledge (Jnana-yoga), the path of work (Karma-yoga), and the path of devotion (Bhakti-yoga). All forms of spiritual elevation fit into one of these three categories.

Commentary

Ultimately, one path leads to God: It is the path of developing a loving mood toward the Supreme and living one's life according to that mood. Because people find themselves at varying stages of spiritual evolution, however, this one process necessarily manifests in diverse ways. Thus, they appear as different processes, with varying emphases. This allows practitioners to develop love for God according to their psychophysical makeup and the conditioning that has accrued over countless lifetimes. All these paths are subsumed in the three mentioned here: Jnana-yoga, Karma-yoga, and Bhakti-yoga, with differences that Krishna will now explain.

7. If one is fed up with material life and thus detached from ordinary, fruitive activities, he may be inclined to Jnana-yoga, the path of knowledge. Alternatively, if one is not yet fully disgusted with material life, and still wants to pursue sense gratification, he could follow the path of Karma-yoga, working for God.

Commentary

Krishna briefly mentions the various motivating factors that determine one's path in spiritual life. The rigorous route of philosophical speculation (Jnana-yoga) usually is instigated by frustration with material existence, in which one wants to renounce all relationship and day-to-day activities in favor of serious scriptural study and the performance of intense austerities. The scriptures include detailed procedures and practices for those inclined to this path.

For those not inclined toward the hard life associated with Jnana-yoga, the scriptures recommend a family-centered life in which one offers the fruits of his work to the Lord (Karma-yoga). In this scenario, one generally lives a "normal" life in the material world—but with the caveat that he acknowledges God as the source of all and the ultimate enjoyer of all work. Consequently, he gradually cultivates detachment, offering his assets to the Supreme. Both paths culminate in Bhakti-yoga.

8. And then there are those who are not particularly attached to material life, nor disgusted by it. By additional good fortune, too, they develop faith in hearing and chanting about Me. These devotees achieve perfection through the path of devotional service (Bhakti-yoga).

Commentary

By the grace of God, one comes into contact with a pure devotee of the Lord. In this way, he develops a taste for hearing and chanting and gradually evolves into the greatest of *yogis*—one who has love and devotion for the Supreme. Such a devotee is distinguished by balance—he has a healthy aversion to all things material, in a simple way, and an attraction to Krishna, the essence of spirituality. He is not particularly consumed by attraction or repulsion, at least for material things. Rather, he is focused on loving devotion and on practices that help him move further on this path.

9. Vedic injunctions must be followed by those who are still inclined to fruitive activities—and especially by those who have not awakened their taste for hearing and chanting about Me.

Commentary

This directly relates to the conversation about good and bad qualities—about who needs to be conscious of such dualities and who does not. Those who do not have a genuine taste for transcendental subjects, that is, hearing and chanting about the name, fame, form, and pastimes of the Lord, must certainly follow the principles of Karma-yoga or Jnana-yoga, with their many rules and regulations predicated on that which is "good" and that which is "bad." Only those who have graduated to Bhakti-yoga, under the guidance of a pure devotee of the Lord, may discard scriptural injunctions in favor of spontaneous devotion. Of course, being situated in pure goodness, such devotees have a natural tendency to follow the rules and regulations of scripture anyway, and usually do so, but this is no longer their focus. Instead, they embrace one simple principle: Accept those things that are conducive to spiritual service and reject those things that are not.

10. A person who performs his prescribed duty according to Varnashram and conducts Vedic sacrifices without desiring the fruitive result of such worship, O Uddhava, will not necessarily go to the heavenly planets. And in a similar vein, one who engages in forbidden activities will not necessarily go to the hellish planets.

Commentary

Those who perform Karma-yoga and Jnana-yoga properly need not go to heavenly planets—even if this is where most practitioners of religious observance hope to go. Through the grace of a pure devotee, such practitioners may be directly promoted to the kingdom of God. In other words, we generally think that those who consistently engage in religious life will go to heaven after death, just as we think that those who act sinfully will go to hell after death. Not necessarily so. By grace, all may attain the supreme destination. True, one's consciousness and intention are factors. But God is merciful and is always ready to bestow His mercy on all souls, if we would but willingly accept it.

11. Those who practice their individual duties, according to the mind and body they've been given—avoiding all sin and free of material inebriety—will certainly develop transcendental knowledge in this life, or, if they are extremely fortunate, attain the platform of pure devotional service.

12. Living beings in both heaven and hell aspire to be born as humans on earth. This is because entities on other planets have numerous distractions, whereas the human form is especially suited to transcendental knowledge and devotion for God.

Commentary

According to the Vedic literature, the earth is part of the middle planetary system, in between the higher planets, where people enjoy inconceivable pleasures, and the hellish planets, where people suffer intense misery. The two extremes of godly delights and excessive misery make it difficult to pursue spirituality in earnest. The entities on higher planets are distracted by amazing joys beyond our imagination; and the beings on lower planets are so embroiled in pain and in the struggle for existence that they, too, cannot focus on the spiritual side of things.

Earth affords a balance—the most intense pleasures here are the most minimal of those on higher planets, while the greatest pains of our planet constitute the most mild form of suffering in hell. Therefore, entities from other galaxies pray for birth on earth, for here they can tolerate the negligible distractions of lukewarm pleasure and pain, using the majority of their time for spiritual pursuits.

13. One who is wise never wants to go to heaven or hell. Nor should he aspire to permanent residence on earth—all material situations are merely distractions from the soul's actual purpose in life.

Commentary

Self-realization means discovering who you actually are. In essence, you are a soul who has an eternal relationship with Krishna in the spiritual world. Therefore, the temporary pleasures of the heavenly planets—however great those pleasures may be—will not satisfy you, for it is not who you really are. Similarly, you are not the tormented person who, because of impious activity, goes to hell, experiencing untold suffering. Nor are you the false identity you have built up for yourself on earth, with pleasure and pain coming in its usual way—whether tepid or intense—leading to inevitable death.

An intelligent, evolved soul, therefore, will not aspire for any material situation, whether in heaven, hell, or on middle planets such as earth. None of these places, he knows, is his real home. They are temporary stopovers on his sojourn in the material world. Rather, he aspires to the spiritual realm, where he can serve the Lord eternally, with a spirit of love and devotion.

14. **Before death rears its head, a wise soul should take full advantage of his material body, which, even though subject to death, can still award the perfection of human life.**

Commentary

Interestingly, the material body, though made only of material elements and created for planned obsolescence, is ultimately a facility given by the Lord to pursue self-realization. A precious gift, the body can be utilized for God's purposes in the world and thereby "spiritualized." Once this is accomplished, it is effectively transformed into a transcendental tool that liberates the soul. The essence of this transformation comes about through sound vibration: If one learns to chant the holy names of God under the direction of a bona fide spiritual master, the bodily vehicle, though material, can transport one to the spiritual world.

15. **Heartless scoundrels, who are like the embodiment of death, sometimes cut down trees where birds live, destroying their nests. Out of necessity and without attachment, the homeless birds easily abandon the tree that housed their nest and settle peacefully in another area.**

16. **In a similar way, everyone's duration of life is being cut down by time, causing intense fear. Knowing this, people should renounce material attachment and the desire for sense gratification, for they can then understand the Supreme Lord and attain lasting peace.**

Commentary

Like birds that fly from tree to tree, making temporary residence without attachment, humans endeavoring for self-realization should realize that their many bodies—from one life to the next—are like temporary homes that they must one day abandon. They are not these bodies any more than the birds flying from tree to tree are the trees into which they fly. Self-realization, at least in its initial stages, means becoming aware of this.

17. The laws of nature automatically award all humans their material bodies—and this particular form is precious and rare. In fact, sages have compared the human body to an expertly constructed boat. The bona fide guru is like a captain, and the instructions of God, as revealed in sacred texts, are comparable to favorable breezes, setting it on its course. With all these assets, a human being is loath to not use his precious human body for crossing the ocean of birth and death. He must even be considered a "killer of his own soul" if he neglects to do so.

Commentary

The *Vedanta-sutra* begins with these words, *athato brahma jijnasa*: "Now one should inquire about Brahman, the Absolute Truth, which is spiritual in nature" (1.1.1). The word "now," in this verse, is key. The implication is this: "*Now* that I have a human birth." The Puranic texts informs us that we have gone through 8,400,000 species of life—insects, aquatics, animals, and so on—without the ability to inquire into the nature of spirit. Thus, the human form is considered special, a gateway, if you will, through which one can enter the spiritual world, our original home, resolving, once and for all, the problem of material existence.

The analogy expressed in Verse 17 is quite beautiful. It tells us that the human form of life is like a superexcellent ship that can take us to the shore of reality—the spiritual world. But we must use it properly. This means taking advice from the experienced captain, the spiritual master. His instructions, in tandem with those gleaned from sacred texts, are like fortunate winds, pushing our sails in the direction they need to go. We are blessed, the sages tell us, to have this ship, amidst the many different species of life, and to have the guidance of both the guru and the scriptures. How, then, can we be so ungrateful as to not use this ship as it was originally intended by God—how can we not use it to get back to Him?

Incredulous that some might in fact misuse their human form in this way, the scripture calls such persons *atma-ha*—"killers of the soul." Of course, the soul is eternal and can never be slain. But the offense of having a human body and not using it for its intended purpose is so heinous that the scriptures consider this a type of death or suicide. One can, of course, always attain the Lord's mercy and spring back from this deathlike situation, but the abuse in this case is so outrageous that it becomes very difficult to do so.

18. A true *yogi*, or spiritualist, sees the futility of endeavoring for material happiness. Accordingly, he learns to control the senses, developing detachment from the world of matter. By constant practice, in due course, he comes to focus his mind on spiritual reality without cessation.

19. While trying to concentrate the mind on spirit, of course, distraction may sometimes occur. If this happens, one should use traditional procedures for again carefully bringing the mind under control.

20. The higher self should always control the mind. One should never forget the actual goal of meditation. Instead, mastering the breath and the senses, with intelligence enhanced by goodness, one should bring the mind under control at all times.

21. To tame an independent horse, the expert horseman might first let his creature have its way for a brief moment. But then he quickly pulls in the reins, forcefully directing his horse to the desired path. In a similar manner, the best form of yoga requires that one first observe the movements and desires of the mind, without making adjustments—but he then brings them under full control.

22. Until one is spiritually satisfied, with the mind focused in meditation, it is important to analyze the temporary nature of all things, observing one's material surroundings with a keen eye. He should note how all things come into being and how they are annihilated in due course.

23. Thus, one eventually becomes disgusted with the temporary, illusory nature of the material world, developing a natural detachment from it. At that point, remembering the instructions of his spiritual master, a person looks deeply at the nature of everything around him, eventually relinquishing his false identification with all things material.

24. There are numerous disciplines and procedures that are effective at this time—logic and spiritual education, yoga, worshiping Me according to tradition—but the central point is to engage your mind in always remembering Me as the goal of yoga. No other means will have the same effect.

25. Sometimes, a sincere *yogi*, due to a momentary lapse, might accidentally commit a reprehensible deed. If this happens, he

should burn away all sinful reactions through the practice of yoga and nothing more.

Commentary

This verse is reminiscent of the *Bhagavad Gita*, wherein Lord Krishna says: "Even if My devotee commits an abominable action, he should be considered saintly because he is properly engaged in My service" (9.30). This is not to excuse irresponsible or repugnant behavior but rather to acknowledge the fallible nature of all souls. Devotees or *yogis*, being human, certainly can falter, but, if they are sincere and well meaning, Krishna will forgive them, especially if they correct themselves as quickly as possible. That is the essential meaning of this verse.

26. Spiritual seekers should be steady in their chosen practice. This is real piety, and the opposite, sinful life, occurs when one neglects his prescribed duty. Following this principle, sincerely avoiding sense gratification, one is able to subdue materialistic desire and its concomitant action, which are both impure by nature.

27–28. My devotee is always happy, worshiping Me with unswerving faith and conviction. He is able to do this because he sings My glories (chanting My names and the narrations of My pastimes), and also because he disdains material activities, knowing that all sense gratification leads to misery. Sometimes, it is true, he finds himself still engaged in some form of sense enjoyment, but, knowing that it will ultimately lead to a miserable result, he sincerely repents and moves on with his life.

29. By constantly worshiping Me through loving service, a wise soul becomes firmly ensconced in My essential nature, loving Me with heart and soul. Because of this, his material desires are effectively destroyed.

30. When one recognizes Me as the Supreme Lord, the knot in his heart is immediately ripped apart and the chain of fruitive actions ceases and desists.

31. Thus, for a devotee engaged in My devotional service, with mind focused on Me, the cultivation of knowledge and renunciation are merely byproducts in achieving yoga's highest perfection.

32–33. My devotee achieves, through serving Me with love, everything that can be had by fruitive activities, austerity, knowledge, detachment, yoga, charity, religious duties and all other means of spiritual practice. Because he is so dear to me, if My devotee

desires promotion to heavenly planets, liberation, or residence in My supreme abode, I will grant him his wish.

34. But know this: My devotees are saintly and their intelligence is deep. Therefore, they dedicate themselves to My service, without any other desire. Indeed, I might at times offer them liberation from birth and death—but they often reject it.

35. One is truly free when he is completely detached from matter. Therefore, if one is disinterested in personal rewards, showing no material desire, he is a prime candidate for My devotional service.

36. The dualities of pious work and sinful action, which reflect the good and evil of the material world, have nothing to do with My dedicated devotees. Because they are free from material desires, they are always focused and steady in their pursuit of the spirit. Indeed, My devotees have achieved the ultimate—Me, the Supreme Lord—and I am beyond anything conceivable, both in this world and in the next.

37. Those who follow My methods of devotional yoga, as I have taught here, will become free from all illusion. And when they reach My spiritual abode, they will have already perfectly understood the highest truth.

Commentary

To sum up Chapters Thirteen and Fourteen: For people on the material platform, life presents numerous considerations of purity and impurity, auspiciousness and inauspiciousness. These are calculated according to one's body, the place of action, the action itself, the time of action, the objects utilized, the performer, and the mantras chanted. This means that, in reality, concepts such as virtue and fault are not absolute but rather are relative to one's particular status in life—and according to one's platform of spiritual advancement.

For example, the *Mahabharata* (*Anushashana-parvan* 116.37) states that nonviolence is the highest duty (*ahimsa paro dharmo*). Upon close study, however, we find that this is true only for Brahmins. If a Kshatriya were to take this to heart, the world as we know it would function ineffectively. This is so because one who adopts the vocation of a police officer, for instance, must sometimes engage in harsh behavior to protect the innocent, abrogating the command to be nonviolent in all circumstances. Thus, scriptural mandates, including its views of right and wrong, are wholly relative, to be applied with wisdom and due consideration.

Ultimately, then, there is little substantial basis for distinguishing between virtue and fault, because these concepts vary and even transform according to time, place, and circumstance. Still, the scriptures make use of our conditioned responses to the world around us—taking into account our reactions to right and wrong and our self-identity. With this as a backdrop, scriptures recommend prescribed religious duties acknowledging different levels of good and evil, allowing for a certain degree of illusory life.

In the final analysis, however, the scriptures seek to enhance virtue and minimize the desire for sense gratification. To accomplish this end, the scriptures recommend numerous actions and proscribe others. Overall, the process works, gradually subduing each practitioner's materialistic propensities. Thus, the lengthy process outlined in the *Vedas* instills a taste for the highest perfection of life, which is transcendental.

Nonetheless, those pursuing spirituality in this way sometimes get waylaid in the middle of the process. Because of inferior intelligence, certain practitioners tend to take the stepwise instructions of the *Vedas* as ultimate truth, and they get caught in a network of inferior religious practices and even in fruitive work, albeit of a more sophisticated nature. In terms of ultimate goals, however, this was never the intent of the *Vedas*, nor is it the goal of any genuine process of religion, which is to link with God (*yoga*). This will be made clear in Chapter Fifteen.

Chapter 15

The Vedic Path

1. **The Supreme Lord said: If one abandons the best methods for achieving Me, i.e., devotional mysticism (Bhakti-yoga), spiritual philosophy (Jnana-yoga), and regulated work according to one's prescribed duties (Karma-yoga), what hope is there for spiritual life? Such a person, captured by the material senses and enamored by sense gratification, will certainly be born repeatedly in the cycle of birth and death.**
2. **Real piety consists of steadiness in one's practice. If one deviates, impious behavior becomes the norm. Distinguishing between these two states of being is actually this simple.**
3. **O sinless one, to understand what is proper and what isn't, it is important to evaluate things according to categorical distinctions. Thus, in analyzing religious principles, for instance, one must consider what is pure and what is not—for this is the standard when it comes to religion. In a similar way, if one is to distinguish between good and bad, or right and wrong, in ordinary, mundane spheres, there are respective standards such a person must consider, even if he still regards one act as auspicious and the other as inauspicious.**
4. **In many ways, the ordinary religious way of life is a burden for people—but it allows them to make gradual progress.**

Commentary

Unless one is a pure devotee of the Lord, or at least following the teachings of a pure devotee in the context of Bhakti-yoga, religious ritual is often a burden. One follows the many rules and regulations, mixing them with ordinary material life, as a way to make gradual advancement, to avoid sin, and to "do the right thing." Since the world leans toward sense gratification, it is often difficult to pursue a religious path with any success, for it always feels like swimming upstream—the current of material life goes the other way.

It is not until one meets a pure devotee of the Lord that a shift in consciousness takes place. At that time, one feels vacant without religiosity, and while rules and regulations may recede into the background, spiritual practices become the basis of one's life. In fact, such spiritual practitioners cannot imagine living without them. But this is a far cry from the mundane religiosity that is a burden for fledgling seekers, the kind Krishna is addressing here.

5. **All material elements—earth, water, fire, air, and ether—emanate from Me. Furthermore, these same elements make up the bodies of all conditioned souls, from Lord Brahma down to the smallest microorganisms.**

6. **My dear Uddhava, even though all material bodies are made of the same five elements, and are in that sense equal, the Vedic literature distinguishes between them, referring to them by various names and forms. In this way, living entities may function according to a hierarchical system and gradually achieve the goal of life.**

7. **O best of the saints, in order to subdue materialistic tendencies, I have declared certain things proper and others improper. The entire world is divided in this way, including time, space and all physical objects.**

8. **Among places, contaminated lands will have the following characteristics: There will be no spotted antelope, nor devotion to the Brahmins; other such places might be inhabited by spotted antelope but not by even one person worthy of respect; provinces like Kikata, where cleanliness and religious rites are neglected, where meat eaters are prominent, or where the earth produces no fruit—these are also polluted places.**

Commentary

In ancient India, Brahmacharis living in their guru's forest ashram would use the hides of spotted antelope as garments and sitting mats. They would never hunt the animals, of course, but would find the remains of the creatures after they had died at the hands of a hunter or for natural reasons. Thus, lands where this commodity was found in abundance were considered auspicious. Conversely, if these necessary accoutrements of spiritual life were *not* available, the land would be considered inauspicious.

An esoteric reading on the "spotted antelopes" phenomenon would be as follows: Places devoid of spotted antelopes are called *akrishna-sara*, even in the Sanskrit of this verse. *Akrishna*, of course, can also mean "without Krishna." Thus, lands where Krishna is not glorified are considered inauspicious or polluted. In addition, lands where He *is* glorified but do not also have bona fide spiritual masters, or "respectable men," can be considered polluted as well, for the conception of Krishna thereby will be compromised.

This verse tells us, too, that a given region should be considered "dirty" if it is difficult to keep clean there, or if there is little facility for performing religious rituals. The predominance of meat eating is also a sign of contamination, for it indicates a lack of *ahimsa*, or nonaggression. This, in turn, indicates a heartless and self-centered state of being, which is "unclean." Modern society, which caters to a meat-eating culture, lacks sensitivity and awareness, blindly killing animals and generally supporting the ill treatment of our four-footed, feathered, and scaly kin. This is all a sign of contamination.

9. Time is relative: It is considered pure when it is used properly, either by providence or because it works in terms of prescribed duty. But it is considered impure if it impedes the performance of that duty.

Commentary

Places are considered pure or impure according to how they affect one's spiritual practices, as indicated in the prior verse. In this verse, the conversation moves to the subject of time, which is similarly defined in terms of how it affects one's duty to God. Such considerations, of course, are mainly a concern in ordinary religiosity. In terms of transcendental religion, or Bhakti-yoga, time and place are largely inconsequential. Chanting of the holy names, for example, can be enacted anywhere and anytime, and those who engage in such practices are therefore transcendental to the dualities of material existence.

10. An object's purity or impurity may sometimes be determined according to its relation to other objects—or by words, rituals, the effects of time, or according to a given object's greatness.

Commentary

Examples are numerous. The body becomes pure, for example, when washed with water—thus, one item's purity is affected by proximity to another. A person's consciousness becomes pure by the preaching of a Brahmin—thus, words can determine purity, too. Religious ceremonies can purify numerous substances, and certain items—like perishable foods—can be polluted in the course of time, showing how time affects purity as well.

11. Impure things may or may not affect a person, depending on his strength, weakness, intelligence, wealth, location, and/or physical condition.

12. There are certain objects that are deeply affected by time, especially in terms of purity or lack thereof: Grains, wooden tools, things made of bone, thread, liquids (like clarified butter or oil), objects derived from fire (gold, etc.), skins, and things from the earth are all purified by time, by the wind, by fire, by earth and by water, either separately or in combination with each other.

13. In general, a purifying agent is considered effective when by applying it one removes a bad odor or a dirty exterior, making the contaminated object resume its original unblemished nature.

14. Similarly, the self, when embodied, can be purified by bathing, giving in charity, performing austerity, aging, developing personal strength, religious rituals, and prescribed duties. Most of all: he is purified by remembrance of Me. Twice-born men, especially, should purify themselves in these ways.

15. When mantras are chanted with proper knowledge, they are considered pure, having their best effect. Similarly, one's work is purified when done as an offering to Me. In this way, by purification of the following six items—place, time, substance, doer, mantras and work—one becomes religious; and by the opposite, they become irreligious.

16. Sometimes ordinary pious behavior becomes sinful, and, conversely, that which is ordinarily considered sinful can be seen as piety—all on the strength of Vedic injunctions. Such exceptional rules have the effect of blurring the clear distinction between good and bad.

Commentary

The basic principle behind the Vedic system is elucidated in this chapter. Distinguishing between proper and improper, pious and impious, and clean and unclean are central to the Vedic paradigm, allowing practitioners to make gradual progress on the spiritual path by adhering to activities that foster "good" as opposed to "bad."

However, students of the Vedic literature—by the processes embedded in the Vedic texts themselves—ultimately come to see all good and bad activities as relative, depending on body, social status, time, place, and circumstance. In this way, they eventually realize that true spirituality—pursuance of the absolute truth—is not dependent on the relative good or bad of the material world but that it exists in a category of its own: It is completely transcendental. This is alluded to in this verse.

17. If one is advanced in spiritual life, he must be cautious regarding activities that are degrading. However, the actions that demote him

will not necessarily do so to those who are already fallen. Indeed, if one is lying on the ground they need not worry about falling further.

Commentary

Again, the duality of material existence is highlighted, with special attention to the relativity of truths that lead up to transcendence. The specific consideration in Verse 17 is in regard to activities that one might consider uplifting or degrading, and how this varies according to just who one happens to be and where they stand in their spiritual journey.

Persons on the spiritual path might be considered cautious or liberal according to their status in life, and there are other considerations as well. A Sannyasi, for example, must scrupulously avoid the opposite sex, for casually associating with women constitutes degradation for him. A Grihastha, on the other hand, is not considered fallen in such association.

Another example: It is said that when a non-Vaishnava chants the holy name with an offensive mentality, he raises himself to the level of a fallen devotee. This shows relativity when considering actions that are either degrading or proper, given one's status in life or level of spiritual advancement.

18. One becomes free from particular kinds of sinful or materialistic activity simply by refraining from its performance. This kind of conscious renunciation lay at the core of religious life, and it serves to extinguish all suffering, illusion and fear.

Commentary

To become a thief, one does not have to meet any specific prerequisite—he simply needs to steal. If you steal, you are a thief. Similarly, to avoid sinful acts, you simply have to stop performing them.

The psychological implications of refraining are deep.

If one ceases to engage in specific forms of sinful behavior, consistently avoiding them over a period of time, he finds that he is progressively less inclined to those acts as life goes on. By refraining from them, he diminishes his taste for their fruits, especially if he develops a higher taste by regular engagement in spiritual practices.

19. If one desires material sense objects, he naturally becomes attached to them. This attachment leads to lust, or intense craving, and this lust forces people to argue and fight.

Commentary

Krishna reiterates his teaching from the *Bhagavad Gita*: "While contemplating the objects of the senses, a person develops attachment for them, and from such attachment, lust develops—from lust, anger arises.

"From anger," Krishna continues, "complete delusion arises, and from delusion bewilderment of memory. When memory is bewildered, intelligence is lost, and when intelligence is lost one falls down again into materialistic life" (2.62–63).

20. Quarrel leads to intolerable anger, which firmly situates a person in the dark hole of material ignorance. This ignorance blocks out any intelligence one might have previously had.

Commentary

Again, this is Krishna's way of paraphrasing His own teaching in the *Bhagavad Gita*. See commentary to prior verse. Such parallel teachings are noteworthy, for they mark a certain consistency between the *Uddhava Gita* and its sister text.

21. If a person is deprived of his intelligence, it is to be understood that he has lost everything of value. For without intelligence one loses track of the actual purpose of life, making him almost inert, like a dead body.

22. Overly absorbed in trying to enjoy the senses, such a person cannot understand who he really is, what to speak of others. His ignorance is comparable to that of a tree, and his breathing is meaningless, like a mechanical apparatus for producing air.

Commentary

Verses 21 and 22 sum up life without spirituality. Intelligence, properly directed, will lead one to inquire about the meaning of life. But if it is misused, or underdeveloped, it will distract one from the spiritual pursuit, becoming a liability rather than an asset. In such a case, from the spiritual point of view, one is considered dead, because his life lacks meaning.

Similarly, Verse 22 tells us that a life dedicated to titillating the senses, without higher purpose, is a sham, a facsimile of real living, for all pleasure ends with the demise of the body, if not sooner, and life's real purpose is wasted. A tree stands senseless, and that is nature's way, but if a human, too, stands senseless, it is a horrible misuse of God's special gift: the human form. Misusing the human body in this way is a travesty of nature, and when one does so, the *Uddhava Gita* tells us, our breathing may be compared to a bellows—for real breathing is breathing for God.

23. Sometimes, religious scriptures promise material rewards for their votaries, but these are not valuable in terms of the ultimate goal of life. Rather, such rewards are merely meant to entice practitioners who are still materially attached. Indeed, this strategy will encourage

fledgling spiritualists to perform beneficial religious duties, just as promises of candy induce children to take healing medicine.

Commentary

Verse 23 summarizes Krishna's attitude not only toward the *Vedas* but also toward ordinary religiosity in general—it serves a purpose, no doubt, for those who still have material desires, but it falls short in terms of the ultimate goal of life. Such systems of religion offer rewards for pious acts, and those rewards include material prosperity, an appropriate spouse, health, and heaven. All these assets are temporary. But they do serve a purpose: They get materially motivated people to embrace religion, the practice of which can then take them to the next level.

If one is dutiful and consistent in religious endeavor, he gradually will see the futility of material existence, along with its duality of good and bad, reward and punishment, and so on. Those who graduate to this level are the real devotees of the Lord. They bid adieu to material life—and that includes even subtle material life as embodied in the higher forms of goodness and religiosity. They want only love of God, the transcendental truth that lies hidden in the deepest recesses of all religious scriptures and in the hearts of all self-realized souls.

24. **Merely by being born into a material body, people become attached to personal sense enjoyment. This includes the desire for longevity, sensual satisfaction, bodily strength, virility, and the love of friends and family. In this way, they become obsessed with those things that eventually lead to their undoing.**

Commentary

Because we have bodies, we naturally are inclined to satisfy the senses and to enjoy bodily relations. This is nature's arrangement for beings in this world. Nonetheless, for an aspiring transcendentalist, such activities must be seen as not only distractions but as detrimental to spiritual life. This is not to say, of course, that bodily pleasure, along with friends and family, must be summarily discarded. No. But one must always be vigilant to guard against their becoming the center of one's life. The overwhelming tendency, due to bodily attachment, is to let these things override our spiritual practices. Krishna therefore warns us, in this verse and in many other scriptural texts, that these very natural feelings, practices, and relationships have a downside, and that, if left uncontrolled, they will lead to the destruction of our spiritual lives.

25. **Being unaware of what is actually good for them, most people traverse the path of material existence, becoming more and more ignorant as time goes on. If this is actually the case, one may**

legitimately ask: Why would religious scriptures encourage people to behave in this dangerous way? After all, the scriptures, too, are offering material rewards.

Commentary

Krishna wants to underline the point that people are naturally absorbed in sense gratification, and that this absorption brings them progressively further from spiritual life. He also points out that, with this as a given, it would seem unnecessarily risky for religious scriptures—whether the *Vedas*, the Bible, the Koran, or whatever—to tempt practitioners with sensual rewards, even if these scriptural traditions are using these rewards like candy-coating on beneficial medicine.

Most religious texts tell us that if you are true to your vows, you will get commensurate rewards for your endeavor. Sometimes one is promised seventy-two virgins, daily bread, or good health. In other cases, one is granted divine knowledge, mystic powers, or a long life, like that of Lord Brahma. In any case, the strategy is risky, and that is Krishna's main point. Nonetheless, religious authorities have determined that, risky though it might be, this is the best way to get embodied beings to embark on the spiritual path. Having begun the journey, they will become purified by the process and by the association of people who are spiritually advanced. And in this way, they will rise beyond the need for material rewards, however subtle.

26. Due to the natural distractions of material life, most people do not understand this actual purpose of Vedic knowledge. Instead, they mistakenly emphasize the flowery statements of the *Vedas* offering material rewards, thinking these to be the ultimate prize of the spiritual pursuit. Those in actual knowledge never make this mistake.

Commentary

Krishna is not only summarizing what He has been saying in this chapter thus far but also is paraphrasing His own teaching from the *Bhagavad Gita*: "Men of miniscule knowledge become attached to the flowery words of the *Vedas*, which recommend various religious rituals for elevation to heavenly planets, good birth, material power, and so on. Being desirous of sense gratification and opulent life, such people think that these things are the highest of achievements" (2.42–43). Krishna, of course, is saying the opposite—that such things are only the beginning, an enticement to get people to approach the real goal: love of God.

But most practitioners will never know this. Their attachment to sense gratification blinds them to the truth and thus to His loving service. As He says in the *Bhagavad Gita*'s next verse: "For those who are too attached to sense enjoyment and material riches, and who are naturally bewildered by such things, the appreciation and determination for My devotional service does not take place" (2.44).

27. **If one is beleaguered by lust, desire, and greed, he tends to mistake dry flowers for succulent fruits. Undone by his inherent illusion, such a person is distracted by the glare of fire, with his ability to breathe stifled by its smoke. In this way, he cannot even understand who he is.**

Commentary

Using poetic language, Krishna indicates that ordinary religionists are blinded by their actions, like one who is in proximity to fire. This blindness actually can cause one's life to end, just as smoke can kill by causing suffocation. The poetry is particularly effective here because it conveys a double meaning: The word Krishna uses for fire is *agni-mugdhah*, "bewildered by fire," and it alludes to the fire sacrifices promoted in the *Vedas*. His implication is that the "glare" of these sacrifices causes a certain kind of blindness in which one misses the ultimate goal of life. To extend the analogy, He indicates that fire causes smoke, which, as we know, can obscure a person's vision. Thus, He is again making the point that ordinary religiosity can be misleading if not downright dangerous.

28. **O dear one, those who honor Vedic rituals in this shallow way, looking for material rewards, cannot understand who I am, situated in everyone's heart. Nor can they perceive how I am the universe, even as it emanates from Me. I must say, they are like people with fog covering their eyes.**

29–30. **Because they are dedicated to sense gratification, they misunderstand the real meaning of religious texts. For example, taking pleasure in the outcome of violence, they slaughter innocent creatures in sacrifice—and in this misguided way they worship demigods, forefathers, and various demonic creatures. Such violent sacrifices, it should be noted, are never really supported by Vedic texts.**

Commentary

As one example of how superficial religionists might use the scriptures for their own sense gratification, Krishna refers to the animal sacrifices mentioned in Vedic texts. Like in the biblical tradition, these slaughtering rituals were meant as concessions for those addicted to violence and the taste of meat. While they indeed constitute a major portion of the *Vedas*, the text is rife with caveats and warnings about the dangers of meat eating. In fact, it is clear that the sacrifices carry with them severe karmic reactions, so much so that the Sanskrit word for meat is *mamsa*, or "me-he," indicating that the priest killing the animal in sacrifice will one day be victimized by the same fate. "What I am doing to you now," he chants in the animal's ear, "you will one day, in another life, do to me."

Killing begets killing, and the karmic reactions for sacrificing an animal were well known in Vedic times. Therefore, the great Vaishnava teachers have recommended vegetarianism, for the outmoded rituals of the *Vedas* are not only harsh and unduly cruel, both to the animal and, in a future life, to the one killing the animal, but they miss the real point of the Vedic texts: love of God. Krishna makes clear here that only lesser universal administrators, such as demigods, might take pleasure in such sacrifices—but He, of course, never does. Rather, if one loves Him, one will offer vegetarian foods instead of meat and take the remnants as *prasadam*, or "the Lord's mercy." Such transformed food is purifying, nutritious, and uplifting. This is the way of the Vaishnava sages.

31. In the same way that a businessperson might make a poor investment, losing his wealth because of bad decisions, unintelligent religionists abandon that which is really valuable in favor of some vague conception of heaven. Such bewildered people think they will achieve a higher level of happiness, but their achievement is simply material.

32. Just as universal administrators and other deities are defined by the modes of nature they preside over, whether goodness, passion, or ignorance, so too, do worshippers of these entities conform to the laws of those same modes. But none of them worship Me in the proper way.

Commentary

Krishna is reiterating the teaching of the *Bhagavad Gita*: "Those who are devotees of lesser gods, worshiping them with faith, are no doubt, in the ultimate analysis, intending to worship Me. But they are doing it in the wrong way" (9.23).

Universal administrators on higher planets, also known as demigods, are like officers and directors in the government of the Supreme. One has to abide by the laws of the government, not worship the officers or directors. In the same way, worship is meant for the Supreme Lord only, which is accomplished by following His ordinances and thereby developing love for Him. If one does this, it naturally will satisfy the many officers and directors who are servants of the Lord.

Demigod worship is like offering a bribe to the officers and directors of a government—it is simply illegal. This is stated here as *avidhi-purvakam*—"but none of them worship Me in the proper way." In other words, Krishna does not approve of this kind of worship. And why would He? As indicated in this verse, the demigods are within the jurisdiction of goodness, passion, and ignorance, which are material qualities. Indeed, ordinary religiosity may fall into this realm, but Krishna wants His devotees to rise beyond this, to become transcendentally situated in His divine service.

33–34. When those who are addicted to sense gratification worship lesser gods, they think, "By our penances we will go to heaven and enjoy like gods there. When our pious credits are used up, we will be born again in this world and enjoy here, perhaps in wealthy families." Indeed, being greedy, they miss the entire point of the spiritual pursuit, for they are bewildered by the flowery words of the *Vedas*. Because of this, they couldn't be less interested in topics about Me.

35. The *Vedas* are divided into three divisions—focusing on fruitive gain, worship of universal administrators, and a philosophical understanding of the Supreme, respectively. All of these texts, however, ultimately reveal the living entity as pure spirit soul. That being said, the Vedic sages compiled their mantras using cryptic language. No doubt, I am pleased by such esoteric descriptions.

Commentary

The *Vedas* offer the world an entire gamut of higher knowledge, from the Karma-kanda section, which deals with fruitive rituals, to the Jnana-kanda section, dealing with the pursuit of knowledge and how to appease universal administrators, and even to the Upasana-kanda, wherein the idea of Brahman, or God, is introduced, as is His service. All three levels of Vedic understanding begin and end with the idea that all living beings are essentially spiritual and that the supreme spirit is God.

Nonetheless, Vedic mantras are expressed in confidential language, and their meaning is hard to grasp, unless one studies under a bona fide spiritual master. Krishna is pleased with this arrangement because He wants people to approach the scripture according to their conditioning and level of realization. If it were written in clear, direct language, it would be impossible to miss the plain conclusion of *bhakti*, or devotion to the Supreme. Because not everyone is ready for this conclusion, Krishna appreciates the stepwise fashion of Vedic revelation, and He expresses this here, in Verse 35.

36. Spiritual sound vibration, as conveyed in the *Vedas*, is extremely subtle, and its meaning is obscure. In fact, it is unfathomable, like the ocean, manifesting on numerous levels in the *prana*, senses, and mind.

Commentary

Continuing from Verse 35, Krishna is explaining why most people misunderstand Vedic texts and religious scriptures in general: In addition to coming to these texts in an already conditioned state, wanting sense gratification and little more, most people cannot penetrate the subtle dimensions of sound found there. Indeed, the texts themselves exist in several categories of sound vibration, with only the grossest level being evident to conditioned souls.

Traditionally, ancient Indic texts divide sound into four distinct levels, and the subtlest of these, known as *vaikhari*, is beyond the ken of the mass of living entities. Thus, the *Vedas* generally are understood in terms of their external meaning, for entrance into their more subtle layers is almost impossible. If, however, one can develop some modicum of genuine spiritual advancement, through practice and through studying under a bona fide spiritual master, one can then pierce through the external coverings, learning how to perceive sound on the purified, mental, sensual, and pranic airwave levels. This leads to transcendental life in the spiritual realm.

37. It is I—the limitless, changeless, and endlessly powerful Lord, dwelling within the hearts of all—who award perception of Vedic sound on the highest level. It thus appears within the core of each person's essence as the mantra OM, or Omkara, just waiting to be awakened. Accordingly, at the right time, one senses it within, like a subtle strand of fiber on a gentle lotus stalk.

Commentary

Krishna tells us that Vedic knowledge, like He Himself, is found in every living being's heart in seed-like form. It is there as Omkara, which is His sound representation. He further tells us that He is the true repository of Vedic knowledge, and that, if a living being is to perceive the *Vedas* on the most subtle of levels—which conveys its deepest, most accurate meaning—it must come from Him, for He awards Vedic understanding to surrendered souls.

The same notion is expressed in the *Bhagavad Gita*: "I am seated in everyone's heart, and from Me come remembrance, knowledge and forgetfulness. By all the *Vedas* I am to be known; indeed I am the compiler of Vedanta, and I am the knower of the *Vedas*" (15.15). In short, Krishna is in the heart, He is the goal of Vedic wisdom, and true awareness of what the *Vedas* have to say will come only by His grace.

38–40. It is said that a spider's web originates from its heart and pushes forward through its mouth. In a similar way, the Supreme Lord manifests as the vital air (*prana*), pleasing and subtle, ultimately projecting Vedic sound through His heart.

This transcendent sound pushes out in countless directions, adorned with the different letters expanded from the syllable Omkara, including its many variations in terms of language. Manifesting in numerous verbal varieties, the *Veda* is expressed in different meters, each having four more syllables than the previous one. In due course, the Lord withdraws the vibrations of Vedic knowledge into His own being.

Commentary

The analogy of a spider is quite apt: The Lord emits Vedic knowledge from the core of His being, like a spider sends out its web. The spider's numerous intersecting silken strands—whether shooting out as a vertical plane (orb webs), a horizontal plane (sheet webs), or at any angle in between, serve several distinct purposes. The web originally manifests from spinneret glands located at the tip of the spider's abdomen, usually to create (1) a trailed safety line, (2) sticky silk for trapping prey, or (3) fine silk for wrapping it. Similarly, from the Lord's essence comes forth Vedic knowledge, in various forms, whether it is the Vedic sound vibration proper or other sacred texts. Alternate sound vibrations are meant for "capturing" different types of "prey"—that is, those who are conditioned in various ways respond to differing spiritual sound vibrations, allowing them tailor-made pathways into spiritual life. This correlates to the spider's web "pushing out in countless directions," alluding to the fact that spiritual sound manifests in different Vedic mantras and also as "different religions."

41. **The Vedic meters are Gayatri, Ushnik, Anushtup, Brihati, Pankti, Trishtup, Jagati, Atich-chanda, Atyashti, Atijagati and Ativirat.**

Commentary

Vedic sound is expansive and profound, and to understand the implications of its various nuances in terms of meters, rhythms, and melodies—what to speak of content or meaning—one must be highly trained in Sanskrit. Here, Krishna gives examples of meters that expand out from the Gayatri meter, which has twenty-four syllables—each one having four more syllables than the prior one, as indicated in Verse 41.

42. **I am the only one who understands the inner meaning of Vedic knowledge. Most people merely subscribe to the ritualistic injunctions of the Karma-kanda section or the intellectual profundity of the Jnana-kanda. At best, they adhere to the principles of worship in the Upasana-kanda. But they do not generally know Me.**

Commentary

Krishna is *veda-vit*, the only true knower of Vedic conclusions, as mentioned in *Bhagavad Gita* 15.15 and quoted above. He sums up in yet another way the unfortunate truth that most followers of the Vedic scriptures—and this applies to all people who emphasize the (1) fruitive work form of religion, (2) the intellectual study of scriptures, along with meditation, or (3) ritualistic worship, regardless of the religious tradition—simply miss the point. *Bhakti* is hard to access through religious texts and mainstream traditions. It is for this reason that Vyasadeva chose to compile the Puranas and the Epics, which strive to reveal the essence of religious truth, picking up where the *Vedas* leave off. It is essential to study these texts and engage in the practice of religion more generally under the auspices of a bona fide spiritual master, who teaches students to go to the heart of the religious quest.

43. The *Vedas* ultimately point to Me as the beneficiary of all sacrifice—for I am the worshipable Deity of all living beings. Know it for certain: I am the ultimate conclusion of each and every philosophical hypothesis, even though intellectual debate is essentially endless. Indeed, I am the conclusive meaning of all Vedic knowledge. The *Vedas*, then, after fully analyzing the material world, finding it to be little more than My illusory potency, move beyond the world of duality and, in the end, refer to Me.

Commentary

In conclusion, though Vishnu (Krishna) is mentioned in the *Vedas*, the texts are unclear as to exactly who He is and why He is to be worshiped. The *Vedas* are, after all, written in cryptic language and must be studied under a teacher who knows Vedic truths, as passed down in one of four authorized lineages. Otherwise, one is likely to get sidetracked with Karma-kanda, Jnana-kanda, and Upasana-kanda conceptions of religion, which exist in abundance in the *Vedas* and in all mainstream approaches to religion.

That being said, the *Vedas* do identify Vishnu with "the sacrifice" (*yajno vai vishnuh*), which is the mainstay and central practice for all devotees of Vedic ritual.

The *Vedas* are accompanied by additional texts known as *Brahmanas* and *Aranyakas*, and in these texts the Lord's position becomes clear: The very first verse of the *Aitareya Brahmana*, which is appended to the *Rig Veda*, says that "Vishnu is the greatest and the oldest among the gods," establishing a sort of monotheistic reality in Vedic parlance. In the *Brahmanas*, then, the supremacy of Lord Vishnu becomes a fact of life.

As Krishna Himself says in the *Bhagavad Gita*: "But it is I who am the ritual, the sacrifice, the offering to the ancestors. I am the healing herb, the transcendental chant. Indeed, I am the butter and the fire and the offering itself.

"I am the father of this universe, and its mother, too," Krishna continues. "I am the support and the grandsire. I am the object of knowledge, the purifier, and the syllable Omkara. Know it for certain: I am also the *Vedas*" (9.16–17).

Chapter 16

The Elements of Material Creation

1–3. Uddhava asked: How many different elements of creation have the great sages revealed to us? What is their estimation on this? I have heard You personally describe a total of twenty-eight—God, the ordinary soul, the subtle basis of creation, false identity, the five gross elements (earth, water, fire, air, and ether), the ten senses (eyes, ears, nose, skin, and tongue, through which we acquire knowledge; and hands, feet, mouth, anus, and genitals, which allow us to perform action), the mind, the five subtle objects of perception (forms, sounds, smells, tastes, and textures) and the three modes of nature (goodness, passion, and ignorance). Nonetheless, some authorities claim that there are twenty-six elements, while others cite twenty-five. Some say there are four, six, seven, nine, or eleven, and still others say that there are thirteen, sixteen or seventeen. Why the diversity in their calculation? Please explain this to me.

Commentary

Uddhava is concerned about the many ways in which one might understand material nature, and he wants Krishna to clearly assert that all of them are legitimate: They are merely different methods of categorizing the same reality.

Still, the diversity can be confusing, just as the *Vedas* themselves are confusing. This is especially true of the Jnana-kanda portion, which attempts to understand how material nature is broken down and categorized. Such an analytical attempt to understand reality will necessarily fall short, for it neglects the essence of essential truth, which is located in the heart.

4. The Supreme Lord replied: It is entirely understandable that learned Brahmins would categorize material elements in different

ways. There are many ways to think about such things and, by My mystic potency, there is truth to all of them.

5. **If learned people debate, saying things like, "I choose to analyze this particular phenomenon in my own way, as opposed to the way you have analyzed it," please perceive My own supernatural energies at the heart of their differences.**

6. **Different opinions arise due to the interactions of My mystic potencies. This is the way of philosophical argumentation in the material world. But for those who focus their intelligence on Me, controlling their senses by engaging in religious practices, all such confusing differences fall to the wayside.**

Commentary

In the *Bhagavata Purana* (6.4.31), Lord Krishna affirms that the consistent wrangling of mundane philosophers is part of His overall plan. Through His own mystic potencies, He gives them the ability to endlessly debate on subjects innumerable, creating a situation in which it is nearly impossible to come to a reliable conclusion. However, He also judiciously places pure devotees throughout the cosmos to take these philosophers to the next level, whereby they eventually can understand Him and thus reach the summit of all philosophical knowledge.

7. **O great one, learned debaters tend to understand and thus explain material elements in various ways, according to the point they are trying to make and according to context. Subtle and gross elements, it should be remembered, manifest variously in different circumstances, with respect to how they interact, and they will be enumerated accordingly.**

8. **It is important to remember the following as well: All subtle material elements are embedded within their gross effects. In a similar way, all gross elements are present, in seed-like form, within their subtle causes. This can be understood by the fact that material creation takes place by a progressive manifestation of elements from subtle to gross. Accordingly, all material elements are actually present in each other, at least essentially.**

Commentary

A common example of how one might see a gross element in its subtle cause: Fire exists, at least in its latent form, in wood. The potential for fire is already there. Similarly, one can see mud in an earthen pot—only desire, time, and endeavor separate one from becoming the other. In this way, causes and effects interpenetrate each other, making all material elements essentially the same (if overtly different).

9. **Thus, each thoughtful person's point of view should be respected, regardless of whether they calculate material elements in terms of their subtle causes or in terms of their gross end products. I accept their conclusions as meaningful, because a logical explanation always supports each of their theories.**

10. **Still, most people have been covered by ignorance since the beginning of time and consequently are not able to realize ultimate truth on their own. They must find some outside personality who has knowledge of the Absolute Truth—only such a soul can impart knowledge to conditioned beings.**

Commentary

Though Krishna is expressing the need to approach an authority within the context of understanding material elements—their number and content—He is giving a general instruction as well. He is talking about the importance of approaching a spiritual master to receive transcendental knowledge. Most people are thoroughly conditioned, birth after birth, and thus cannot extricate themselves from material conditioning. They are like the man who falls in a deep well—unless someone comes from above and throws him a rope, he is destined to stay in his dark hole, without hope of getting out.

In the *Bhagavad Gita*, too, Krishna teaches: "One should attempt learning truth through the grace of a spiritual master. Ask him submissive questions, and serve such a guru faithfully. He is a self-realized soul and can impart knowledge unto you because he has seen the truth" (4.34).

11. **When one sees through the lens of goodness, he does not perceive qualitative distinctions between God and self. Indeed, he sees such differences as imaginary.**

Commentary

When some philosophers enumerate the elements of creation, they consider that there are twenty-five as opposed to twenty-six elements, for they include God and the living entity in the same category. Krishna accepts this perspective because there is a way in which the Lord and the living beings are in fact one: They are one in quality but not in quantity.

The traditional example is that of a gold earring in relation to a goldmine. In the same way that the quality of gold in a gold earring is equal to the quality of that in a goldmine, we are qualitatively equal with Krishna. The quantity of gold in the mine, however, is infinitely greater than the quantity in the earring.

That is to say, Krishna is great and we are small. In other words, we are fragmental parts and parcels of Krishna, while He is the "complete whole."

Another example is that of an entire ocean in relation to a drop of water from that same ocean—chemically analyzed, they are the same. That is, in terms of salt content, for instance, they are one. However, this is just a "qualitative" consideration. In terms of quantity, there is a vast difference.

Therefore, Krishna speaks of "seeing through the lens of goodness (*sattva*)." Through this lens, the qualitative aspect is highlighted, and oneness with God is clearly perceived. If one graduates to pure goodness (*vishuddha-sattva*), which is a more advanced spiritual perception, the duality is emphasized—one worships God as a distinct being, and the oneness recedes into the background.

12. Originally, material nature functions through a balancing of the three material modes, goodness, passion, and ignorance, which doesn't really touch the soul. These modes impact the creation, maintenance and destruction of all material universes, affecting everything in the material world.

Commentary

This informative verse tells us about the power of the three modes. These modes are essentially a transformation of the Lord's inherent qualities—eternity, knowledge, and bliss—and, as such, wield tremendous power. They virtually control all living beings, at least in the latter's conditioned state, and dictate how they act. Once a given living entity overcomes conditioning, the modes step aside, and he becomes situated in his constitutional position in the spiritual world, where the modes have no sway.

The modes of material nature are calculated as part of the elements of creation, and therefore Krishna mentions them here.

13. The mode of goodness is characterized by knowledge, the mode of passion by fruitive activities, and the mode of ignorance by foolishness. This is how the modes are to be understood in the material world. The sum total of material elements remains inert until they are agitated by time, which is effected by the modes in the subtlest of ways.

14. Previously, I have described the nine basic elements as the soul, nature, nature's primeval manifestation (known as the *mahat-tattva*), false identity, ether, air, fire, water and earth.

Commentary

Krishna lists the basic elements from most subtle to most gross. All other elements have some relation to these, as He will now show.

15. Hearing, touch, sight, smell, and taste are the senses through which we acquire knowledge, while our five working senses include speech, the hands, the genitals, the anus, and the feet. The mind certainly has a place in both these categories.

16. The knowledge-acquiring senses have sound, touch, taste, smell, and form as their objects. And the working senses are concerned with movement, speech, excretion, and the ability to make things.

17. In the beginning of creation, I—the Supreme Lord—do not directly deal with material manifestation. Rather, I merely glance upon nature and invest it with My energy. Through this action, I bring into existence the modes of goodness, passion and ignorance, which in turn spark off all subtle causes and gross manifestations within the cosmos.

18. As the aggregate of material elements undergoes its primeval transformation, it receives special mystic potency from My glance. At that time, nature works its magic, combining all of this into a universal egg.

19. Some philosophers say that there are basically seven elements, namely earth, water, fire, air, ether, and also the soul and God, the latter of whom is the source of all the others. According to this theory, these seven elements are responsible for the body, the senses, the various life airs, and all other material phenomena.

Commentary

Krishna explains His own point of view but, as we have seen earlier and as expressed in the next few verses, also gives credence to that of other philosophers.

20. Some thinkers talk about six elements—the five gross ones (earth, water, fire, air, and ether) and the sixth, or God. That Supreme Lord, taking full advantage of the elements that issue forth from Him, creates the universe with the specific purpose of entering into it.

Commentary

Krishna reiterates the perspective described in Verse 11, wherein God and the living being are merged into one category.

21. Others say that there are four basic elements, beginning with fire, water and earth—these three arise from the self, which is

spiritual. Coming from that divine source, the three material elements produce the cosmic manifestation.

22. Still others proffer that there are seventeen basic elements—the five gross elements, the five objects of perception, the five sensory organs, including the mind, and the soul.

23. Then there are those who calculate sixteen elements, differing from the previous theory only in that the soul is seen as nondifferent from the mind. Or one can think in terms of thirteen elements as well: the five physical elements, the five senses, the mind, the individual soul, and the Supreme Lord.

24. If one starts with the premise of eleven elements, one could include the soul, the gross elements, and the five senses. Or nine would run as follows: eight gross and subtle elements, along with their source, the Supreme Lord.

25. My point is this: The great teachers throughout history have analyzed material elements in numerous ways and much of what they say should be seriously considered. After all, their presentation is usually based on sound logic. Nothing less would be expected of those who are truly wise.

Commentary

Krishna sums up by essentially repeating what he had said in Verse 9.

26. Sri Uddhava said: We see a natural distinction between material nature and the living being within the body, O Lord Krishna. And yet it seems as though there is no difference between them, because one resides in the other. In this way, the soul appears to be within nature, even as nature appears within the soul.

Commentary

Verse 26 reveals why detailed knowledge of material elements is necessary for one on the spiritual path: By analytically exploring the nature of matter, one can come to see the distinction between the body and the actual self, and this is the beginning of spiritual life proper.

Uddhava realizes that many will not understand this point, and so he asks the Lord for clarification on behalf of others. Krishna, too, sees this issue as pivotal and therefore He devotes the next thirty or so verses, until the end of the chapter, to explaining it.

The living entity's identification with the body is so immediate, so intense, and so fundamental, that Krishna's words will do little more than provide an intellectual basis for further exploration. True, He will use logic and reasoning to cut the knot of material conditioning, affording readers a chance to enter into the truth of their actual spiritual identity. But it takes consistent religious practice and deep meditation to actually untie the ropes of ignorance that bind one to the bodily concept of life. What follows, then, might be seen as an introduction to the topic, preparing readers for a journey that will establish them in existential reality—knowledge of the actual self.

27. O lotus-eyed Lord, O omniscient one, please cut this terrible doubt from my heart with Your words, which show Your sharp skill in the realm of logic.

28. You are the source of all knowledge, and, by Your potency, that same knowledge can be stolen away in due course. Indeed, only You have the power to overcome Your illusory potency.

Commentary

With Verses 27 and 28, Uddhava beseeches the Lord, as the source of all knowledge, to answer this most vexing of questions: How is it that we are not our bodies, even though bodily identification seems so certain, so undeniable?

A huge factor in this mystery is the illusory energy, which keeps all living beings in a sort of materialistic stupor, allowing us to forget our constitutional position in the spiritual world, where we originally serve the Lord in a spirit of love and devotion. This illusion facilitates our sojourn in the material world. Without it, we would see the stark reality of material existence, which then would thwart our enterprise of imitation Lordship, wherein we try to enjoy our senses as if we were God.

In short, we need to learn certain lessons that only life in the material world can provide, thus helping us to grow spiritually mature. The illusory energy allows us to do that. Therefore, Uddhava prays to Krishna as the possessor or originator of this energy—indicating that He, God, is ultimately responsible for our plight in the material sphere. Such beseeching, Uddhava hopes, will instigate compassion, encouraging Krishna to lift the veil of illusion, at least temporarily.

29. The Supreme Lord said: O best of men, the material body and the possessor of that body are definitely distinct. This visible creation—which people mistakenly identify as the self—undergoes consistent transformation caused by the modes of material nature.

30. Varieties of creation and variations of consciousness come about through My material energy, which is comprised of the three modes of nature. These give rise to three aspects of transformation, known as *adhyatmam, adhibhutam*, and *adhidaivam*.

Commentary

This complex subject might be summarized as follows: Numerous forms reveal various aspects of the Lord's creation. For example, birds fly in the air; fish exist in water; and insects are found within the ground. Thus, astute observation of these various forms can tell us much about the world around us. Form is chiefly understood through the medium of the eye and the other senses, and therefore the word *adhyatmam* is used; perception takes place within the material world, and it is dependent on the existence of tangible objects all around us—this is *adhibhutam*; and our ability to perceive things occurs by the grace of higher beings, the demigods, which is what *adhidaivam* means. In simple terms, these three refer to: sense, object of perception, and presiding deity.

31. **Sight, that which is visible, and the reflected light in the eyeball itself all work together to reveal tangible things in the material world. But the sun, appearing in the sky, exists of its own accord, whether we see it or not. Similarly, the Supreme Lord, the cause of all living entities, is self-illumined by His own spiritual essence, and He is not dependent on those who see Him or on those who do not.**

32. **The sense organs, too, and by this I mean, the skin, ears, eyes, tongue and nose—as well as the functions of the astral body, that is, conditioning, the mind, the intelligence, and false conceptions of the self—can be understood in terms of *adhyatmam, adhibhutam*, and *adhidaivam*.**

33. **Generated from the *mahat-tattva*, the subtle cause of creation, which comes from unmanifest material elements, the three modes of nature combine in a particular way, creating various false conceptions of the self. These false conceptions—whether influenced by goodness, passion, or ignorance—are the instigators of all material illusion and duality.**

Commentary

According to psychologist William James (1842–1910), whenever two people meet, in fact at least six people are present: There is each person as he sees himself; each one as the other person sees him; and each person as he really is. Present, too, are all the people and actions that have influenced each of them throughout their lives. Thus, it is virtually impossible to know who we really are until we become accomplished in the process of self-realization.

34. **When philosophers argue about whether the material world is real or not, they do so with incomplete knowledge of the Supreme. As a**

result, they merely bicker about material dualities, without a genuine notion of transcendent truth. Because they have turned their focus away from Me, such people cannot understand that their arguments are a waste of time, and they are unable to abandon them.

35–36. Sri Uddhava said: I know, my Master, that such people focus on fruitive activities, allowing their minds to wander from Your grace. Their fate is thus uncertain. Please tell me how they accept various kinds of bodies as a result of their materialistic activities—and how they eventually relinquish their bodies. O Govinda, this is a difficult topic for ignorant people to grasp. Totally ensnared by the illusions of this world, they are usually oblivious to ultimate truth.

37. The Supreme Lord said: If one is materialistic, his mind is formed by the reactions of his fruitive work. Because of his five senses, his subtle body, which includes the mind, travels from one physical form to another. And the spirit soul—which is clearly different from the mind—follows along, establishing a new bodily residence according to desire and taste.

38. Conditioned by past fruitive work, the mind always focuses on the objects of the senses, whether those objects are actually perceivable in the material world or just heard about from various authorities. Because of this, the mind seems to appear and disappear like other objects of perception. Accordingly, it is unable to remember its past or to anticipate its future.

Commentary

It is here, in Verse 38, explained how the mind loses its ability to remember previous lives, or to plan for future ones. Because it is completely ensconced in its current physical form, conditioned by the modes of nature and by its attachment to fruitive activities, it cannot break the illusion that binds it to its current life. In this way, it travels from body to body, carrying the soul, which learns from mistakes in a cumulative way, if not consciously.

Only through the trials and tribulations of material life does the mind one day start to question the viability of material existence, and then, due to prayer and good fortune, God sends one of His pure representatives to carry the aspiring spiritualist further, giving him food for thought in various ways. He trains him, and nurtures his mind and heart, giving him the tools for pursuing advanced spirituality at his own pace.

39. Each living entity's body, then, is created by his own karma, i.e., his previous actions, and when he passes from his present body to the next one, he becomes absorbed in the joys and pains of his

new bodily vehicle, completely forgetting the sensations of his previous body. This forgetfulness is facilitated by death.

Commentary

Krishna elaborates on just why one forgets his previous life: The mind is not only absorbed in its new set of senses and their concomitant conditioned responses to the outer world, but the trauma of death, too, has an impact on the mind's function. In addition, modern science reveals that birth also causes forgetfulness—during the last stages of pregnancy, the mother's womb is flooded with oxytocin, a natural mammalian hormone that also acts as a neurotransmitter in the brain. In fact, it is best known for its role in female reproduction: The baby, it is said, forgets the trauma of childbirth because of the presence of this particular hormone. No doubt, this is God's kindness upon the newborn.

40. That which is called birth, O most charitable of people, is merely this: It is complete identification with a new body. This illusion is all encompassing, much in the way one experiences a dream—while immersed in it, it seems as though it is absolute reality.

41. While residing in a given body, a person thinks that he has only recently come into existence, even though he has had many such bodies before. Again, it is similar to one's experience of a dream, or daydreaming—while so absorbed, one does not think of previous dreams or daydreams.

42. In each life, through the agency of the senses, the mind creates an illusory identification with a new body, believing that it fits into high, middle or low class. In this way, the self becomes deluded by materialistic duality, just as a good person's offspring might have inferior qualities.

Commentary

The analogy found at the end of Verse 42 is interesting. The soul, by its very nature, is eternally good, that is, it is transcendental to duality and to superficial class distinctions. However, due to association with inert matter and the conditioning that comes from desire and the three modes of material nature, it inherits lesser qualities—qualities that are alien to the soul in its original form.

In a similar way, a hard-working, ethical person sometimes might have a child that does not represent him properly. Although coming from his seed, with a genetic connection that cannot be denied, the offspring may exhibit all inferior qualities, indicating little connection between child and father. This is the position of the pure soul—it takes on a body that is anything but pure. Once born in the material world, such a soul is usually given to conditioned behavior and even degraded acts, far from the characteristic loving purity of one's original identity in the spiritual world.

43. Material bodies are always created and destroyed as time moves on, and this happens more quickly than most people can imagine. Indeed, time is so subtle that it passes by imperceptibly, eluding the average person.

44. In time, each body goes through predictable stages of transformation—a similar principle can be observed in the flame of a candle, the current of a river, or fruits on a tree.

Commentary

Krishna refers to the inevitable plight of all embodied beings—impregnation, life in the womb, birth, infancy, childhood, youth, middling years, old age, and death—nine transformations all material bodies must go through, if they are allowed their natural life cycle and do not die prematurely. He will mention this catalog of transformations specifically in Verse 47. But before that, He will briefly elaborate on how these transformations are similar to the flame of a candle and the current of a river. He does not develop the "fruits on a tree" analogy because its correlation to human life is self-evident—fruits are born, grow, ripen, sweeten, rot, and die.

45. A flame's light consists of innumerable rays, constantly regenerating itself, through being, transformation and destruction. But if an ignorant person sees the light shining before him, he will misconstrue it as one consistent flame. A similar analogy: One in knowledge can understand that a flowing river consists of water that is ever replacing itself, always flowing in, passing by, and going to destinations unknown. Even so, one without knowledge will see the river and think it is all one body of water, without renewal, without change. These phenomena point to the following truth: Even though the material body is undergoing endless transformation, ignorant people tend to think that each particular stage of bodily development is who they really are.

46. In reality, a person does not actually take birth because of his past actions, and, since he is an eternal soul, he doesn't die, either. It is illusion only that makes birth and death appear as real, just as the element of fire, already existing in firewood, gives the appearance of coming into being and then vanishing.

47. Impregnation, gestation, birth, infancy, childhood, youth, middling years, old age, and death are the nine transformations of the body.

48. Make no mistake: The material body is distinct from the actual self. But because of ignorance, those in illusion falsely identify themselves with higher and lower bodily conceptions. If they are fortunate, however, they can rise beyond this fundamental misconception.

49. By the very fact that one's father and grandfather have died, one can anticipate one's own death. Similarly, by the birth of one's own son, or by witnessing the birth of other children, one can understand the nature of one's own birth. Thus, by deeply reflecting on the creation and destruction of material bodies in this way, one can rise beyond such dualities.

50. Look intently at the life of a tree, from its birth as a seed to its ultimate demise—though you may watch it closely, you still remain merely an observer, distinct and separate from the tree itself. Similarly, you may witness the birth and death of a material body—but know for certain that you are separate from it.

51. Due to a lack of intelligence, one is unable to distinguish oneself from material nature, thinking his body to be himself and the illusions in his midst to be real. Because of this, he is fundamentally bewildered, inadvertently initiating his journey into the cycle of birth and death.

Commentary

Ultimately, whatever our beliefs, something separates living beings from inorganic matter. Something is present in life that is absent in death. The physical, chemical components of the body remain in place at death: heart, brain, skeletal structure, and every chemical present in the body during life; but something else, something nonphysical has been lost. Whatever one chooses to call it, this nonphysical life force distinguishes a living body from an inert chemical shell. An intelligent person, one who is spiritually evolved, can see this—and that is Krishna's main point.

In fact, what do we know about this unique element that pervades the body? We know that classical science rejected it along with religious dogma—at least when referred to as "the soul"—and we know it has been accepted by religionists throughout history, with few exceptions. In the interest of finding terms acceptable to both classical science and religion, we will speak of "consciousness," for science studies consciousness as at least a potential nonmaterial force within the body, and religionists often accept consciousness as synonymous with or at least symptomatic of the soul, which is eternal.

This conception is consistent with the First Law of Thermodynamics, or the Law of Conservation of Energy. Basically, this law says that energy cannot be created or destroyed. If it exists, it continues to exist. Likewise, if the "soul" exists at all, as Krishna says it does, then it must subsist in sustained existence. As the *Bhagavad Gita* tells us: "For the existent there is no cessation, and for the non-existent—like a dream or an illusion—there is no endurance" (2.16).

Where does the energy within the body go at the time of death? Nature supplies numerous hints that suggest a sensible answer. Consider, for example, the changes of the body we undergo in this one life, from childhood, to youth, to old age—changes that occur while the person remains in the same body. Physiologically, the cells of our bodies constantly deteriorate and die so that after approximately seven years the cellular structure of the body has been completely overhauled. Our bodies do not contain a single one of the molecules that it contained seven years ago. In this sense, the body can be compared to a whirlpool. The essential form appears the same, but all the ingredients stream through at a dizzying pace.

In a seventy-year lifetime, a person physiologically "dies" and is "reborn" ten times; and while these intermediate "deaths" do not involve reincarnation as such, they allow us the remarkable experience of looking back, in this lifetime, to previous lives: as infants, children, youths, and grown-ups. These are not—strictly speaking—previous lifetimes: The evidence available suggests that reincarnation permits us only rarely to carry the recollection of our previous life into our new one. They are, nonetheless, past physical selves that no longer exist. Different bodies, same person—a simple exercise in seeing the difference between the physical and spiritual self, in seeing who we appear to be and who we really are.

52. Wandering aimlessly in the material world because of his desire for sense gratification, the conditioned soul may eventually come into contact with the mode of goodness, taking a birth among the sages or demigods. However, the more common scenario is this: Because of contact with the mode of passion, he becomes a demon or, at best, a human being, and by association with the mode of ignorance, he takes birth as a lower being, in a ghostly body, or in some animal species.

53. Although he is never actually entangled in material activities, the soul becomes captivated by sensual engagement and bewildered by a network of illusions. In that sense, he is similar to a person who sees others dancing and singing and starts to imitate them.

54–55. In the same way that a tree's reflection may look like the tree itself is quivering when seen in the ripples of a river, or just as the earth may appear to spin if one focuses one's eyes in a particular way, or like the world of a fantasy or dream—the soul's involvement in material life, in the realm of sense gratification, is actually false, without any substantial reality.

56. Because conditioned souls focus on sense gratification—which is at the heart of all materialistic life—it will always be a part of them, even though it lacks existential substance, just like a nasty dream.

57. Therefore, O Uddhava, please try to avoid sense gratification, for it will prevent you from realizing the self.

Commentary

Thus, for some thirty verses, Krishna elaborates on the nature of the self and the difference between the soul and the body. Indeed, the importance of this subject is highlighted earlier in the *Bhagavad Gita*, too: "Just as in this life we reincarnate through childhood, youth, and old age, similarly we transmigrate into another body at the time of death" (2.13). "But know that the real entity who pervades the physical body is indestructible. No one is able to cause the destruction of the imperishable soul" (2.17). "The soul never takes birth and never dies at any time, nor does it come into being again when the body is again created. The soul is birthless, eternal, imperishable, and timeless, and it is never terminated when bodily existence comes to an end" (2.20). "As a person gives up old and worn-out garments and accepts new apparel in due course, the embodied soul similarly abandons old and worn-out bodies only to accept new ones" (2.22). "For one who has taken birth, death is certain, and for one who has died, birth is certain" (2.27).

Thus, in His instructions to Arjuna, Krishna elaborates on many of the truths we also find in the *Uddhava Gita*: The soul is eternal and can never be slain; it is who we really are, even though we now identify with our current material body; we transmigrate through the various species of life, according to our desire and karma; we gradually achieve a human form, and even then we travel through numerous bodies, from those in ignorance, into passion, and then finally into goodness. When ready, we come in contact with a self-realized soul, who helps us achieve love of God, at which time we may return to our original position as eternal loving servants in the spiritual realm.

58–59. One who desires the highest goal in life, that is, self-realization, should undergo any and all difficulties to keep oneself safe on the spiritual platform. And this holds true even if people foist upon you neglect, insult, ridicule, envy, physical expulsion, prejudice, and so on—even if they spit on you, urinate on you, or whatever.

Commentary

Unfortunately, history is replete with such reprehensible behavior. We need merely remember how the vast majority of Jesus' contemporaries mistreated and eventually killed him.

60. Sri Uddhava said: Because You are the best of all speakers, I know You will help me understand [how people can mistreat loving devotees].

61. O soul of the universe, conditioning is very intense, and it is therefore quite difficult for even wise people to tolerate harshness when directed against them. But, I must say, Your devotees, who are established in Your loving service and who are peaceful because of residence at Your lotus feet—they are able to tolerate such decadent behavior, indeed, and so much more.

Commentary

Uddhava is at first amazed that the Lord's devotees would be mistreated in the ways described above. But then he realizes something even more important: Ordinary people cannot tolerate mistreatment and, in fact, often want to be treated like kings and queens. Not so for Krishna's devotees. They are naturally humble, and, because they are innately peaceful and happy, they are able to tolerate all forms of mistreatment, accepting it as the Lord's mercy.

Chapter 17

The Avanti Brahmin

1. **Sri Uddhava, most venerable among all devotees, thus respectfully asked Lord Krishna about how to deal with harsh words and reprehensible offenses committed toward His devotees. The Lord first expressed appreciation for Uddhava's inquiry and then began to reply.**

Commentary

It is Shukadeva Goswami, the narrator of the *Bhagavata Purana*, who utters this first verse, telling us that this chapter will pick up where Chapter Sixteen left off. Lord Krishna had mentioned that worldly men often mistreat His devotees, for they do not understand the devotees' glorious status. In response, Uddhava asked how this could be so.

2. **Lord Krishna said: O disciple of Brihaspati, even saintly people are naturally disturbed when insulted by thoughtless men, and it can upset their usually settled mind.**

3. **Even when sharp arrows pierce the chest, entering the heart, the resultant pain does not equal that coming from the arrows of harsh, insulting words perpetrated by thoughtless men.**

4. **My dear Uddhava, for you to truly grasp this, you will need to hear a well-known, auspicious story. Please listen carefully.**

5. **Long ago, there was a renunciant who was continually insulted by a group of impious men. Though the disparaging words went on for a long period of time, he always tolerated it, for he considered that the criticism was the result of his own previous karma. Please hear his story.**

6. **In Avanti country, long ago, there lived a Brahmin who was very rich and gifted in many ways. Although a successful businessman, he was also a miserly person, given to lust, greed, and anger.**

Commentary

Ujjain (also known as Ujjayini and Avanti) is an ancient city of central India, in the Malwa region of Madhya Pradesh. The first significant kingdom in the region was Avanti, an important power in western India by around 500 B.C.E., when the Maurya Empire annexed it to the region in question. Thus, the reference to Avanti indicates that the story may have a basis in historical fact, rather than just being told for instructive value.

7. **His stinginess made his home a hellish place, devoid of religiosity. Harsh words were frequently heard in his household, where family members and guests were commonly mistreated, verbally and otherwise.**
8. **Because of his miserly nature, his entire family, including his sons, daughters, in-laws, wife, and servants, became disgusted with him, never treating him with any affection.**

Commentary

As expressed more clearly in Verse 9, auspicious interaction with these five types of family members is said to be governed by five higher beings, who allow success in family relations or disallow it, depending on one's *karma* and attitude.

9. **His thoughtless ways angered the five demigods responsible for family relations. They watched as he guarded his wealth like a demon, losing all focus in life. Because of his selfish preoccupation, he inadvertently deprived himself of both religiosity and sense enjoyment.**
10. **Through his neglect of these higher beings, as seen in his mistreatment of all five types of family members, he brought ruination upon himself, losing all his wealth. Everything was soon lost.**
11. **My dear Uddhava—his own relatives absconded with a large portion of his wealth. The balance left him by way of thieves, and also because of fate, the effects of time, and through taxation.**
12. **In due course, his money and property were gone, and his family members abandoned him. As a result, there was no end to his anguish.**
13. **With nothing left, he lamented piteously. He cried countless tears, and he thought deeply about all that had happened. Just then, he was overtaken by a sense of renunciation.**
14. **The Brahmin articulated his plight: O what a terrible calamity! I've spent my life in vain, working hard for money but without**

reason: I never used my earnings for religiosity nor even for material enjoyment.

15. The wealth of the miserly brings little happiness. Indeed, it is the very source of their torment, and when death comes, it forces them to the most hellish of destinations.

16. Just as physical beauty is thoroughly diminished by even a trace of white leprosy, greed is known to destroy the fame of the famous and the superior qualities of those who are virtuous.

17. Successful men work very hard in the pursuit of wealth, experiencing fear, anxiety, and delusion in the process. This is true while earning, attaining, increasing, protecting, losing, and enjoying their money.

18–19. There are fifteen unwanted qualities that overtake people who have greed for wealth: thievery, violence, telling lies, duplicity, lust, anger, confusion, pride, quarreling, enmity, faithlessness, envy, and the dangers caused by the opposite sex, gambling and intoxication. Although these qualities are clearly undesirable, people foolishly chase after them while in pursuit of earning money. There is no question that one should avoid these things, and instead focus on the good things in life.

20. Those who are closest to you—your brothers, spouse, parents or friends—will lose interest in you and become your enemy over a single coin.

21. Indeed, even a small amount of money is enough to make relatives and friends angry, their forgiveness a thing of the past. Becoming like an opponent, they lose all sense of camaraderie, developing total disregard for those who are near and dear—even to the point of taking a life.

22. Although it is rare to become a human—a type of birth that is prayed for even by beings on higher planets—it is even more rare to become a Brahmin. Thus, if one is fortunate enough to achieve Brahminical status, and then to disregard the opportunity by behaving in non-Brahminical ways, he is the greatest of fools, unaware of his own self-interest. Truly, such a person will lack fortune in this life and his demise, too, will be inauspicious.

23. Having achieved this special human frame, which leads to both heaven and liberation, one would be foolish to squander it. Yet attachment to the worthless commodity that men call material property is certainly doing just that: wasting the human form of life.

24. Using wealth properly means sharing it with the appropriate people—the higher beings who enable us to earn it, sages, forefathers and the people around us, including immediate relatives and in-laws. In addition, of course, one must take care of his own needs with his money. But if one neglects to do all of the above, he is using his wealth in the mood of an unfortunate rogue and he will develop reprehensible qualities as a result of it.

25. People with discriminating intelligence are able to make use of their money, youth, and strength for higher purposes. But I have wasted all three just trying to enhance my wealth. Now I am old, and I wonder—what purpose did it all serve?

26. An intelligent person should avoid suffering by abandoning vain efforts to acquire wealth. Indeed, the entire world is within the grips of an illusory potency that virtually forces them to run after money.

27. Consider this: Death is coming to each of us in due course. Given this inescapable fact, what is the use of wealth or of those from whom we might acquire it? Of what value is sense gratification or those who offer it to us? And, for that matter, what is the value of any type of fruitive gain—for each variety simply causes us to again take birth in the material world?

28. Now I know: The Supreme Lord, known as Hari [Krishna], who is the abode of all higher beings, should be satisfied with my life. Nothing else matters. Indeed, it is He who has led me to my current pitiable condition, forcing me into a mood of detachment. Yes! This, indeed, is the boat that will carry me through this turbulent ocean of birth and death.

29. I will not waste another moment. If there is any time left, I will perform religious rituals and practice severe austerities, pushing my body to the limit. No longer confused about the purpose of life, I will pursue that which is really in my self-interest, finding satisfaction only in the self.

30. With this determination, I am praying that all higher beings shower their mercy upon me. Indeed, Maharaj Khatvanga was able to achieve the spiritual world in a single moment.

Commentary

The Avanti Brahmin recalls the example of King Khatvanga, from the *Bhagavata Purana*, Book Two. This king diligently fought on behalf of the demigods, winning the boon that he could have whatever he wanted. His one desire: He wanted to know when his life would end. Unfortunately, he found out that he had barely a moment left. With that information, he immediately surrendered to Krishna and attained the supreme destination.

Our once-wealthy Brahmin wanted this same good fortune. He was old and regretful, and he knew he had squandered his life. Still, he now had a new passion: detachment and a clearer view of what life was really all about. He therefore prayed that, like Maharaj Khatvanga, he could quickly accomplish the supreme goal of life.

31. The Supreme Lord spoke: Focusing on his new goal, the determined Avanti Brahmin cut through the knots of material desire within his heart. He then became a renunciant, a Sannyasi, both peaceful and silent.

32. Without any attachments, he wandered far and wide, always keeping control over his intelligence, senses and internal life air. Living on charity, he became a loner, traveling to various cities and villages begging alms just to stay alive. He never spoke of his advanced spirituality, and others were thus naturally unaware of who he was.

33. Because of this, O kind one, people saw him as just a dirty old beggar, without purpose or goal. And those that were particularly cruel tended to ridicule him, harass him, and insult him.

34. Some of them would grab his Sannyasi rod, while others would take away the waterpot he was using as a begging bowl. When he wasn't looking, they would steal his deerskin seat, or his chanting beads, or even his torn, worn-out clothing. Often, they would tease him, pretending to offer back what they had just taken, but then they would run off again, laughing and saying unkind things.

35. Even when he sat peacefully on the bank of a river, preparing the food that he had collected through his begging, they would sneak into his camp to urinate on his edibles, and they would sometimes spit on him as well.

36. They would often try to make him speak, knowing that he had taken a vow of silence. If he would not oblige them, they would beat him with sticks. Some falsely accused him of being a thief, while others would bind him with a rope, shouting obscenities and enjoying his torment.

37. Accusing him of hypocrisy, they would say, "He is just a cheater, using religion to make money—having lost his wealth and being abandoned by his family, he's trying to earn an income by pretending to be a holy man."

38–39. They would often joke at his expense, saying things like, "Look at this great sage in our midst! He is as powerful as the Himalayas. His vow of silence shows his great accomplishment—making him just like a duck." Others would pass gas in his presence, trying to disturb him—and sometimes they would bind him in chains, keeping him captive like a forgotten pet.

40. As a true Brahmin, however, he never took offense. Rather, he understood that all suffering in his life was meant to be, whether inflicted by other living beings, natural calamities, or as a result of his own body. It was assigned to him by fate.

41. True to his status as a Brahmin, he remained determined in his spiritual duties, even while being harassed and insulted by these obviously inferior men. Well established in the mode of goodness, he began to sing the following song.

42. The Brahmin sang: The people in our midst are never the cause of our happiness and distress, nor are the demigods, our own body, the planets, our past work (karma), or time. Instead, it is the mind alone that causes happiness and distress and perpetuates the cycle of birth and death.

Commentary

As the *Bhagavad Gita* tells us:

> For the person who has conquered his mind, it is the best of friends; but for one who has failed to do so, it will certainly be his greatest enemy. Indeed, for one who has conquered the mind, the Lord in the heart is already achieved, for such a person has attained inner tranquility. For him, happiness and distress, heat and cold, honor and dishonor are all the same. (6.6–7)

These are the truths being expressed by the Avanti Brahmin, and he will elaborate on them in upcoming verses.

The mind's central role in the experience of both pleasure and pain should not be underestimated. In fact, an uncontrolled mind is the root of all worldly affliction (*klesha*), which Indic texts tell us exist in three basic categories: (1) *adhidaivika-klesha*, or suffering brought on by higher beings, who instigate natural calamities, such as droughts, earthquakes, and storms; (2) *adhibhautika-klesha*, which refers to suffering caused by other living entities, such as insects, enemies, and so on; and (3) *adhyatmika-klesha*, which are the more immediate pains caused by one's own body and mind. In fact, however, close inspection reveals that all of these forms of suffering, as well as their opposites—that is, those things that bring us pleasure—come down to our own mental disposition, for whatever happens to us in the external world will be experienced in light of what we feel and think. And this will determine whether we enjoy what happens to us or whether it affects us adversely. In this way, the mind is central in our experience of pleasure and pain.

This is not to say that *adhidaivika, adhibhautika*, and *adhyatmika* do not have objective reality—these are the sources through which pain comes to us. Nonetheless, if this received pain is not filtered through a receptive mind, it cannot take hold or affect the living entity in any way. Therefore, Krishna says in the *Bhagavad Gita*, "O Arjuna, the nonpermanent appearance of heat and cold, or happiness and distress—and their disappearance in due course—are like the appearance and disappearance of winter and summer seasons. They arise from sense perception only, and one must learn to tolerate them without being disturbed" (2.14). That is to say, in the summer months, cooling water may create a pleasurable sensation on the body, but in the winter, this same water may be shunned for being too cold. In either case, the water is the same, but we perceive it as pleasant or unpleasant due to its contact with the body at different times. *It is our perception that makes it pleasing or painful.* This is the point.

43. **Because the mind is so powerful, it brings to life the material modes of nature, which spark off various kinds of material activities in goodness, passion, and ignorance. Corresponding statuses of life arise due to actions perpetrated in each of these modes.**

44. **The Supersoul, or God in the heart of all living beings, is not performing action as such, because He is already transcendentally situated, although He is indeed present along with the soul and the struggling mind within the material body. He is the dearest friend, witnessing all our actions from nearby. The tiny spirit soul—you and I—on the other hand, tend to identify with the body and mind, which is like a mirror reflecting who we really are. But it is inverted, creating the image of the material world. This is why we become engrossed in enjoying objects of desire and entangled in material life.**

45. **There are many practices for those who pursue higher reality: charity, ritualistic duties, religious principles, studying scriptures, pious works, and purifying vows. All such acts, however, lose meaning if they are not directed toward controlling the mind. Though many people are unaware of this, focusing the mind on God is what yoga is all about.**

46. **When the mind is focused and at peace, there is little need for ritualistic charity and other religious practices. Conversely, if the mind remains uncontrolled, such pious acts will not have their desired effect.**

47. The senses are always under the control of the mind, while the mind itself is often independent. In fact, at times it seems stronger than just about anything, and its power is awesome. Therefore, if one can bring the mind under control, he becomes the master of all the senses.

48. If one does not get this formidable opponent—the mind—under control, then its intolerable urges, which pull at the heartstrings, will leave him fundamentally confused, provoking anger and a tendency to quarrel with others. Because of the mind, people conclude that someone is either their friend or enemy and that still others are merely indifferent to them.

49. Identifying with the body, which comes about because of the mind, most people lack even rudimentary intelligence, thinking in terms of "I" and "mine." Because of this illusion, they feel separate from everyone and everything, and they exist in the darkness of ignorance.

50. If you think that the harsh people around me are the cause of my happiness and distress, then you are not considering the spiritual element. Such happiness and distress do not pertain to the soul; they are functions of the material body and mind. If you bite your tongue with your own teeth, to whom can you reasonably direct your anger?

51. Similarly, if you think that the higher universal administrators of the cosmos cause our suffering, then, still, you'd have to explain how this relates to the spirit soul. Entities who perform action in this world—and also those entities that are acted upon—merely have bodies and minds that are subject to material conditions and their presiding deities. But it is not who they really are. Thus, who is to blame if one limb of the body attacks another?

52. If happiness and distress were coming from the soul, those experiences would be our original nature, and so we wouldn't need to commend or blame anyone for what happens to us. And if it is *not* the soul itself that causes happiness and distress, then we need not blame others anyway, since both happiness and distress would be illusory. In the end, then, only the soul actually exists, and if we were to perceive something outside the soul, that perception would certainly be an illusion. Consequently, since happiness and distress do not actually refer to who we really are—the soul—why should we become angry with ourselves or with others?

53. And if we lean toward the astrological idea that the planets cause our happiness and suffering, we are then, again, leaving the soul

out of the equation. It is well known that the planets only have influence on entities that have taken birth, but we should remember that we are not the material body—the body takes birth but the soul remains aloof. In any case, should we direct our anger to the stars?

54. **Sometimes we say that our own work (karma) is the cause of our happiness and distress, but this still neglects the soul. Material work arises because there is a spiritual agent, one who acts through a body, who is conscious. Happiness and distress, as a reaction to such work, affect the body. But since the body is not the living being inside the body, it is not the actual recipient of happiness and distress, nor is the soul, who is completely spiritual and is ultimately unaffected by the material body. Thus, since karma does not impact on either the body or the soul, at whom can one become angry?**

55. **If we think of time as the cause of happiness and distress, we are still forgetful of the spiritual soul—time is a manifestation of God's energy, as are the multitudinous living entities, both manifesting through time. Therefore, just as it would not be said that fire burns its own flames, or that cold might harm its own snowflakes, time cannot affect the soul. Overall, then, let it now be said: the spirit soul is completely transcendental, meaning that it is beyond both happiness and distress, at least the material variety. Why, therefore, should we become angry at anyone?**

Commentary

The Avanti Brahmin should be clearly understood. In the preceding verses, he was not really talking about how happiness and distress actually arise, although this certainly seemed to be his subject. Rather, he was talking about who we really are.

Happiness and distress, in fact, will arise for all the reasons he mentioned in these verses, but his real point is this: We should not take this happiness and distress seriously, because it does not really affect the soul, who we really are. And because it does not affect who we really are, we need not get angry at anyone or anything, because they cannot truly accost the soul, they cannot hurt a transcendental entity. In our enlightened state, we remain untouched. This is why he was able to remain tolerant, despite the volumes of abuse inflicted upon him.

56. **Our conception of the self forms our illusory material existence, and this gives rise to our experiences of happiness and distress. But the spirit soul, it bears repeating, is transcendental to**

material nature—he is never actually affected by material happiness or distress in any place, under any circumstances, or through the actions of any person. If one could understand this simple truth, he need not fear anything in the cosmos.

57. I shall cross the fathomless ocean of ignorance by being steady in my devotion to the Supreme. This is the method given to us by the previous lineage holders, the great teachers in disciplic succession, who were unwavering in their devotion to Mukunda (Krishna).

Commentary

The Avanti Brahmin's song ends at Verse 57, with Krishna adding a few words below.

58. The Supreme Lord said: And so the loss of his wealth and property was a great boon for the Avanti Brahmin. In his heart, he had found the bliss of detachment, which freed him from all unhappiness. Leaving behind everything he once knew, he adopted the Sannyasa order of life, journeying to many distant places. And when he was harassed or insulted by heartless fools, which happened frequently, he remained steadfast in his duty, for he was inwardly happy, always singing his song as expressed in these verses.

59. It is the souls' own inner confusion—and nothing else—that makes him experience happiness and distress. It is ignorance only that informs his perception of friends, neutral parties and enemies. In fact, material life in general is like a dark cloud created from a fundamental illusion: mistaking the body for the self.

60. This is why I say, O Uddhava, that you should focus your intelligence on Me, completely controlling your mind. This is what the science of yoga is really all about.

61. Anyone who listens to or recites to others this song of the famed Avanti renunciant, which thoroughly analyzes the nature of the self, meditating on it without distraction, will never again find himself confounded by the dualities of happiness and distress.

Chapter 18

Sankhya Philosophy

1. **The Supreme Lord said: The great sages of the past have given us the science of Sankhya, which helps one distinguish between matter and spirit. By thoroughly comprehending this science, in a mood of devotion, one can overcome the illusion of material duality.**

Commentary

In Chapter Seventeen, focusing on the teachings of the Avanti Brahmin, Lord Krishna conveyed the importance of understanding the distinction between the body and the self, and how this distinction affects our conceptions of happiness and distress, ultimately allowing us to transcend both and to attain a state of blissful spirituality. Now, in this chapter, He will elaborate on Sankhya, the distinction between matter and spirit, expressed through analytical categories and a thorough exposition of material elements. Lord Kapila had explained this science in the *Bhagavatam*'s Third Book, and Krishna had touched on this earlier in the *Uddhava Gita*, but here He will summarize it for context in terms of what He has been telling Uddhava about the nature of the self. His purpose is self-evident: By understanding the distinction between matter and spirit, it becomes easier to understand the differences between the body (matter) and the self (spirit), which has been the subject of the last couple of chapters.

2. **There was time—during the Krita-yuga, also known as Satya-yuga, millions of years prior, when all people were evolved spiritually—when seer and seen existed as one.**

Commentary

At the dawn of creation, and for the first world age, known as Krita-yuga, all living beings were spiritually realized, aware of their connection to the Lord. They understood both their oneness with Him and their difference as well, relishing a sweet relationship with the Absolute Truth. But in due course, as the world ages trudged forward, realization diminished, and living beings were not as spiritually equipped as they once were. Krishna implies that when this natural spiritual evolution wanes, it is necessary to find various means to distinguish between matter and spirit, an understanding that was innate in prior ages. Sankhya is one such way to cultivate this realization.

3. **Although the Supreme Truth is one, free from material dualities and beyond experimental knowledge, He became manifest in this world as two—material nature and the living beings who attempt to enjoy that nature as part of life.**

Commentary

Although the Lord's energy expands as both material nature and as all living beings, He remains a separate entity, a distinct Person, eternally existing as the sum and substance of all reality.

4. **One can understand these two categories in the following way: Material nature embodies both the subtle causes of matter and its manifest products, i.e., material substances (*prakriti*), while the conscious living entity, all living beings, are thought of as "the enjoyer" (*purusha*), or those who use material substances.**

5. **I brought material nature into existence through My glance, and the three material modes—goodness, passion and ignorance—which are part of material nature, appeared in this world to fulfill the desires of innumerable conditioned souls, who also come from Me.**

6. **The first transformation of material nature arose from the modes, along with the *mahat-tattva*, the primary elements of the material universe. From this came the false ego, which is a sense of identity that is separate from God—this is the underlying illusion permeating each and every conditioned being.**

7. **False ego is responsible for physical sensation, the senses, and the mind, involving both spirit and matter. It manifests in three varieties: goodness, passion and ignorance.**

Commentary

Although the soul ultimately is untouched by anything material, she becomes implicated in the physical world through a desire to enjoy without reference to God and through an erroneous identification with the body. In due course, material conditioning overtakes her, and, depending on just how this occurs, she will lean toward action in one or another of the three modes—all the modes will affect her life in numerous ways, but one mode will predominate.

8. Perception of the body and its sensations arise from false identification (*ahankara*, false ego) in the mode of ignorance, and from this the gross elements come into being. The senses themselves arise due to false ego in the mode of passion, and from false ego filtered through the mode of goodness we get the eleven universal administrators.

Commentary

Verse 8 summarizes a complex outline, originally detailed by Lord Kapila, of how material existence is initially created. The specifics are too elaborate to go into here, but the mention of eleven "universal administrators" should briefly be addressed. The entities referred to are Brahma, Chandra, Mitra, Upendra, Agni, Indra, the Ashvin twins (counted as one), Varuna, the deities of the four direction, and the wind and the sun. Many other universal administrators are mentioned in Vedic texts, but these were the initial demigods who played distinct roles in cosmic creation.

9. Through My energy all these elements came together and functioned in a systematic way, giving birth to "the egg of the universe." Just see: This egg has become My unsurpassed home as well.

Commentary

When Krishna creates the cosmos, He enters into it as Vishnu, and it thus becomes His dwelling place as well, as He will explain in the next verse.

10. I manifest Myself within that egg, floating on an ocean of causal water. While in that restful position, a universal lotus arises from My navel—this is the birthplace of Lord Brahma.

Commentary

Unlike many denominations of Hinduism, which ascribe to Narayana or Vishnu the categorical distinction of being the source of all incarnations, the *Bhagavatam* (1.3.28) is clear in saying that Krishna is actually the source (*krishnas tu bhagavan svayam*), even if Vishnu, as Lord of creation, appears earlier in manifest history. The Gaudiya Vaishnava tradition endorses and develops this point of view. Just because Krishna incarnates in the visible world at a later date (merely 5,000 years ago), they say, does not mean that He is not prior in both a spiritual and an ontological sense. Indeed, He is the source of all manifestations of the Supreme.

Although Krishna is the original Personality of Godhead, He has many manifestations and incarnations. This truth unfolds in the context of our present discussion on creation as follows:

(1) Mahavishnu, also known as Karanadakashayi Vishnu, lies on the causal ocean, which appears in one corner of the spiritual world. He manifests the

mahat-tattva (or the sum total of material energy). It is into this *mahat-tattva* that He exhales all of the seed-like universes through the pores of His skin. These seed-like universes then expand as the different material elements, forming coverings around them. Each of the coverings is ten times thicker than the previous covering and eventually manifest as a shell-like enclosure. When Mahavishnu impregnates the living entities by His glance into material nature, it begins to manifest its various energies.

(2) When the universes have thus developed in the womb of material nature, Mahavishnu expands as Garbhodakashayi Vishnu, who enters into each universe with the living entities assigned to that particular region, thus activating each universe by His presence. This is the manifestation of Krishna referred to in this verse. He lies down on Ananta Sesha, a form of Balaram, Krishna's elder brother and first expansion, who, in turn, lies on the Garbha ocean—a body of liquid composed of the Lord's divine perspiration, which fills half the universe. From His navel comes a lotus bud, which, it is said, represents the total form of all living entities' fruitive activity. The lotus blossoms and in so doing dissipates the darkness of the as yet unformed universe.

On top of the lotus, Brahma, the first living being, appears. Situated on the lotus, Brahma has no sense—at least not yet—of what goes on around him. He begins entering the stem and climbing down to find its origin. Not finding anything, Brahma again returns to the top of the lotus where he hears the Sanskrit word, *ta-pa* ("austerity"), obviously a hint from Vishnu as to what must be done.

Hearing this sound, Brahma undergoes penance for 1,000 celestial years, which is described as being 6 × 30 × 12 × 1,000 earthly years. A very long time.

Being pleased with Brahma's *tapasya*, or austerity, the Lord gives him a vision of the spiritual planets. Seeing Vaikuntha, the Supreme abode, Brahma becomes happy and bows to God in full surrender. Satisfied with Brahma's devotion, the Lord expresses His glee by revealing how to create the universe.

(3) To maintain the universe, Garbhodakashayi Vishnu expands as Kshirodakashayi Vishnu, who is the all-pervading Supersoul (Paramatma). By entering into every atom and into the hearts of all living beings, He maintains the whole universe as a loving witness and dearest friend.

11. By My mercy, Lord Brahma, the first created being, used his passion in a constructive way—he performed great austerities, creating the three planetary divisions, Bhur, Bhuvar and Svar, along with their presiding deities.

Commentary

The three broad planetary divisions, Bhur, Bhuvar, and Svar, refer to earthly planets, hellish planets, and heavenly planets, respectively. This is further divided into fourteen divisions: Patala, Rasatala, Mahatala, Talatala, Sutala, Vitala, Atala, Bhurloka, Bhuvarloka, Svargaloka, Maharloka, Janaloka, Tapoloka, and Satyaloka. Vaishnava texts elaborate on the different types of planets and the living beings who reside there.

12. **Svar was established so that the demigods might have a heavenly region to enact their work; Bhuvar was created for ghostly spirits; and Bhur, the earthly or middle planetary system, facilitates humans and other mortals. Those transcendentalists who strive for Me, attaining ultimate liberation, go far beyond these three levels.**

Commentary

This interesting verse draws a distinction between heavenly planets, Svarloka, and the kingdom of God, which is the destination of pure devotees. Generally, when one practices religion—and this includes Vedic religion—one seeks godly enjoyment and various rewards for his pious work. Such rewards are enjoyed on upper material planets, subtle though these planets may be. But for those who seek no reward, wanting only to serve God with a pure heart full of love and devotion—these souls journey to a world far beyond the three divisions of material planets, rising above even heaven to Krishna's world, known as Vaikuntha.

13. **The region below the earth was created for demons and Nagas, various kinds of serpents. Thus, the three worlds correspond to the types of work various people tend to perform, especially in conjunction with the three modes of material nature.**

14. **Through the practice of ordinary religion, mystic yoga, severe austerities, and the renounced order of life, the upper planets of Maharloka, Janoloka, Tapoloka and Satyaloka are attained. It is only through Bhakti-yoga, the yoga of devotion, however, that one can achieve the Supreme destination.**

Commentary

Again, Krishna underlines the difference between attaining heavenly planets and reaching His Supreme abode.

15. **As the ultimate source of everything, including time, I am responsible for awarding the results of all fruitive work. Accordingly, I allow some people to rise up toward the surface of that vast river known as the modes, while others tend to be hopelessly submerged.**

Commentary

Lord Krishna reveals His part in the placement of living beings within the three established planetary systems: According to their work within the three modes of nature, they in a sense determine their own placement. Krishna is the overseer, however, and He ensures that the system works properly, usually through His universal administrators.

The analogy of a river is fitting here: When people act in the mode of goodness, it is like rising to the top of the river, where one can breathe and exist peacefully. However, if one acts in passion, and, worse still, in ignorance, it is like being caught at the bottom, where suffocation is likely and darkness takes precedence.

16. The visible features of this world—small or great, thin or stout—reflect a given thing's essential nature and also that of its enjoyer, the spiritual person within.

17. With gold and earth as raw ingredients, one can construct golden ornaments, such as bracelets and earrings, and clay pots and saucers, respectively. The original ingredients exist prior to the products made from them, and when the products eventually cease to be, the original ingredients—in this case, gold and earth—will continue on. In this way, essential ingredients are present in the beginning and at the end, and also in the middle phase, though at that time they take on a particular form. It is to this form that we assign a particular name for convenience sake, such as bracelet, earring, pot or saucer. With this as a backdrop, we can understand that, as a general rule, essential ingredients must exist before the creation of a given product and after that product's destruction, too. Moreover, the same ingredients will also be present during a particular product's manifest phase, as the substance of its existence.

18. Each material object, which is naturally composed of a basic ingredient, can be turned into another material object through a process of transformation. In this way, one created object tends to become the starting point for another. A given thing is thus considered real if it possesses the basic ingredients of another object, as seen in its origin and final state.

Commentary

The traditional example is that of a clay pot, which is considered real because its ingredients are real both before and after it is a clay pot. In other words, clay comes from the earth, which is real. Real begets real, and false begets false. The traditional example of falsity is a dream. No matter what products are built or created in a dream, they are to be considered imaginary, because both before and after those products come into "existence," they are part of a dream, which is false.

19. Understanding this truth, we can see that the material universe is real, having nature, which comes from God, as its original ingredient and its final state. In this way, O Uddhava, please see nature, the Supreme Enjoyer, and time as not different from Me.

Commentary

A class of philosophers in India claim that the material universe is unreal—a mere illusion that has no substance. Krishna refutes this view with strong logic. However, it must be understood that the "reality" of this universe is different than that of the spiritual realm. Matter is temporary—real but lacking the eternal feature of the transcendent realm. This makes it *illusory*, perhaps, but not *illusion* as such. Because it comes from Krishna, who is real, it must also be real, even if the nature of how and to what extent it is real might be negotiable.

20. The world's continued existence comes about through the glance of God, which is reflected in procreation, allowing us to participate in the supreme and diversified flow of life.

21. The Universal Form (Virat-rupa) comes from Me, and it is with that manifestation that I display variety, exhibiting countless nuances. This variety is seen in the world through My ongoing creation, maintenance and destruction of the various planetary systems. My Universal Form accomplishes all this by coordinating limitless combinations of the five elements.

Commentary

The *Bhagavatam*'s Second Book, Chapter One, explains "the Universal Form"—it is God as the manifest universe. Since it is a given that He exists, in some sense, as everything, there are legitimate ways to see Him in all of nature. These multifarious manifestations of the Supreme, taken together, constitute the Virat-rupa, and meditating on Him in this form, under proper direction, is legitimate.

This confidential form was shown to Arjuna in the *Bhagavad Gita*, and to others at different times throughout history. Arjuna claims to have seen "everything at once, all in one place" (11.13). This is how he defines the Universal Form. Mother Yashoda, who, according to tradition, appeared as Krishna's mother in the material world, some 5,000 years ago, saw a similar vision. This is the dynamic aspect of Krishna's Godhood, and it is inconceivable.

How does it apply in the present context? The *Bhagavatam* tells us: "When the twenty-three principal elements were sparked into action by the will of God, the gigantic Universal Form, or the Vishva-rupa, came into existence" (3.6.4). "As God, in His plenary portion, entered into the elements of the universal creation, they transformed into the gigantic form in which all the planetary systems and all movable and immovable creations find their resting place" (3.6.5). Thus, the Universal Form plays an essential role in creation.

Ultimately, the *Bhagavatam* tells us that,

> The conception of the Virat-rupa, as appearing in the material world, might be seen as imaginary. Its purpose is to enable those who are not yet spiritually evolved to adjust to the idea of God as having a form. In point of fact, however, the Lord has no material form. He is totally spiritual. (1.3.30)

This is to say that the Virat-rupa, the Universal Form, serves a specific purpose, but in the end, one should develop love for Krishna, the person—this is the goal of yoga and of religion in general.

22–27. When the world is annihilated, all mortal bodies go back to the earth, merging into food. Food manifests as grains, which comes from the ground. The ground is subsumed into its subtle sensation, which is smell. This merges into water, and water further merges back into its own essential quality: taste. Taste in its turn blends back into fire, which merges into form. Form merges into touch, and touch into ether. Ether then merges back into sound, at which point the senses all merge into their own origins, including the demigods that preside over them. It is these great personalities, O gentle Uddhava, who merge into the overarching mind, which itself merges into false ego in the mode of goodness. Sound, too, goes back into the false ego, but in the mode of ignorance—and this all-powerful false ego, the first of all the physical elements, also merges into the totality of material nature through passion. This total material nature, which is the resting place of the three basic modes, loses its existence in the modes themselves, which then merge into the unmanifest form of nature, the *mahat-tattva*. This, of course, merges into time, and time into the Supreme Lord, present in the form of the omniscient Vishnu, the original source of all living beings. That origin of all life merges into Me, the original, unborn God, who remains alone. Although established within Myself, it is from Me that all creation and annihilation come into being.

Commentary

Krishna explains the process of annihilation, which is, in effect, a reversal of the process of creation, wherein all the material elements as listed here emanate out from Him, into Vishnu, into time, into the *mahat-tattva*, and so on. In the end, everything merges back into the prior element until everything merges back into God.

28. This detailed knowledge of universal annihilation can destroy the illusion of duality, just as the rising sun removes darkness from the sky.

29. For this reason, I, who know all truths, both material and spiritual, have explained Sankhya to you, My dear devotee. By this systematic analysis of creation and annihilation, you can destroy the illusion of doubt.

Chapter 19

Beyond the Three Modes of Material Nature

1. The Supreme Lord said: O Uddhava, please hear from Me how each living being acquires his distinct nature through the material modes: goodness, passion, and ignorance.

Commentary

Though the Lord already has referred to the three modes in several places in the *Uddhava Gita*, He now explains them more fully, especially because His explanation of (1) Sankhya, wherein material elements are analyzed to distinguish between matter and spirit, (2) the creation of the material world, along with its annihilation, (3) and the distinction between the body and the self are dependent on a more thorough understanding of how the modes work.

2–5. The mode of goodness fosters the following qualities: Control of the mind and senses, tolerance, intelligent discrimination, consistent adherence to one's prescribed duty, truthfulness, compassion, deep awareness of the past and future, general satisfaction, a giving nature, the ability to renounce, faith in one's teachers, shame during improper behavior, charity, simplicity, humility, and inner peace. People in the mode of passion, on the other hand, will have these characteristics: Selfish desire, the tendency to over-endeavor, audacity, never satisfied (even when they obtain something they want), pride in material acquisitions, praying for mundane benefits, considering oneself unique and more important than others, ever thirsty for sense gratification, quick to fight or argue, a fondness for hearing one's own praise, the tendency to criticize others, broadcasting one's own prowess, and overpowering others with superior capabilities. Those in the mode of ignorance will display the following: Intolerance, anger, a lack of generosity, the tendency to speak without

intellectual or scriptural basis, thoughtless violence, hatred, living at the expense of others, hypocrisy, constant fatigue, a quarrelsome nature, the tendency to lament, delusion, sadness, depression, an inclination to oversleep, unrealistic expectations, fearfulness, and intense laziness. But these modes usually combine in various ways, and you should hear about this.

6. **When people think in terms of "I" and "mine," O Uddhava, the combination of all three modes are necessarily present. They are there, too, in all worldly phenomena, but in people, particularly—they are there in the mind, in the objects of perception, in the senses, and in the very life airs of the physical body.**

Commentary

As sure as one identifies with the body, thinking in terms of "I" and "mine" and thus separating oneself from others in a materialistic way, he will exhibit a combination of the modes in every aspect of his being. Those trained to recognize the modes and how they work on a particular individual will be able to distinguish reality from illusion and to see just how a given living entity is conditioned.

7. **Whatever a person does—whether endeavoring for religious practice, economic development or sense gratification—the faith, wealth, and sensual pleasure resulting from his efforts will show a certain interaction of the modes.**

8. **These modes manifest whenever a person desires sense gratification. In relation to those who live in the world, attached to family life and engaging in conventional religious and occupational duties, it is easy to see.**

Commentary

For those trained in understanding the modes, the common person is virtually transparent when it comes to his motivation and consequent course of action. For example, if one looks at mainstream religion and its adherents: A person primarily affected by goodness might selflessly contribute to charity and religious causes, thus assuring himself that he is a good person; people in passion are anxious to be recognized for their contribution and enthusiastically look forward to the results of their practice; and people given to ignorance are lazy, with a tendency to find excuses for not attending services or contributing in any way.

9. **If one exhibits qualities like self-control, the mode of goodness predominates in his life. Along similar lines, lustiness is the hallmark of a passionate person, and a preponderance of anger can be found in one governed by ignorance.**

10. If a man or woman worships Me in a mood of devotion, using their skills in My service, without material attachment—this is the pinnacle of true goodness.

11. Sometimes, however, a person may worship Me with the hope of gaining something material—this is worship in the mode of passion. And one who worships Me thoughtlessly, who commits violence against others, is worshipping in ignorance.

12. These three modes, it should be known, can only influence ordinary living entities—they have no effect on Me, because I am the Lord, creator of the modes. They instigate attachment to material bodies and other created objects. Because of this, the living entity becomes embroiled in a network of illusion.

13. If in a given person's life the mode of goodness—which is illuminating, pure, and full of auspicious omens—predominates over passion and ignorance, he will embody happiness, virtue, knowledge, and other desirable qualities.

14. If the mode of passion—characterized by attachment, divisiveness, and restlessness—outweighs ignorance and goodness, one will find oneself working relentlessly for fame and fortune. This leads to constant endeavor and endless anxiety.

15. The mode of ignorance is seen to predominate, outdoing both passion and goodness, when a person is consistently unwise and dull-headed. Those in ignorance are given to a host of illusions and lament about nearly everything; they aspire to hopeless goals and tend to think of violence as a viable solution. They enjoy sleep and engage in it as frequently as possible.

16. There is a fortunate situation wherein one's consciousness becomes clear, enabling the senses to detach from matter. In this state of being, one experiences fearlessness and becomes aloof in regard to both body and mind. This is a mindset in which the mode of goodness predominates, for here one can gain realization of Me.

17. The mode of passion, too, can be understood by its symptoms, whether it is jumbled intelligence due to hyperactivity, the inability to divorce oneself from the desire for mundane sense objects, ill health due to the abuse of one's body through excessive sense gratification, or just overactive mental attitude.

18. Ignorance predominates when progressive awareness recedes into the background, ultimately disappearing altogether and leaving one in a state of total lethargy. Unable to focus his attention, such a person's mind loses its ability to function properly, resulting in chronic depression.

19. As the mode of goodness increases, the strength of the demigods becomes enhanced in a commensurate way. When passion predominates, the demoniac, who oppose the demigods, rise to the fore. And with a preponderance of ignorance, O Uddhava, the strength of monster-like people conquers all.

Commentary

This interesting verse indicates that large groups can be affected by overpowering ratios in regard to the modes. In previous ages, for example, when goodness predominated, the demigods were able to wield their power more effectively. This facilitated positive situations in which people in general were healthy and happy, with long lives, and nature abundantly provided all their needs. As the ages wore on and passion predominated, wars became commonplace and competition became the order of the day. Life span diminished, as did health and happiness. Now, in the age of Kali, ignorance predominates, and people are therefore short-lived, unhappy, and always quarrelsome. In other words, the general ethos of the time is affected by an overall predominance of one mode over another.

20. If one is alert and fully conscious, he is in the mode of goodness; if while in a sleeping state, dreaming predominates, he is governed by the mode of passion; and if he falls into a deep, dreamless sleep, he is overtaken by the mode of ignorance. The fourth state of consciousness, rarely attained in this world, transcends these three and yet engulfs them as well.

21. If one becomes learned, dedicating oneself to spiritual principles, the mode of goodness is allowed to act, elevating such a person to progressively higher levels of consciousness. In opposition to this, the mode of ignorance forces one into lower and lower births, while the mode of passion instigates continual transmigrating through human incarnations.

22. If one dies while predominantly in the mode of goodness, he will go to a heavenly planet. Those who leave their body while in the mode of passion tend to remain in the middling world of human beings. And those dying in the mode of ignorance must be born on a hellish planet. But those who are free from the influence of all modes of nature, O Uddhava, will come to Me.

Commentary

This is a general outline of the respective destinations of those who die while a particular mode dominates their lives. However, extenuating circumstances and numerous factors dictate where and how one is born. For example, one in goodness may be born in a family of religionists on an earthly planet, depending on his level of piety and his needs in terms of moving forward in spiritual life. A person in passion—depending on the intensity of this quality—might take birth as a lion or tiger or as some other creature in which passion predominates. And an ignorant person may be reborn as a slouch on earth, with another opportunity to move forward, or as a tree or some other entity that favors life with covered consciousness.

23. Again, when one performs his activities as an offering to Me, without consideration of what he gets in return, he is working in the mode of goodness. But if he desires to enjoy the results of his endeavors, he is working in the mode of passion. And if he is directed by violence and envy, he is in the mode of ignorance.

Commentary

One might legitimately query the distinction between work in the mode of goodness, as depicted here, and pure devotional service, which is free from the material modes. Indeed, the sacred texts of India sometimes refer to this kind of activity—working for Krishna, without expectation of return—as Karma-yoga, and it is often seen as transcendental to material nature. But just as often a distinction is made, as in this verse, demoting such work to the mode of goodness. The reason for this is to show that true transcendence must include the element of *bhakti*, or devotion—merely working for Krishna is indeed a step in that direction, but until one does so with a heart steeped in love, the modes remain present and affect one's service.

24. Non-dual, otherworldly knowledge is said to be in the mode of goodness, and when knowledge is based on duality, it is in the mode of passion. Misinformation and knowledge of materialistic phenomena is understood as being in the mode of ignorance. There is a form of knowledge, however, that transcends all three: this is when knowledge focuses on Me alone.

Commentary

In addition to its direct meaning, Verse 24 hints at the truth of transcendental knowledge: It is not merely non-dual (monistic), nor is it understood solely in terms of duality (theism). The last word in transcendental knowledge must encompass both. Therefore, the Vaishnava conception of reality rings true: It is simultaneously one and different (*achintya bhedabheda tattva*). Although this idea usually applies to the relationship between God and His offshoot living entities, it also can be applied to His self-existent nature—He is one with everything, exhibiting no duality (Brahman), and yet He is also a distinct person (Bhagavan), worshiped by all.

25. Living in the forest is in the mode of goodness, while city-life is in the mode of passion. If one's dwelling is in places where people gamble or drink, or in other, similarly dark environments, he is said to be living in the mode of ignorance. Great fortune embraces those who reside in a place where I exhibit My transcendental pastimes (*mat-niketam*).

Commentary

Verse 25 indicates that various dwellings lend themselves to the enhancement of certain modes. However, there are exceptions, as always. For example, trees, insects, and various animals also live in the forest, but they do not necessarily partake of the mode of goodness. Nonetheless, a bucolic environment generally offers peace and tranquility, especially for humans—a situation fostering a solitary, contemplative lifestyle, which allows for the mode of goodness to develop. To cite another example: Sometimes people find themselves living in cities, which generally are overrun with the mode of passion, but they perform welfare work and are fortunate enough to have a peaceful environment even in the midst of chaos. This can, in certain circumstances, allow for goodness to develop, despite many disadvantageous factors.

As an addendum, the Lord adds the Sanskrit word *mat-niketam*, which refers to "My residence." This is sacred space, transcendental to the three modes. In essence, this refers to His spiritual abode, far beyond the material world. But the word also can refer to sanctuaries here on earth and on other material planets. Ashrams, temples, and other places where people devote their lives to chanting His glories may be included in *mat-niketam*, for material modes become conspicuous by their absence in such places, allowing one to achieve transcendence.

26. Simply put, if one works free of attachment, he is in the mode of goodness. However, if he is deluded by personal desire, he is functioning in the mode of passion, and if, in his work, he has lost track of right and wrong, he is in the mode of ignorance. But beyond all this: If one works while taking shelter of Me, he is acting in a transcendental mode, free of material influences.

27. Indeed, if one has faith in spirituality, he is in the mode of goodness; if he has faith only in what he can gain from his work, he is in the mode of passion; and if his faith brings him to irreligious activities, he is in the mode of ignorance. But faith in serving Me—that goes beyond the modes.

28. Food that is wholesome, nutritious, and easily obtained is in the mode of goodness; food that gives immediate pleasure, agitating the senses, is in the mode of passion; and food that is dirty, causing distress and illness, is in the mode of ignorance.

Commentary

As we can see, in this section of the *Uddhava Gita*, Krishna is enumerating various aspects of life and how they are affected by the modes. In fact, the modes affect every facet of our being, and one who understands how they work will gain insight into who people are, what motivates them, and why they do the things they do. This knowledge, moreover, will facilitate self-reflection, promoting inner awareness and the ability to transcend the modes by spiritual practice.

Krishna's analysis of food, in Verse 28, brings to mind his more elaborate discussion on this subject in the *Bhagavad Gita*:

> Foods in the mode of goodness increase longevity and purify a person's existence, affording strength, health, happiness and satisfaction. Such nourishing foods tend to be sweet, juicy, fatty and tasty. But if foods are too bitter, sour, salty, pungent, dry or spicy, they are representative of the mode of passion. Such foods cause pain, anxiety, and disease. Finally, food cooked for more than three hours before being eaten, which is tasteless, stale, rotting, decomposed and unsanitary, is the preferred food for people in the mode of ignorance. (17.8–10)

29. If one's happiness comes from the self, it is in the mode of goodness; happiness that is dependent upon sense gratification is in the mode of passion; and happiness based on illusion, misconception, and degrading activity is in the mode of ignorance. Happiness found by absorption in Me, on the other hand, is transcendental.

30. From all of the foregoing, you can see that three modes of material nature are impacted by material substance, residence, results of action, time, knowledge, work, the performer of work, faith, state of consciousness, particular species, and destination after death.

31. O best of My devotees, it is easy to see that life is really about the interaction of the enjoying soul (*purusha*) and material nature (*prakriti*). And no matter how one views this—whether one sees it directly, hears about it, or merely has a mental conception of it in his mind—the modes of nature play a prominent role every step of the way.

32. My dear devotee, the many different phases of life experienced by conditioned souls stem from work that is influenced by the modes of material nature. If one can rise beyond these modes, by conquering the mind, he can become My devotee, and eventually develop love for Me.

33. This, therefore, is the ultimate conclusion: Those who have achieved the human form of life, which allows the mind higher knowledge, can, by developed intelligence, free themselves from the degrading modes of nature. And by this freedom they can realize that My loving service is the only activity worth engaging in.

34. One who is wise, separating himself from all material association and thus freeing himself from illusion, should conquer his senses by worshiping Me. This begins by rising beyond the modes of passion and ignorance, and by engaging only in those things that are characteristic of the mode of goodness.

35. At that time, a wise soul can also move beyond the material mode of goodness, entering a world of spiritual service. Here he will find Me. As a result, he will know complete peace, being freed from the dictates of the modes of nature, which were the very cause of his conditioned life in the first place.

36. Thus, he will find himself not only transcendental to the modes but free from the subtle conditioning of the mind, which comes from material consciousness. His entire focus will be My spiritual service, which is so fundamentally satisfying that he will no longer contemplate material enjoyment in any way. Indeed, he will find no pleasure in even casually remembering this type of enjoyment, for it will have totally evaporated from his heart and mind.

Chapter 20

The Aila Gita

1. The Supreme Lord said: Graduating to the human form enables a person to realize Me in his heart of hearts. By engaging in spiritual activities, one comes to My abode in the end, and in this way attains happiness—for I am the source of all pleasure and the Supreme Soul of all.

Commentary

Krishna is affirming that the human form of life is meant for self-realization. His initial words are reminiscent of the *Vedanta-sutra*'s first verse, quoted earlier, which states that "Now one should inquire about Brahman—the absolute truth, or transcendental, spiritual subjects in general" (*athato brahma jijnasa*). This aphorism is particularly dependent on the term "now" (*athato*), which refers to graduating to the human form after going through countless species to get here.

In lower forms of life, intelligence does not facilitate anything beyond life's primary necessities—eating, sleeping, mating, and defending. Dogs, cats, and other animals, for example, are always engaged in trying to find food or a place to sleep, defending their terrain, and looking for sexual encounters, for sheer pleasure. But in the human form of life, one begins to inquire: "Who am I? What is life? Why am I here? Is there a God?"

In the *Bhagavad Gita,* Lord Krishna says, "I am seated in everyone's heart, and from Me come remembrance, knowledge and forgetfulness" (15.15). It is He that causes the animals and other creatures to forget who they are, but in due course they remember—the human form is created as a gateway, facilitating this remembrance.

Once remembering who we are in relation to the Lord, we experience an inner happiness unknown to other species. Indeed, it is unknown to humans who are not sufficiently evolved—if one misuses the special prerogative of this human form, neglecting to inquire about the Absolute Truth, he or she will remain far away from the happiness of self-realization. But for those who begin asking the questions peculiar to the human form, and act on the answers that come in due course, spiritual happiness awaits.

2. **One who has true knowledge feels free from all hindrances, both physical and mental, because he has given up his identification with the material body. Aware of all illusions associated with material existence, he bypasses the modes of nature, even while living in a world that is composed by them. Seeing clearly that these modes and their byproducts are like mere dreams, he does not take them seriously.**

Commentary

Krishna teaches that an enlightened soul is just like a lotus flower, which has the peculiar trait of being in the midst of a muddy river while remaining untouched by its mud—the flower's long stem allows it to rise up above the dirty water serving as its home.

In a similar way, the wise transcendentalist can remain "in the world but not of it," as it is said, for while the illusions of material existence may exist all around him, he remains untouched by them, functioning as part of society for society's betterment. He gives his association to all and sundry, enabling people to benefit from his clarity and from his pure company. Because he is free from illusion and the influence of the modes, those who associate with him also gradually become free.

3. **A great danger lies in associating with the common person, or those who value the temporary things of material existence—they are preoccupied with satisfying their genitals and filling their stomachs. By such association, one falls into a deep ditch of darkness, like the blind leading the blind.**

Commentary

Thus begins the main teaching of the *Aila Gita*, a holy text embedded in the *Uddhava Gita*, which centers on the importance of association. The right kind of company can take you to God, whereas the wrong kind can trap you in the material world. This verse focuses on avoiding bad association. Similarly, Lord Krishna says in the *Bhagavad Gita*:

> One who is equal to friends and enemies, and equal-minded while experiencing either honor or dishonor, heat or cold, happiness or distress, fame or infamy, who is always free from contaminating association, always silent and satisfied with anything that comes his way, who is indifferent to his residence, who is fixed in knowledge and who is engaged in devotional service—such a person is very dear to Me. (12.18–19)

The pertinent line here bears repeating: "One who is always free from contaminating association" is very dear to Lord Krishna.

4. **Please listen to the *Aila Gita*, originally sung by the famous Emperor Pururava. When he lost his wife, Urvashi, he was naturally upset and confused—at first. But in due course he controlled his sadness, and, with a little distance, was able to feel detached.**

Commentary

Aila refers to a descent of Ilaa, which is a female name. Ilaa was the mother of Pururava, through Budha, traditionally indicating the planet Mercury. Thus, another name for Pururava is Aila. This sort of patronymic is common in Sanskrit—increase the length of the initial vowel to its maximum grade, as in i > ai, u > au. The same phenomenon is found in the *Bhagavad Gita*, as when using the name Kaunteya for Arjuna, son of Kunti.

The word "*aila,*" then, is a synonym for Pururava. Thus, this particular *Gita* refers to the story of the great king who was known by that name. His interaction with his wife is instructive in numerous ways, a tale also told in the *Bhagavata*'s Ninth Book.

5. **As she left him, he ran after her like a madman, wearing no clothes. Lost in thoughts of their relationship, completely distraught, he called out, "O wife, O terrible one! Go no further!"**

6. **They had spent their nights together enjoying sex, but he was never satisfied. Still, totally absorbed in thoughts of his wife, he neglected to notice how one night turned into two, with time inexorably marching on.**

7. **King Pururava said: I was so deluded! Because she was such a goddess, she had me totally in her grip. I was completely distracted by lust—so much so that, although life was passing me by, I neglected to see it.**

8. **I was so enamored by her beauty that the rising and setting of the sun became meaningless to me. In this way, I passed my days in delusion, year after year.**

9. **Just look at me! People think of me as a mighty emperor, the best among all kings to have ever walked the Earth. Yet, in reality, I am like a bewildered toy animal—I was a plaything in her very capable hands.**

10. **While it is true that I was a supremely opulent king, a powerful lord with dominion over so many others, she easily rejected me like an insignificant blade of grass. And I, like a fool, naked and without shame, followed her, begging her like the lost soul that I am.**

11. **So what is the value of my great influence—what is the real extent of my power and sovereignty? Rather, I am like a donkey being**

kicked in the face by his she-ass. I ran after her, even though she had already rejected me.

Commentary

The graphic example of the donkey is appropriate. In India, it is frequently seen that a male donkey will approach a she-ass for sex, as she kicks him in the face repeatedly each time he tries. Nonetheless, he keeps coming back for more, so attached is he to the act of sex. King Pururava compares himself to such an ass, and the analogy is made all the more poignant because of his status as a great and powerful emperor.

12. **Of what value is good education or the benefits that come from austerities and renunciation—and what is the use of studying religious scriptures, of living in solitude and silence—if, after all that, a woman steals your mind?**

13. **What an idiot I was, unaware of what was actually good for me! How foolish: I arrogantly deemed myself highly intelligent, having achieved the exalted position of a demigod. But in the end I was conquered by a woman, as if I were a common bullock or jackass.**

14. **Even after kissing her sweet lips for many years, my lusty desires just kept increasing, never knowing satisfaction. It is reminiscent of a fire that can never be extinguished because of the clarified butter consistently poured on its flames.**

15. **No one but the Supreme Lord, who exists far beyond material conceptions and is the cause for the self-satisfaction of sages, can possibly save me now, for my heart and mind have been completely stolen by this wayward woman.**

16. **Due to my dull intelligence, fostered by uncontrolled senses, my attachment and confusion just increased with each day—and this is true even though Urvashi herself warned me that women are not to be trusted.**

Commentary

This reference to Urvashi refers to a conversation related in the *Bhagavata*'s Ninth Book, wherein she eloquently warns the king about the perils of attachment to the opposite sex.

17. **It is no doubt incorrect to blame her when I myself should have been more conscious of my real, spiritual nature. Because I did not control my senses, I am like the foolish person who mistakenly thinks a harmless rope is a snake.**

Commentary

In Verse 17, King Pururava importantly admits that the fault lies with him alone. In life, it becomes convenient to blame others for our deficits and inferior qualities. But looked at carefully, it is our own unwillingness to control our senses, and our own lust for pleasure, in both gross and subtle forms, that keeps us from bettering ourselves or from achieving the ultimate goal of life. Intelligent readers should deeply consider this abiding truth: We are in charge of our own destinies, and with some effort, we should be able to overcome all attachments and base desires in favor of a righteous life in God consciousness.

18. It all makes me reflect on the strangeness of the bodily tabernacle—what is this flawed container, which is unpleasant, often emitting foul odors? To think: I was attracted by the fragrance and beauty of a material body, albeit a woman's. But what, really, are those characteristics we find so attractive? They are simply a false coating prepared by the illusory energy of the Lord.

19–20. And while we're thinking about it: How can we decide just whom the body really belongs to anyway? Does it belong to one's parents, who are its biological source, or to one's spouse, who gives it pleasure? Does it belong to one's employer, for whom one works, or is it the property of the funeral pyre—or of the dogs and jackals that may one day use it as food? Is the real proprietor the indwelling soul, who benefits from its happiness and distress, or would you say it belongs to the intimate friends who support and help it throughout life? In the end, it is difficult to ascertain to whom the body belongs, even though each of us is so attached to it. If we think about it, the material body is a tainted material container, fated for ill fortune and death. Yet when a man looks into the eyes of a woman, he thinks, "How attractive! What charming features she has, from her hair to her beautiful smile!"

21. Is there really a difference between ordinary worms and people who try to squeeze pleasure from this material body, which, in reality, is merely composed of skin, flesh, blood, muscle, fat, marrow, bone, stool, urine and pus?

22. If a man even theoretically understands the actual nature of the body, he should be on guard: never associate with women or with men attached to women. After all, the contact of the senses with their objects inevitably agitates the mind, causing one to forget reality in all its forms.

Commentary

Naturally, as a man, the king is speaking from a man's point of view. However, a woman similarly should be on guard in relation to the opposite sex. The point is this: When one is enamored by physical attraction, he or she loses all sense of reality, thinking the perishable, flawed material body is in some sense desirable.

23. Those things that one neither hears nor sees cannot perturb the mind. Therefore, if one restricts the mind and senses, he will automatically have less engagement in the material world, allowing his mind to become pacified.

24. With this understanding, one should never allow his senses to freely focus on women or on men who are attached to women. Indeed, even the truly wise cannot trust the mind's six enemies—and this is even more the case when it comes to fools like me.

Commentary

Renunciation and detachment are important lessons, and the king expresses his realizations in this regard. He acknowledges how difficult it is to control the mind, which is essential in the act of renouncing or in becoming detached. He notes that even great sages struggle with this, and that, therefore, as an ordinary person, he too will struggle. The process is made even more difficult, he tells us, by the mind's six enemies: desire, anger, greed, delusion, arrogance, and jealousy (*kama, krodha, lobha, moha, mada*, and *matsarya*). If we fully surrender to the Lord, however, He promises to "carry what we lack and preserve what we have" (*Bhagavad Gita* 9.22), allowing all sincere souls to actually rise beyond the mind and to become established in transcendence.

25. The Supreme Lord said: Singing his *Aila Gita* in this way, the qualified King Pururava was able to abandon the world of Urvashi—the world of women and attachment. Thoroughly cleansed by transcendental knowledge, he understood Me as the Supreme Soul within his heart, allowing him the inner peace he so richly deserved.

26. One who is intelligent, therefore, will reject the detrimental association of worldly people and instead associate with My devotees, whose example and words serve the purpose of destroying the mind's material attachments.

27. True saints focus their minds on Me, never depending on anything material. Moreover, they are always peaceful, equally disposed to all, and free from possessiveness, duality, greed, and false conceptions of the self.

28. O greatest amongst the devotees, such saintly people are always discussing My glories—talking, chanting, and singing with great relish. Both those who engage in uttering these sound vibrations and those who hear them are relieved of all sins, and they are established in true spirituality.

29. Know it for certain: Whoever hears, chants, and deeply relishes these topics about Me will in due course develop dedication to the spiritual path, thus achieving the platform of devotional service (*bhaktim*).

30. This is the ultimate goal of life: devotional service unto Me, the Supreme Absolute Truth, whose qualities are endless and who is the embodiment of bliss.

31. When one approaches an area where a sacrificial fire is taking place, qualities such as cold, fear, and darkness gradually dissipate. In a similar way, those who serve My devotees invariably lose all lesser qualities.

32. My saintly devotees, peaceful souls with abundant knowledge, provide shelter for the masses that tend to remain on a tottering platform in the frightening ocean of birth and death. The devotees might be compared to a strong boat, plying along just to rescue the fallen souls who are drowning in that ocean.

33. In the same way that food sustains all creatures—as I am the ultimate refuge for the downtrodden and as those preparing to die tend to value religion—My devotees are the only resource for the fearful of this God-forsaken world.

34. The devotees allow people to see through divine eyes, whereas the sun allows only conventional vision—and that only when it is high in the sky. Therefore, My devotees are worshipable, the real family of all living beings. Indeed, they are the very self of all selves. Ultimately, they are nondifferent from Me.

Commentary

For the last nine verses or so, the Lord glorifies the association of devotees, which is the real purport of the *Aila Gita*. Although ostensibly focusing on giving up bad association, or association that distracts one from the ultimate goal of life, the teaching here, in the end, is about the importance of something positive: associating with Vaishnavas. Indeed, if one gives up bad association but neglects to then adopt good association, one will not achieve the ultimate goal of life. One must benefit from the purity and knowledge of the saintly, as Verses 25–34 show.

The importance of this instruction should not be underestimated. The entire Vaishnava tradition rests on the urgency of saintly association. As the seventeenth-century text *Sri Chaitanya-charitamrita* states, "The verdict of all revealed scriptures is that by even a moment's association with a pure devotee, one can attain all success in spiritual life" (2.22.54). The company of exalted devotees is indeed a precious thing.

35. In this way, King Pururava transcended the world of Urvashi, wandering the earth freely, without attachment for anyone or anything. He knew only the complete satisfaction of the self.

Chapter 21

The Process of Deity Worship

1. Sri Uddhava said: My dear Lord, please explain to me how one might connect with You in this age, specifically through Deity worship (*archanam*). What are the needed qualifications to do this properly, how does one establish such worship, and what are the details of the specific method? Please reveal this to me, O master of the devotees.

Commentary

For people in this age, a very specific form of worship is recommended, especially for those who live in the world (as opposed to renunciants and others who may retire to the forest). To facilitate meditation on God's form, carved images and their veneration are authorized when performed under the direction of a pure devotee. Moreover, in contradistinction to other forms of worship, such as meditation and ordinary yoga, this method enables one to easily develop a personal relationship with the Lord: the deity is visible to the senses, and the devotee may "care for" the Lord in this form in a variety of ways—by "feeding" Him, "dressing" Him, and otherwise showering Him with service and affection. This leads to a sense of intimacy with the divine unavailable in other forms of worship.

This is not idol worship as commonly understood in the Western Hemisphere. Indeed, idol worship refers to the veneration of concocted images and deities other than the Supreme. This principle is considered an abomination not only in biblical literature but in Vedic and post-Vedic texts, too. However, these latter writings, sacred to millions, establish an alternate if similar form of worship in which visible images—deities (*archa vigraha*), not idols—are constructed for the benefit of the worshipper. The difference is that these images are not the product of human imagination but rather stem from the revelation of the Vedic literature and the realizations of purified souls, whose vision of the divine comes from Krishna Himself. Thus, the principle of Deity worship, which Krishna will now explain, stands a long distance from the idol worship eschewed in both Western and Indic scriptures.

2. **This form of worship, Uddhava continued, brings a special kind of ultimate benefit. Narada Muni, the great Vyasadeva, and my own spiritual master, Brihaspati, all say so.**

3–4. **It was You, O compassionate Lord, who initially revealed this process of Deity worship to the world. After Your original revelation, the great Lord Brahma explained it to his sons, including Bhrigu, and then Lord Shiva to his wife, Parvati. Now, time has passed, and this process is still valued and accepted by all, regardless of their particular station in life or spiritual predisposition (Varnashram). It is for this reason that I consider worship of Your Deity form to be among the most important of all spiritual practices, for everyone and at all times.**

5. **O lotus-eyed Lord, God of gods, please thoroughly explain to me, Your devotee (*bhaktaya*), this superior way of attaining liberation from the bondage of work.**

Commentary

The implications of this important word *bhaktaya* should be clearly understood. Uddhava hints that to truly understand the principle and secrets of Deity worship, one must be a devotee of the Lord. Otherwise, the subtle nuances of the system will be missed and unauthorized derivatives will rise to the fore. Accordingly, many people engage in compromised forms of Deity worship, all of which are tantamount to the idol worship proscribed in the Western Hemisphere's biblical literature and in various Eastern Hemisphere books.

6. **The Supreme Lord said: The Karma-kanda section of the *Vedas*, O Uddhava, thoroughly delineates this process of Deity worship. Still, because you have asked, I will briefly elaborate in a methodical way.**

7. **However one worships Me is fine, but in general devotees must choose between three methods: Vedic, Tantric, or a combination of these.**

Commentary

Verse 7 is primarily about authorization, particularly about the texts to which one might refer for worshiping properly. First, of course, there are Vedic texts, meaning the original *Vedas*, the Brahmanas, the Aranyakas, and the Upanishads. The Tantric literature, on the other hand, refers to the Pancharatra tradition, especially the "how-to" manuals among the sacred texts of India. "Mixed" literature means all sacred texts that are based on the prior two, including the Epics and the Puranas.

8. I will now explain exactly how a Brahmin should worship Me with devotion.

Commentary

Though a Deity of the Lord can be worshipped by anyone, in any status of life, and spiritual advancement will result, a formal practice—usually conducted in temples—is best left to those with Brahminical training. It is this that Krishna indicates in Verse 9.

9. A Brahmin should worship Me without being two-faced in any way and without any form of deceit. With genuine devotion, he should offer appropriate items to My Deity form. If no such form is available, the offering can be made to Me upon the ground (marked in sand, for example), in fire, in the sun, in water, or within the worshiper's own heart.

Commentary

The *Bhagavad Gita* says, "Peacefulness, self-control, austerity, purity, tolerance, honesty, knowledge, wisdom and religiousness—these are the natural qualities by which Brahmins are identified" (18.42). A Brahmin is particularly characterized by honesty, or truthfulness (*arjavam*), which is also indicated in Verse 9. Thus, he should not be "two-faced," but rather simple and pure, without any sense of guile or deceit.

It is with these qualities as a backdrop that he should worship the Deity, without doubt or the desire to impress others. He should do so in a simple-hearted and innocent way.

Verse 9 also indicates that the principle of Deity worship is so important that if a *murti*, or form, is not appropriately carved, then the devotee can learn methods to see the Lord in nature and worship Him accordingly. It is the "tangibility" of Deity worship that makes it distinct—it is a way to use one's body and mind in God's service and therefore it is irreplaceable in cultivating devotional intimacy.

10. First, one should become thoroughly purified through cleansing, with body and teeth being immaculate. After this, a second cleansing should take place, in which the body is smeared with earth, and a third—with the chanting of mantras to cleanse one's heart.

Commentary

In addition to thoroughly cleaning one's body, in an external sense, sacred earth can be applied in the form of *tilak*, marking the body's energy centers as the abode of Vishnu. One can then chant various holy names of the Lord, purifying one's consciousness. This is the best cleansing to prepare for Deity worship.

11. With mind focused on Me, one should certainly engage in his prescribed duties, and he should also chant the Gayatri mantra three times each day. The *Vedas* make these activities obligatory, for they purify the worshiper of all sinful reactions.

Commentary

The indication is that life should go on and one's occupational and spiritual services should be maintained. That being said, all Brahmins, especially, should add Deity service to their regular activities, thus acquiring closeness with the Lord. The Gayatri mantra is a sacred chant known to all Brahmins, which they utter at sunrise, midday, and at sunset. All such obligatory activities should continue, but Deity worship can and should serve to enhance the spiritual quality of all that one does.

12. The Deity of the Lord appears in the form of eight elements—stone, wood, metal, earth, paint, sand, jewels, or the mind.

Commentary

The Lord now commences to explain Deity worship proper, first by mentioning the elements usually used in the construction of said forms.

13. The carved Deity, who is the resting place of all souls, can be formed in two ways: as a temporary image or as a permanent one. And know this, O Uddhava: Those forms that serve as permanent Deities, having been called to reside in an apparently material form, should never be sent away or discarded.

Commentary

Sometimes the Lord's form is made of sand, or other constantly changing elements, so He can be worshipped in a temporary way for specific situations, usually while the practitioner is on the move. This is legitimate and there is a proper way to do this. However, "established" Deities are meant for more than temporary purposes, such as the Deities usually found in temples. These forms should always be given respect, for the Lord is "called" to dwell in these forms eternally. The term used in the Sanskrit is *pratishtha*, "installation," a ceremony in which the Lord is formally asked to reside in the *murti*. When a Deity is so installed by a pure representative of Krishna, all devotees are obliged to honor that Deity because the Lord Himself will always be present in that form—indeed, the Deity becomes "nondifferent" from the Lord Himself—and He effectively uses this image to receive worship from all sincere souls.

14. If a Deity is specifically meant for temporary worship, He can be called forth and asked to leave with the proper mantras. In fact, these mantras should always be chanted when the Deity is in the form of indentations or markings on the sand. In addition, the Deity should always be bathed with water, unless He is made of clay, paint or wood, for in such a case this bathing would be detrimental.

15. One should try to use only the best items when worshiping Me in My Deity form. That being said, a devotee who is free from material desire can use whatever is readily available. He can even worship Me within his heart using the facility of his mind.

Commentary

Generally, in Deity worship, one is encouraged to use expensive or quality paraphernalia in his offerings and rituals, just to show the Lord how highly He is regarded. However, if the devotee is actually advanced in spiritual life, with no material desires, then the Lord wants his offering no matter how minimal or modest the offering might be. Because the essential ingredient in any offering is love, a pure devotee has this love in abundance. Therefore, whether a devotee is offering a fruit, a flower, or simply some kind thoughts, the Lord is anxious to receive it, because it is offered with the correct mood—it comes from a heart filled with love and devotion.

16–17. O Uddhava: When a Deity is worshiped in a formal setting, as in a temple, bathing and decoration are important offerings for the Lord. For the Deity drawn in the sand or on sacred ground, the process of chanting special mantras is most wanted. Ritualistic fire sacrifice is best conducted with offerings of sesame and barley soaked in clarified butter, whereas worship consisting of yogic *asanas* and libations to the gods is preferred for the sun. One can worship Me in the form of pure water by making a simple offering of the water itself. In the end, whatever is offered to Me by My faithful devotee—even if only a little water—is the best of all offerings.

Commentary

Krishna's main point, again, is that from complex Vedic sacrifice to simple offerings to the Deity in a temple—the main ingredient is *bhakti*, or devotion.

18. If even the best of offerings are given to Me by those who are not truly devoted, I consider them pointless and dissatisfying. On the other hand, I am deeply pleased by anything given to Me by My loving devotees, no matter how humble the offering may be. Overall, I really appreciate nice gifts of fragrant oil, incense, flowers, and palatable foods—but only when they are offered with love.

Commentary

As Krishna says in the *Bhagavad Gita*, "If one offers Me with love and devotion a leaf, a flower, fruit or water, I will accept it" (9.26).

19. After duly cleansing himself and gathering the various elements needed for ritual worship, keeping it all nearby, My devotee should arrange his own seat with blades of *kusha* grass whose tips point toward the east. He should then sit facing either east or north, or, if the Deity is located in one particular place, he should sit so he can easily see Him.

20. Before beginning his worship, the devotee should sanctify various parts of his body by chanting the appropriate mantras. He should also do this for the Deity, and immediately afterwards he should clean the Deity of remnants from prior offerings. With all of this in place, he should arrange, just for this purpose, a special pot with various auspicious substances, and a vessel, which contains water for ritual washing.

Commentary

One of the cleansing procedures mentioned in these verses is the Sanskrit *arghya*, which refers to the purifying water offered to a guest, usually poured directly into his hand, or sometimes sprinkled over the head. In worshipping the Deity, *arghya* water usually is poured out of the two palms and offered to the sun three times with recitation of the Savitri Gayatri mantra (twice at noon). The offering is accompanied by the meditation that this water forces the demons (*asuras*), known as the Mandehas, back to their island home, called Mandeharuna. Each day, these demons are said to attack the sun, only to be repelled by devout Brahmins, through the offering of this *arghya*. The inner meaning is that the sun is the locus of light, representing knowledge. The Mandehas, for their part, represent demoniac qualities (*asura gunas*), like lust (*kama*) and anger (*krodha*), which effectively block the practitioner's path to knowledge (*jnana*). Such knowledge, it is said, is needed to attain liberation (*moksha*).

21. At this time, he should take the water from that special vessel and sprinkle the area where the Deity is being worshiped. He should

similarly pour water on the offerings or paraphernalia that he is planning to present to the Deity, and on his own body. After this, he should decorate three vessels filled with water, making them auspicious by adding various sacred elements.

Commentary

All of these instructions come from sacred guidebooks and the traditions of the sages in ancient India. They can be adjusted by one's guru or by stalwarts in the lineage in which one is trained. A particular, long-established method is followed to appease the Deity, and this is not done whimsically or according to popular fashion. Rather, it is based on scriptural wisdom and the directions of self-realized souls.

22. The three vessels should then be purified by sprinkling water on them and by chanting the appropriate mantras. The vessel containing water for washing the Lord's feet is sanctified through the chanting of a special "heart" mantra; the vessel containing water for libations to the gods by chanting a special "head" mantra; and the vessel containing water for washing the Lord's mouth by chanting a special "crown" mantra. In addition, the Gayatri mantra should be chanted over all three containers.

Commentary

These highly technical procedures are actually quite simple and, under the tutelage of one who knows, a priest or guru, they become second nature for a sincere practitioner, especially those properly trained as Brahmins.

23. In addition to worshipping the Deity externally, an accomplished worshiper knows how to see My supreme form, the source of all living beings, in his heart of hearts. This form is situated in the practitioner's body—and in all bodies, everywhere—sanctified by air and fire. But it is only seen by realized souls as they chant the sacred syllable OM for purification.

Commentary

Although the Deity in the temple is nondifferent from the Lord Himself, He exists in His original form as a spiritual entity, only perceived by souls who are completely surrendered to Him. They chant the sacred syllable OM, and experience Him in that way, or chant His holy names, thereby entering into a loving relationship with Him. Deity worship is especially meant for fledgling spiritualists who cannot see the Lord's invisible spiritual form. Nonetheless, having seen His manifest form in the person of the Deity, such devotees become purified and move ever closer to perceiving His original form in the spiritual world.

24. **The pure devotee, according to his level of realization, can see how I pervade his body, and how My presence energizes his very being. Because of this, he worships Me fully, absorbing his mind in Me at all times. He engages this realization by touching the various limbs of the Deity while chanting numerous mantras, all the while inviting Me to enter the Deity's form.**

Commentary

In one sense, the worshipper of the Deity sees the Lord in His own heart and meditates on how this manifestation of the Lord is in fact nondifferent from the Deity standing before him. In this way, the visible and the invisible merge in a loving realization that the Lord pervades all.

25–26. **In his mind's eye, the worshiper should visualize my sitting place, seeing it decorated with the world's well-known personified deities, including knowledge, renunciation, opulence, and My nine spiritual energies. It is an elegant throne, looking like a lotus with eight petals, glowing with saffron threads within its whorl. Envisioning Me sitting in this way—following the regulations of both the *Vedas* and the Tantric literature—the worshipper should offer Me water for washing My feet and My mouth, gradually offering Me other items of worship, too. He will no doubt enjoy this process greatly and, in the end, achieve liberation.**

Commentary

The classical commentator Shridhar Swami tells us that the Lord's throne is held up by four noble legs: religion, knowledge, renunciation, and opulence. The nine energies of the Lord, he writes, are Bimala, Utkarshini, Jnana, Kriya, Yoga, Prahvi, Satya, Ishana, and Anugraha. These are the goddesses described in the Vedic literature who embody various aspects of the Lord's potency.

27. **Consecutively, moving from one to the other, the Deity worshipper should honor the Lord's Sudarshan disc, His Panchajanya conch, His club, sword, bow, arrows, and plow. In addition, His Mushala weapon, His Kaustubha gem, His flower garland, and the Shrivatsa curl of hair on His chest should all be worshipped in order.**

Commentary

These are all symbols of Vishnu, the Supreme Lord, and by worshiping these individual items, in a particular order, one develops the realization not only of their inner purpose but also of the supreme entity who wields these items: the Supreme Godhead.

28. One should similarly worship the Lord's close associates: Nanda and Sunanda, Garuda, Prachanda and Chanda, Mahabala and Bala, and Kumuda and Kumudekshana.

Commentary

These personalities all are closely associated with Vishnu, and their stories are found in Puranic and Epic texts.

29. With purifying water offerings one should worship Durga, Vinayaka, Vyasa, Vishvaksena, one's spiritual masters and the numerous demigods. Such great personages should be placed in positions facing the central Deity, who is God Himself.

Commentary

Naturally, it is not possible to have pictures or deities of all great personalities and universal administrators—there are literally millions of such entities. Rather, tradition allows for a picture or *murti* of one's spiritual master, who is considered the sum total of all the demigods, to represent all the rest. Indeed, worshipping the spiritual master is tantamount to worshipping Lord Vishnu.

30–31. Proper worship involves daily cleansing of the Deity, as thoroughly as possible. To this end, the worshipper should use scented waters, with added sandalwood, *ushira* root, camphor, *kumkum* and *aguru*. He should also chant various Vedic hymns, such as the Svarna-gharma, the Mahapurusha-vidya, the Purusha-sukta, and various songs of the *Sama Veda*, such as the Rajana and the Rohinya.

Commentary

The Deity should be worshipped with regularity—this is essential in Deity worship and is indicated with the Sanskrit word *nityada*, which means "always." If one worships sporadically, the full results of Deity worship—love of God—will not manifest.

It is important to have in one's mind the "pleasure" of the Deity. To this end, one should bathe Him with the delicious scents of the spiritual world, as Mother Yashoda did 5,000 years ago in Vraja. One should chant mantras with which He would be familiar, such as the Vedic hymns mentioned in this verse.

32. I may then be dressed with clothing, as My loving devotee adorns Me with a Brahmin thread, decorative ornaments, *tilak* markings, and garlands. He should also apply to My body fragrant oils, all according to the directions of previous authorities.

Commentary

A large part of Deity worship is either sewing or purchasing appropriate clothing for the Lord, and then dressing Him at regular intervals throughout the day. This instills in the worshipper a sense of duty and intimacy, in which one feels a nurturing mentality toward God and becomes committed to "taking care of Him." In pursuance of this sentiment, one applies the markings of Vishnu (*tilak*) on the appropriate places of the Deity's body, particularly on the forehead, and otherwise adorns Him with jewelry and scented decorations, all for His pleasure. To make certain that one is performing this service for God's pleasure and not according to the conditioning or taste of the worshipper, the devotee must follow standard guidebooks and traditions passed down by lineage holders.

In general, Deities are worshiped properly if the devotee taking care of them is mindful of four principles: cleanliness, punctuality, and opulent food and dress. In addition, the devotee must have the appropriate mood—that he or she is in fact caring for God and not some lifeless statue. This latter point is most important of one is to actually benefit from Deity worship.

33. One who worships Me in the form of the Deity should, with great devotion, offer water for washing My feet and mouth, as well as fragrant oils, flowers, whole grains, incense, flames, and other appropriate items.

34. According to his ability, the worshipper should offer Me sweet candies, the preparation known as sweet rice, clarified butter, rice-flour cakes, sweet cakes, steamed rice flour dumplings with a filling of coconut and sugar, wheat cakes made with clarified butter and milk (covered with sugar and spices), yogurt, vegetable soup, and other delicious edibles.

Commentary

Vishnu and other divinities, such as the demigods, are known to appreciate several traditional food preparations. Others are found in guidebooks such as the *Hari-bhakti-vilasa*.

35. As one's facility allows, if not every day, the Deity should receive a pleasing massage and a mirror should be brought before Him

(so He can appreciate His own beauty). Additionally, He should be offered a eucalyptus stick for brushing His teeth, bathed with five kinds of nectar, offered all kinds of palatable foods, and entertained with singing and dancing.

36. A special arena should be constructed according to scriptural injunctions, and there the worshipper should perform a fire sacrifice. According to tradition, there should be the wearing of a sacred belt, and special use should be made of the sacrificial pit and the altar mound. Igniting the sacrificial fire with wood piled up by the worshiper's own hands, he should establish a strong flame.

Commentary

Having given some background on how the Deity Himself is to be cared for and maintained, Lord Krishna now describes the general arena for sacrifices made in the Deity's honor. The details are culled from traditional Vedic sacrifices as conducted in days of yore.

37. Spreading *kusha* grass on the ground and sprinkling the entire area with water, the worshipper should perform standard Vedic rituals according to the scriptures. After this, he should prepare all scheduled items to be offered as oblations, purifying them with water from the specially prepared vessel. Most importantly: The worshiper should meditate upon Me, seeing My essence within the fire.

38–41. The Lord's form is like molten gold, with four beautiful arms holding conch, disc, club and lotus flower. He is envisioned as always peaceful, dressed in a garment that is reminiscent of a lotus flower. His helmet, bracelets, belt, and elegant arm ornaments glisten brightly, as does the Kaustubha gem on his chest, showing off His Shrivatsa mark as well. The worshipping devotee, seeing this magnificent form before him, throws pieces of firewood, made especially flammable with clarified butter, into the sacrificial pit. He performs other related rituals, too, such as throwing into the fire other items of oblation similarly prepared with clarified butter. He then offers mantras to the demigods, beginning with Yamaraj, lord of death, and recites the Purusha-sukta hymn. After each line of this prayer, he offers one oblation after the other, naming each demigod as he does so. This is how the intelligent soul meditates on the Lord.

42. After duly worshipping the Deity through the sacrificial fire, the devotee should offer his formal respect to the Lord's personal

associates by bowing down and offering gifts to them. He should then quietly chant the root-mantra of the Deity, i.e., the mantra specifically designed for the Deity in question, fully conscious that He is the Supreme Lord, Narayana (Vishnu).

43. Repeating procedures from earlier in the worship, he should offer the Deity water for cleaning His mouth, giving the remnants of all food offerings to Vishvaksena, the Lord's doorkeeper and personal assistant. After this, he should give the Deity fragrant wash for the mouth as well, for the breath, prepared with betel nut.

Commentary

Betel nut is still popular in India, but it is often abused—though it is refreshing for the mouth, it is a mild stimulant and can be used for intoxication purposes. It is usually identified with the Areca nut in other parts of the world—the seed of the Areca palm (*areca catechu*), which grows in parts of the tropical Pacific, Asia, and east Africa. Usually chewed like tobacco, a few slices of the nut are wrapped in Betel leaf, often with added lime and sometimes clove, cardamom, *kattha*, and so on, for additional flavoring. Betel leaf has a peppery taste, but it can be bitter, too, depending on which variety is being used. It is called "Thamboolam" in Sanskrit, but "Paan" in Bengali and Hindi.

44. In addition to Deity worship, the devotee should regularly absorb himself in festive acts such as these: Singing My glories with others, chanting My names aloud, and dancing in ecstasy. Indeed, My devotees should dramatize My manifest activities, discussing and hearing various stories about Me.

Commentary

Whatever else one does as service to the Lord, or as a method of yoga, they must also perform the special process for this age (*yuga-dharma*), which is chanting the holy name. This should be done with great determination, as indicated in the next verse (Verse 45), proclaiming His glories loudly, with song and dance.

45. One should glorify the Lord with a variety of hymns and prayers, both from the ancient scriptures and from more modern sources. Asking the Lord for His mercy, a devotee should prostrate himself like a rod, offering his most profound respects.

46. After placing his head at the feet of the Deity, in a mood of deep respect, he should then stand erect with folded hands (*anjali*),

praying, "O my Lord, please give me your protection, for I am surrendered unto You. I am terribly afraid of this ocean of material existence, especially since I know I am about to die."

Commentary

Bowing down is a sign of respect, and putting the palms together indicates reverence—this is a hand gesture known in India as *anjali*. Both are recommended when one prays to the Deity. In addition, prayers should show wisdom and realization. For this reason, devotees often extract their prayers from established scriptural texts, as indicated in the prior verse. But they also compose their own, as in the example given above. The wisdom shown in this prayer is that everyone is about to die, although most act as though they will live forever. The wise devotee who prays here acknowledges the common fear that his life is coming to an end, and it surely will, if not next year then twenty years hence. In either case, death is nearby. Therefore, he rightly fears material existence, which will separate him from all that is near and dear in due course. Realizing this, he surrenders to the Lord, who will accompany him birth after birth and live eternally with him in the spiritual kingdom.

47. After uttering such prayers, the devotee should respectfully accept any remnants I offer to him. And if the particular Deity he worships is of the temporary variety, the appropriate mantras should be chanted, all the while contemplating God's presence in the lotus of his heart.

48. In whatever form one has faith in Me, whether it be in My Deity form or in some other, one should pursue Me at all costs. I certainly exist everywhere—both within all created beings and also as a separate person. Indeed, I am the Supreme Soul of all that is.

49. If one worships Me in any authorized way, as prescribed in the *Vedas* and other sacred texts, one will achieve perfection, both in this life and in the next.

50. Devotees should think about how to establish the worship of My Deity on a grand scale—such as constructing temples with beautiful gardens. The flowers from these gardens could then, in turn, be used for the regular worship of the Deity, as fragrant offerings, and special processions and holiday observances could be held in the temple complex.

51. One achieves opulence not unlike My own by serving the Deity nicely. By giving gifts of land, markets, cities, and villages so that regular daily worship and special festivals can go on—all people can reach perfection.

52. **By establishing the worship of My Deity, one becomes just like a king of the entire earth; by building a temple for this worship, one becomes like a ruler of the galaxy; by worshiping and serving the Deity, one can attain the planet of Lord Brahma, chief of the higher beings and creator of the universe; and by performing all three of these activities, one achieves total transcendence.**

53. **All of this being true, know the following as well: One who simply engages in My devotional service with no consideration of what he gets out of it—in other words, one who serves Me selflessly—will attain Me in due course. Thus, whoever worships Me according to the Deity process I have just described will ultimately attain pure devotional service and come to Me in the end.**

54. **If one steals from higher beings or Brahmins, whatever his excuse may be, he must live as a lowly worm in excrement for an incalculable period of time.**

55. **This not only applies to the thief himself but also to anyone who assists him, who instigates the theft, or simply if one approves of it. All must share the reaction that awaits in their next body. Depending on just how involved a person is, he will suffer a proportionate consequence.**

Commentary

Verse 53 sums up the value of Deity worship, which leads to selfless service and the ultimate perfection of life: love of Krishna. Rendering this service, however, requires much facility and paraphernalia. Therefore, in the final two verses of this chapter, Verses 54 and 55, Krishna issues a serious warning: Those who are inclined to abscond with this facility and paraphernalia are destined for hellish existence, even as those devotees who lovingly serve the Lord in His Deity form approach the highest realm.

Chapter 22

Jnana-yoga: The Yoga of Knowledge

1. **The Supreme Lord said: The nature and activities of people in the material world deserve neither praise nor criticism. Instead, everything that goes on in this world should be seen as a natural course of events—the inevitable result of combining material nature (*prakriti*) with enjoying souls (*purusha*). Indeed, it is all part of one reality, even if manifested in different ways.**

Commentary

Krishna is summarizing how to see beyond the illusions of material life. This is Jnana-yoga, the yoga of knowledge. It is meant to help one go beyond the material world through discrimination and insight, using the mind and the intellect for higher, spiritual purposes.

According to Verse 1, the modes of material nature and the inherent desires of living beings instigate various kinds of actions. These actions appear diverse even though they are all based on one thing: material desire.

One might compare this phenomenon to electricity, which can be used to heat a home, light a stove, cool a refrigerator, and so on. Though the manifestation of electricity differs depending on how it is used, the essence or source is always the same. Material activities are like that, and thus the wise see through them, always aware that—good or bad—they are based on materialism, that is, on being separate from God. Therefore, enlightened souls do not praise or disparage material activity, but rather they merely see it in perspective: as nonspiritual.

2. **By acknowledging diversity in the qualities and behavior of conditioned souls—finding them to be praiseworthy or the subject of criticism—one has already fallen into illusion, being distracted from higher reality and entangled in everyday falsehoods.**

Commentary

Krishna underlines the point that He makes in the previous verse, stating that those who indulge the apparent diversity of material phenomena found in conditioned beings have already succumbed to illusion, forgetting that it is all one—all various permutations of matter and nothing more.

3. **In the same way that all embodied beings lose external consciousness when in the process of dreaming or when lost in deep sleep, so, too, do those who think in terms of material duality become subject to illusion and death.**

Commentary

Krishna explains the severity of material illusion. One who knows his existence as spirit-soul, who has risen beyond the dualities of material life—who does not see good or bad in the material world but instead sees all material interactions as nonspiritual and thus as a distraction from the goal of life—has risen beyond illusion and death. Indeed, realizing his existence beyond the body, which is simply dead matter, he experiences eternity, knowledge, and bliss, relishing existence with Krishna in the spiritual realm. Conversely, if one does not attain this level and instead gets caught up in the dualities of material life, his identification with his body naturally engulfs him in the world of birth and death, in which illusion and ultimate demise arise as a matter of course.

4. **Gross material words—and thoughts produced by the material mind—do not represent ultimate truth. For this reason, the so-called good and bad of this dualistic world lack substance, without any relation to that which is real.**

Commentary

While, as a general rule, the words and thoughts of this world are material and have no relation to that which is spiritual, there is a process of transformation, or spiritual alchemy, which is what practitioners of religion and yoga hope to achieve.

Just as an iron rod placed in fire takes on all the qualities of fire, such as heat and light—indeed, it will burn you if you touch it—so, too, will words and thoughts, when given spiritual dimension, take on the qualities of spirit, manifesting the virtues of eternity, knowledge, and bliss.

Kirtan is a good example—though words are generally material, when God's names are evoked, we hear their essential spiritual quality loud and clear, for they purify the chanter in every way. In fact, these names, properly recited, are fully spiritual, bearing little relation to their material counterparts, which, to the untrained ear, may sound the same.

5. People react to shadows, echoes and mirages, even though these are only illusory reflections of real things. Similarly, although living beings are not their material bodies, through a process of false identification they experience fear and death as though it was actually happening to them.

6–7. Nothing exists except the Lord Himself, who is the ultimate controller and creator of this world. He indwells all and is thus both creator and created, maintainer and the maintained, withdrawer and the withdrawn. Everything is contained within Him, and yet He is distinct from everything and everyone else, inconceivably. Of all the illusions that appear within Him, the three modes of material nature are among the most mysterious. But, in the end, they are simply products of His illusory potency.

Commentary

Krishna says that nothing exists outside the Lord—that He is simultaneously everything and distinct from everything. He is the ultimate reality, and although all things are one with Him, some things partake of His nature whereas others do not, being illusory. The three modes, whose jurisdiction is within the material world, are among these latter phenomena, temporary and limited.

8. If one understands the process of attaining both ordinary and realized knowledge, as I am now describing it to you, he sees the material world for what it is, without considering it worthy of criticism or praise. He is like the sun, shining his rays on everyone equally.

Commentary

Again, it is underlined that the vision of duality that gives birth to praise and criticism in the material world is illusory, and that enlightened beings are not distracted by such illusions. They view all material phenomena equally, as the sun shines its rays without discrimination. Rather, they focus their attention on the spiritual element and use their discriminative abilities in this way, so they can make progress on the spiritual path and help others to do the same.

9. If one applies direct perception, logical deduction, scriptural evidence, and personal realization, he can understand that this world has a beginning and an end, with no abiding reality. Consequently, he can be detached from it, knowing it to be unreal.

Commentary

As Lord Krishna says in the *Bhagavad Gita*: "Seers of the truth have concluded that of the existent there is no cessation, and of the nonexistent there is no endurance. They have drawn this conclusion by studying the nature of both" (2.16). In other words, the material world is like a dream, which exists in some form but only in temporary fashion. Because dreams are in fact temporary, we commonly understand them to be a falsehood, and rightly so, for we awaken and the "truths" of our dreams exist no longer. Thus, the wise know that if something does not endure, it should not be considered real. Only the eternal is real—God, the living being (not the body), and the spiritual world.

10. Sri Uddhava inquired as follows: It seems that neither the soul nor the body—the seer nor the seen, respectively—can experience material life. On the one hand, the soul is innately endowed with perfect knowledge, perceiving the spiritual realm, and on the other, the material body is not a conscious, living being, and is thus unable to perceive at all. Who, then, experiences the material world?

Commentary

This brilliant question shows the depth of Uddhava's thinking and realization. He knows that the soul, originally, is composed of eternity, knowledge, and bliss, and thus has nothing to do with the material world. He further knows that the body is just a machine made of material elements, its apparent conscious life dependent on the presence of the soul. So the natural question arises: If the soul, who could perceive material existence, has its life and interests elsewhere, and the body, who cannot perceive anything, is basically inert, who or what perceives the material world?

Ultimately, of course, material existence is experienced by the soul, and yet, it also can be said that the soul does not experience the world at the same time. This philosophical conundrum is not meant to evoke the confusion of a Zen koan but rather to express the soul's actual position in the spiritual world contrasted with its temporary stay in the world of matter. While here, it functions according to the dictates of the conditioned intelligence, mind, and senses, while subsisting in a sort of dormant state in the spiritual realm.

How can this be practically understood? Consider what your body is doing while you dream at night: When you dream, are you experiencing the events taking place in your mind or not? In a sense, yes, you are; but in another way, no, you are not. You are not really walking, talking, eating, or interacting with others as your dream would indicate, even if the dream has a subtle reality of its own.

Consider another analogy: When you watch a movie, are you experiencing the events on the screen or not? In a sense, you are; but in another way, you are not. You feel the characters' emotions through identification and attachment, but you are not really involved in the life and actions depicted in the film, even though it seems as though you are. Your actual life is in a dormant-like state while you become absorbed in a dream or in a good movie.

In this way, the soul is accepted as the "experiencer" (*bhoktri*) in the material world. This is the case not only in the *Uddhava Gita* but also in the *Bhagavad Gita*, the Puranas and in most forms of Vedanta. "Experience" is another way of referring to "awareness" or "consciousness" (*chiti-shakti, chetana*). This is the symptom of the soul, which is never truly in a dormant state and is constitutionally and metaphysically incapable of dormancy (although for all appearances while in the material world its original life with Krishna is halted).

The soul's pristine place is with Krishna in the spiritual realm, and when pure, its consciousness is absorbed in its identity in that higher realm. Therefore, a type of apparent dormancy exists when the soul is here, in the material world, experiencing its conditioned life divorced from ultimate reality. Nonetheless, the soul is always completely aware, even if that awareness is covered by goodness, passion, or ignorance. A 100-watt bulb emits the same light irrespective of its covering—whether covered by a dense cement box (ignorance) or a see-through box made of glass (goodness). Likewise, the soul, underneath its coverings, is eternally and irreducibly aware, never unconscious or dormant.

The problem is that we often confuse the bulb with the box that covers it. In other words, the box is responsible for what we see, even if the bulb remains the same. The *Bhagavad Gita* hints at this when it says, "Nature is said to be the springboard of all material causes and effects, whereas the living entity is the cause of the various sufferings and enjoyments in this world" (13.21).

One might understand this in terms of playing a computer game: The doer or the "experiencer"—the one who acts—is the person playing the game. But all the action, if you think about it, is done by the hardware, software, electricity, and so on. The player is, in a sense, simply an observer, if also the cause of the happiness and distress derived from the game. This is so because the player is communicating his or her desires via computer interfaces.

Another example would be a book or, again, a movie. One chooses to buy a particular book or view a particular movie depending on desire, availability, and resources. However, it is the author or the producer, director, and actors, who control the story and, thus, to an extent, the experiences of the person reading or watching. This latter person is, therefore, only a passive observer and not the doer. Nonetheless, this observer has thoughts, feelings, and desires, and therefore suffers or enjoys based on his conditioning.

Accordingly, it may be ascertained that the soul is the knower and the one who experiences all acts in the material world. That being said, he is, in a sense, dormant inasmuch as his attributive consciousness is not always in a manifest state. According to Vaishnava terminology, while one is awake, his "knowledge of reality" (*dharma-bhuta-jnana*) may be functional, based on his specific frame of reference, as is his "self-awareness" (*dharmi-jnana*). At the same time, however, he may be unaware of his real nature, at least until self-realization takes place.

The *Srimad Bhagavatam* attempts to clarify this complex subject:

> When one's consciousness is completely purified of the contamination of material existence, gross and subtle, without being agitated by working and dreaming states—or when the mind is laying dormant, as in deep sleep—one comes to the platform of mystic trance. At that point, one's material vision, along with the memories of the mind, which functions according to the names and forms of this world, are transcended. Only in such a trancelike state is the Supreme Lord revealed. Thus, let us offer our respects unto God Himself, who is seen in that uncontaminated, spiritual state. (6.4.26)

Verse 10, which, in addition to other things, answers Uddhava's question, indicates that it is the same "experiencer" from beginning to end—the soul views the world, colored by conditioning, while contaminated by material existence. This represents a clouded view of what actually exists and constitutes a kind of dormancy. But then, through spiritual practices, he experiences the Supreme Lord and the spiritual element proper. In this case, he functions on an entirely transcendent level of perception, one that accurately conveys both seer and seen. This occurs when he achieves the ultimate trancelike state of spiritual existence.

11. **Indeed, the soul is without end, spiritual, pure, self-luminous and never influenced by matter in any form. It is vibrant, like fire, whereas the essentially dead material body is more like firewood, dull and unconscious. Given this state of affairs, who is it that actually experiences life in the material world?**

12. **The Supreme Lord begins to answer: For the entire period that deluded souls remain enamored by their body, senses, and power of action, their material existence continues in full force, even if it is ultimately without reality.**

13. **In actuality, the living being is spiritual, transcendental to material existence. But because he wants to control material nature for his own enjoyment, his life in the material world seems substantial. Accordingly, he identifies with all that transpires here, just as one who dreams thinks his dream is real.**

Commentary

This very important verse is repeated several times throughout the *Bhagavata Purana*, either verbatim or in essence. Essentially, Krishna's answer to Uddhava's question is that the soul, in illusion, identifies with all that occurs in relation to his body and mind. In the stupor of material identification, he misperceives illusion for reality, thinking his actual home is here, in the dreamlike state of material existence. Temporarily, then, he forgets his real life in the spiritual world and experiences material life here—but through a glass darkly, as it were. Thus, he experiences the world of matter, as said previously, and he does not experience it, at the same time.

In essence, the confusion arises because Uddhava's initial question presupposes only two possible candidates when it comes to experiencing the material world: the pure soul, who is beyond matter, and the material body, which, being inert, cannot experience anything. The Lord's teachings, however, reveal another element, that is, the "false ego," or a dreamlike conception of the self that is divorced from ultimate reality. This third element (soul in false ego) undergoes material experience, as already suggested in the commentary to Verse 9.

When the soul becomes free of illusion by spiritual practices, it wakes up from its dreamlike state and, instead of seeing the compromised reality of material nature, begins to perceive things as they are—as they exist in the spiritual realm.

14. In dreams, one often experiences harsh, undesirable mental images, but upon awakening one can usually see them for what they are.

15. The following qualities are products of the dreamlike existence known as material life—they have nothing to do with the actual person, the spirit-soul within: Lamentation, elation, fear, anger, greed, confusion, and hankering, as well as birth and death.

16. Most beings of this world foolishly identify with their body, senses, life air, and mind, with these coverings fully engulfing them. Thus, they find themselves appearing like a product of material energy, and, under the undeviating control of time, they are forced to experience the numerous dimension of mundane existence.

17. False conceptions of the self (false ego) have no basis in reality, even if they are perceived in forms that appear to have substance, such as the functions of the mind, speech, and various bodily actions. These illusions can be cut away with the sword of true knowledge, which is sharpened by proper devotional worship. This allows one to live a detached life while still in this world, free from all illusion.

Commentary

Verse 17 embodies the second part of Krishna's answer to Uddhava's question, for He mentions *upasana* ("devotional worship"). By regulated practice, one can gradually become free from spiritual amnesia and remember one's eternal identity as a loving servant of the Lord. Concomitantly, one becomes free of his attachment to his false identity, and sheds the various illusions surrounding his day-to-day life. "The highest devotion," says the *Brahma-samhita*, "is attained by slow degrees by the method of constant endeavor for self-realization with the help of scriptural evidence, theistic conduct, and perseverance in practice" (5.59). The reference to "constant endeavor" is *upasana*, or regulated worship.

18. **Real knowledge is acquired through scriptural evidence, penance, direct perception, historical narrations, and logical inference. The goal of such knowledge is the Absolute Truth, who was present before the creation of the universe and who will remain after its destruction. He is time itself and the ultimate cause of everything. Even in the middle stage of creation—when everything takes place—He alone constitutes all that is real.**
19. **Before gold products can be manufactured, one must have an original piece of gold, and the products themselves are not yet a reality—only the gold exists. Similarly, after the products' destruction, only the original gold remains. Thus, gold alone is the essential reality, even if in an interim state it was known by various names. In the same manner, I, God, alone exist before the creation of this universe—and this is also true during its maintenance and after its destruction.**

Commentary

Verse 19, by way of analogy, shows how only God exists and nothing else. He may expand into numerous manifestations, such as the world and its multifarious living entities—and they are all apparently real enough during their manifest existence—but, in the end, only He exists, with everything and everyone else in a subservient position.

20. **The three modes of material nature allow the mind to manifest in three phases: wakefulness, sleep, and deep sleep, corresponding to goodness, passion, and ignorance, respectively. The mind further divides into three separate categories—the perceiver, the perceived and the regulator of perception. All that being said, it is the fourth factor, which is beyond the modes, the mind, and their subdivisions, that alone constitutes the real and the true.**
21. **If a given thing did not exist in the past and will not exist in the future, how can we say it exists during some temporary interval, even if it appears to do so? Rather, such momentary allusions to existence are only superficial, unreal and insubstantial. In My opinion,**

whatever is created and existing due to its dependence on some other thing, is ultimately only that other thing and nothing else.

Commentary

Verse 19 helps clarify the confusion expressed here, in Verse 21. Krishna is saying, analogically, that, really, only gold exists, not the various objects made from gold. True, such objects may have temporary value and exhibit a sense of reality for a short time; ultimately, however, it is the gold that is of value and that really exists. Similarly, God and the spiritual element are, in fact, valuable and real—even if the various facets of material life, which are dependent on spirit for their existence, seem to have redeeming qualities for some temporary period of time. Ultimately, all material things succumb to planned obsolescence, and fall into a state of nonexistence—to a point at which one may wonder if they indeed existed at all. This is a hint of their illusory nature, diminishing their value in due course.

22. **Transformed manifestations in the material world certainly seem real, created, as they are, from the mode of passion. But this is only so because they stem from something that *is* real: the self-manifested, self-luminous Absolute Truth, who exhibits Himself in numerous ways. This is why material variety, in the form of the senses, the sense objects, the mind, and the elements of physical nature appear to be real.**

Commentary

This truth is fundamental: All material things are real, if only in a very particular sense, because they have their root in something real: God and the spiritual element. In other words, because all phenomena come from the Absolute Truth, such phenomena must be real in some way. This is what Krishna expresses in Verse 22.

23. **In this way, by clearly understanding the unique nature of the Absolute Truth, using discrimination and logic, one should thoroughly dismantle one's misidentification with the body, cutting to shreds all doubts about the true identity of the self. Experiencing the satisfaction of the soul's innate bliss, one will naturally desist from trying to enjoy the inefficient material senses.**

24. **None of these can be called the true self: the body, the senses, the demigods (who control our acts from above), or the air of life; nor are the other elements—air, water, fire or one's mind—to be considered the actual person within. All these are simply**

matter, gross and subtle. Consider it carefully: One's intelligence, material consciousness, false identity, elements such as ether or earth, the objects of sense perception, and even the original state of natural phenomena—none of these can be considered the actual identity of the conscious individual.

25. I so cherish one who has properly realized Me as the Supreme Person. Such a first-class devotee might engage his material senses in meditation, or his senses might become distracted with something else altogether. What does it matter? Indeed, why should the sun be concerned if dark clouds sporadically cover it?

Commentary

The pure devotee is described here. Krishna feels such love for His intimate servitor that, even if such a person is temporarily distracted, or otherwise seems to have some other interest, their relationship goes on unimpeded. Additionally, this is a lesson in how to view Krishna's devotees. Their minds are absorbed in the Lord, but their actions are not always easily understandable, and so they should not be judged. Rather, one should view the overall tenor of such a devotee's life—if he is fully dedicated to the Lord and His mission, momentary deviation or inexplicable actions should be overlooked in favor of the devotee's greater purpose in life.

Needless to say, this principle should not be abused, and lesser devotees should not simply pursue sense gratification while expecting others to honor them as great servants of the Lord. No. The devotee always thinks himself fallen, and will humbly try to do his service to the best of his ability. Still, his actions are between him and the Lord, and others should not attempt to evaluate him in terms of their own conditioned responses or expectations.

26. Consider the sky: It often carries the qualities of air, fire, water and earth, which pass through it as a matter of course. Sometimes the sky carries heat and cold, repeatedly appearing and disappearing with the seasons. Nonetheless, the sky is never truly defined by any of these qualities, which come and go. Similarly, the Supreme Absolute is never actually associated with goodness, passion, and ignorance—material qualities—that cause the material transformations of the illusory self.

27. That being the case, until one has completely eliminated from his mind all contamination of material qualities, especially passion, one must very carefully avoid associating with the modes, which are produced by My illusory energy. The only way to accomplish this is by steadily practicing devotional service to Me (Bhakti-yoga).

Commentary

The open secret of the *Uddhava Gita*: It is easy to rise beyond the modes of material nature and material conditioning, but one must do so by learning the art and science of Bhakti-yoga (the theme of the final chapter, Chapter Twenty-three). Through this method, all problematic material qualities naturally fall to the wayside, almost incidentally. If one tries to conquer one's conditioned mind or the modes on one's own, however, one is bound to fail, for the Lord's illusory potency is inconceivably vast. Only by taking shelter of God Himself, through the yoga of love, can one hope to overcome the intricate network of illusion that engulfs us all.

28. In the same way that an inadequately treated disease tends to recur, giving repeated distress to its victim, the mind that is not thoroughly cleansed of its material tendencies will remain attached to things of this world, repeatedly tormenting the imperfect *yogi.*

Commentary

This effective analogy facilitates understanding of a very important teaching, namely, that one must comprehensively cleanse the mind of material contamination, lest he risk falling back into the material whirlpool. Again, this is best accomplished by focusing on Krishna and His esoteric activity, as described in the *bhakti* scriptures. By absorbing oneself in such meditation, one naturally relinquishes all things material, whereas endeavoring to wipe the mind clean of material contamination separately, without the meditation techniques prescribed in the process of Bhakti-yoga, will leave residue, causing the fledgling devotee eventually to fall from the path.

29. Those who are imperfect on the path of yoga are sometimes stymied by attachment to family members, students, or others, who are sent by envious beings from higher planets specifically for that purpose. Nonetheless, because of their prior efforts, such imperfect practitioners eventually resume their practice in the next life. If they are sincere, they will never again be trapped in the network of their illusory desires.

Commentary

Verse 29 is reminiscent of the *Bhagavad Gita*: "The unsuccessful *yogi*, after many years of enjoyment on the planets of the pious, is born into a family of righteous people, or into a family of rich aristocracy" (6.41). In other words, Krishna gives all souls the opportunity to pick up in their next lives where they left off in this one. And so, for those sincere on the path, there is no loss or regret. Krishna also says this in the *Bhagavad Gita*: "In this endeavor there is no loss or diminution, and a little advancement on this path can protect one from the most dangerous type of fear" (2.40).

30. Normally, living beings perform material action and, throughout life, they are transformed by that action, both by the doing of it and what comes to them by way of reaction. In this way, they cultivate various desires and attachments that virtually force them to continue such action until they die. A wise person, however, having experienced the bliss of his own real self, gives up all materially infected work, including desire and the so-called assets of material life.

Commentary

The natural course of events in the material world is that people are attracted to some form of work because of conditioning from previous lives and desires accrued over many births. This work further entangles them in a web of material illusion, making them reach their last days wanting more. The intense desire forces them to take birth again, so that they eventually may achieve their unfulfilled goals.

Rarely, a soul comes along who has a glimpse of reality, and he or she enlightens others, helping them break free from the vicious cycle of birth and death. When this happens, either through grace or through practice, the newcomer soon experiences his existence as separate from the body, as a spark of the Supreme. This experience allows him to abandon his desires and attachments. The experience is essential. Otherwise, one's attachment to material things will once again manifest in his heart. As Krishna says in the *Bhagavad Gita*:

> The embodied soul may be artificially restricted from sense enjoyment by withdrawing his senses from their objects, but his taste for sense objects will remain. However, one who experiences a higher taste will not have this problem, for he is fixed in consciousness. A devotee of the Lord automatically refrains from sense pleasure because of superior taste. (2.59)

Thus, one must experience "the bliss of his own real self," as Krishna says to Uddhava, for this will establish as an irrevocable fact not only a sense of detachment and steadiness but a genuine taste for all things spiritual.

31. The enlightened person, whose consciousness is absorbed in truth, cares little for his own bodily activities. While standing, sitting, walking, lying down, urinating, eating, or performing other bodily functions, he sees the body as a machine, functioning according to necessity.

32. When such a soul sees something mundane, characteristic of the material world, he accepts it as a compromised form of reality. Because his understanding and realization reveal it as a sort of material illusion—he sees it as distinct from anything of substance. Such material things, in his view, are as ephemeral as a fading dream.

33. The conditioned soul wrongly thinks that material nature, with its various permutations dictated by the modes, is connected to the actual self. However, through the cultivation of spiritual knowledge, this ignorance can be conquered, allowing one to achieve liberation. It should additionally be understood that the eternal self is not something you one day become, nor is it an entity that you will eventually abandon.

Commentary

Aside from identifying with the body, which is a falsehood that one can overcome through the cultivation of spiritual knowledge, foolish souls think that they are a body who has a soul, or that they become a particular entity from life to life. Krishna wants Uddhava to know that he *is* a soul, not a body that has one. Furthermore, the soul is not an entity that one becomes, or a persona that one loses over time. *It is who you are, eternally and without change.* The living being simply forgets this fact and identifies with a material body or mind. But his identity as spirit-soul is changeless and abiding.

34. The sun rises and thus eliminates the darkness covering one's eyes. This makes it appear as though the sun creates the objects one sees around him. In fact, these objects were there all along, but it was too dark to see them. In like manner, realization of Me puts an end to the darkness covering one's consciousness.

35. I am self-luminous, unborn and unlimited. I am pure spirituality, perceiving everything, at every moment. In fact, I stand alone, realized by others only after ordinary material sound comes to an end. Indeed, it is I who bring about the power of speech and the life airs themselves.

36. There is no duality to be perceived in the self—as if a living being is only partly the soul and yet also somehow the body and mind as well. Any such perception of duality in regard to the self is merely delusion. You are the soul only.

Commentary

Krishna is addressing various philosophical systems, prevalent even in India, that attempt to explain the soul as part of the body, or, more specifically, the mind. This is not uncommon. There are those who see the self as a sort of hybrid entity, combining body, mind, and something yet more subtle. Around the world, in fact, the soul remains a vague notion, explained in various ways. The Platonic idea of the soul, for example, views it as having three parts: the mind (*logos*), the emotions (*thymos*), and desire (*eros*), even if the actual soul's identity, or where these components come from, is unclear. Similarly, in the Jewish tradition, various philosophers have presented the soul in like manner. Saadia Gaon, for instance, writes in his classic work *Emunoth ve-Deoth* (6.3) that the soul is essentially a mental apparatus, giving us desire, emotion and thought. The Church of the Latter-day Saints, too, believes that the living being is a kind of merger between body and soul. Finally, when modern scientists speak of the soul, they generally refer to it as a poetic synonym for the mind. Krishna will have none of this. He asserts quite clearly that the living being is solely the soul, so to speak, quite divorced from body, mind, or anything material.

37. The dualities established by the five material elements—earth, water, fire, air, and ether—are understood in terms of names and forms, but they have no ultimate substance. Those who think there is any truth to these dualistic entities are people who foolishly pose as being learned while in fact they are ignorant.

38. The fledgling practitioner may find that his body will give him difficulty. Consequently, I offer the following advice.

39. One may try yogic meditation or sitting postures, practiced in conjunction with concentration on controlled breathing. Alternatives would include special austerities, mantras, or medicinal herbs.

40. Ultimately, these troubling disturbances of the body and mind are conquered by remembering Me without deviation, by hearing and chanting My holy names in the company of others, or by following the traditions of the great masters.

41. Using these various methods, practitioners free the body from disease and old age and keep it youthful for a very long time. In this way, one can engage in yoga for the purpose of achieving mystic powers.

42. Those who have actual knowledge do not consider such mystic powers to be particularly important. In fact, they consider them useless, since the soul is permanent as opposed to the body, which is destined for destruction no matter how long one might preserve it through the methods described here. In this sense, the soul is comparable to a tree, and the body to its fruit.

Commentary

This is the essence of Jnana-yoga, the theme of this chapter: Actual knowledge allows one to understand that the spiritual pursuit is not about acquiring power but about using one's knowledge, heart, and action for the Supreme.

43. **One who is actually intelligent dedicates his life to Me, without putting his faith in trying to perfect the physical body through yoga. Indeed, although physical dexterity and health can be enhanced through the various processes of yoga, the wise in fact give up all such practices in favor of My service.**

44. **Experiencing the happiness of his own soul, the *yogi* who has taken shelter of Me remains free from desire and attachment. In this way, while executing the various techniques of yoga, he is never thwarted by setbacks or difficulties.**

Chapter 23

Bhakti-yoga: The Yoga of Devotion

1. Sri Uddhava said: My dear Lord Krishna, You describe a method of yoga that can only be troublesome, for it is difficult to control the mind. I therefore submit a humble request: Please explain a simpler process by which one can attain You.

Commentary

Krishna has just explained Jnana-yoga, in which one must cultivate an elaborate understanding of the self, become detached, austere, and removed from all things material. In previous chapters, He has explained Raja-yoga, complete with sitting postures and breathing exercises, and Sankhya-yoga, in which one analyzes all material elements, trying to distinguish them from the spiritual element, thus developing higher vision and realization. But all such processes of spirituality, including several others that Krishna had explained in this text and in the *Bhagavad Gita*, are detailed and complex, grueling with goals that are nearly unattainable. In fact, say the Puranas, these processes were best practiced in previous ages, when people lived for many hundreds of years and had superior powers of intellect and stamina.

Uddhava echoes the words of Arjuna, who said in the *Bhagavad Gita*:

> My dear Lord Krishna—the yoga system that You've described appears impractical and virtually impossible to me, for the mind is restless and unsteady. In fact, it is turbulent, obstinate, and very strong, O Krishna, and to subdue it, I think, would be more difficult than controlling the wind. (6.33–34)

These words were uttered by the highly gifted Arjuna—a great prince, personal associate of the Lord, and a man with enviable qualifications, both of the intellectual variety and in terms of physical ability.

Five thousand years ago, Arjuna had much better facilities than we do now, yet, in the end, like Uddhava, he rejected the conventional system of yoga as too difficult, asking for a more practicable alternative. In fact, history does not record either Arjuna or Uddhava as adhering to any of the traditional forms of yoga at any time. Stalwarts in the *bhakti* tradition therefore have concluded that these techniques must be considered nearly impossible in this Age of Kali. Of course, those who feel they must, certainly can try.

But Krishna proposes a different solution. In the *Bhagavad Gita*, He offers the following:

> A *yogi* is greater than the ascetic, the empiricist, and the fruitive worker. Therefore, O Arjuna, in all circumstances, be a *yogi*. But know this: Of all *yogis*, the one with great faith who always abides in Me, thinks of Me within himself, and renders transcendental loving service to Me (Bhakti-yoga)—it is this soul who is most intimately united with Me in yoga and is the highest of all. That is My opinion. (6.46–47)

In other words, real yoga in the age of Kali means becoming Krishna's devotee, and this means chanting His names, associating with other devotees, worshiping His deity, offering one's food in sacrifice, studying *bhakti* scriptures, and following the regulative principles mentioned therein. This is what He expressed to Arjuna, and it is what He will now tell Uddhava.

2. **We have seen *yogis*, O lotus-eyed Lord, who try to steady the mind. But they usually experience frustration because of their inability to attain perfect *samadhi*, the trancelike state of absorption in the Divine. Because of this, they become slack in their attempts at spiritual life.**

3. **It is for this reason, O lotus-eyed Lord of all, that the best practitioners take shelter of Your lotus-like feet, the source of all spiritual pleasure. Unfortunately, the same is not true for those who take pride in their yogic or karmic accomplishments. Such unwise souls fail to take shelter of You, thus defeating themselves by surrendering to Your illusory energy.**

Commentary

In life, one either surrenders to the external illusory energy or the internal spiritual energy of the Lord. There is no middle ground. In each tiny act, we are either moving further away from God or closer to Him, revealing our preference and level of conditioning in the process. When we are materialists, this manifests in a gross way, with most of our decisions and actions leading us further away from the Divine. As we mature spiritually, we see these decisions and acts manifesting in more subtle ways, as in exactly which religious practices we adhere to and why we adhere to them. Are we looking for the best way to serve the Lord, or are we considering ourselves first? Are our motives pure, or are we considering our "likes" and "dislikes" before those of the Supreme?

People attached to a particular process of religion or yogic path might have difficulty with the teaching of surrendering to Krishna in lieu of mystic yoga, and, in fact, with this entire section of the *Uddhava Gita*. Attachment to a particular path can be more difficult to give up than the material sense gratification one had to abandon for the spiritual pursuit in the first place. "The best practitioners," as Uddhava says, take shelter of the Lord, without consideration of what they like or do not like, without thinking of their own inclinations and tastes. This is not an easy thing to do.

For example, if one becomes accustomed to a particular yogic regimen, or even to certain powers—physical, intellectual, or otherwise, developed through one's practice—can attachment to these things be overcome just because Krishna says there is a more effective way to attain Him? Will it be easy to abandon one's habitual procedures just because the goal is more likely to be had through a simple process of surrender, as espoused by the Lord's greatest devotees? One should ask such questions. This is the beginning of Bhakti-yoga.

4. **O infallible Lord, it is not surprising that You fully avail Yourself to those who have taken exclusive shelter at Your lotus feet. It is clear to me that You would rather give Your affection to various creatures, even monkeys, like Hanuman, than to great demigods, if those lesser beings take full advantage of Your mercy.**

Commentary

Hanuman, too, learned this lesson well, when he thought his service more important than that of a lowly spider: Both the spider and Hanuman were engaged in building a bridge made of rocks, so that Rama's army of monkey warriors might retrieve Sita for Lord Rama by marching to Sri Lanka. Of course, the spider, being tiny, was able to carry only small pebbles, whereas Hanuman was throwing big boulders in the water. "Get out my way," Hanuman said to the spider, "I am serving Lord Rama and you are just being a nuisance." But Lord Rama interceded, telling Hanuman that the spider was doing as much service as he was. Rama saw the spider's intention, not its power or accomplishment.

5. **Because You are so loving and compassionate, who would even consider abandoning You, the most dear object of worship and the Supreme Lord of all? You award all possible perfections to the devotees, merely because they take shelter of You—how could anyone be so ungrateful, especially if they are even slightly aware of this simple truth? Who would replace You with material enjoyment, which simply leads to forgetfulness and misery? Indeed, we who engage in Your divine service want for nothing, and we feel no lack whatsoever.**

6. O Supreme Lord! The best of poets and those learned in spiritual truths cannot adequately express their debt to You, even if they lived as long as Brahma (millions of years). Indeed, Your compassion is overflowing, and thus You come to us in two features—externally as the perfect teacher and internally as the Lord of the heart—just to give us a chance to come to You.

Commentary

Uddhava feels deep appreciation for the Lord's compassion, and he expresses it beautifully in these few verses. Starting with Verse 4, Uddhava acknowledges that Krishna does not focus on one's external service but rather on the heart of the person serving Him. God is not interested in elaborate sacrifices, even though they are recommended in the *Vedas*; in great intellectual prowess; meditation expertise; or mastery over the body and mind. No. His main interest is in how much we love Him.

In Verse 5, Uddhava is aghast at the thought that some might abandon the Lord in favor of material sense gratification—this includes inferior systems of religion, too. The Lord Himself says what He prefers: A simple heart engaged in His service (Bhakti-yoga). Uddhava is amazed that such ungratefulness could exist in the person of spiritual practitioners, especially because Krishna has made the process of perfection so simple for them out of His compassion.

Finally, in Verse 6, Uddhava reveals just how compassionate God really is: So we have a chance to really approach Him and to develop our love through the process of Bhakti-yoga, He descends as a perfect master, or someone with whom we can relate—an adept who guides us, purifies us, and teaches us in a practical way. The scriptures tell us that such a perfected soul is Krishna's very self. Furthermore, Krishna descends as the indwelling soul, the Paramatma—or the Lord of the heart. In this form, He accompanies us, birth after birth, until we learn to see material life in perspective and feel the inner longing that is our birthright: to surrender unto Him with love and devotion.

7. Sri Shukadeva Gosvami [the narrator of the *Bhagavata Purana*] said: Because His affectionate devotee Uddhava questioned Him in this pleasing way, Lord Krishna, the supreme controller, who enjoys the universe in His own inimitable way, as Brahma, Vishnu and Shiva, began to reply, showing His all-attractive smile.

Commentary

Shukadeva reminds his audience that Krishna is in fact the Lord of all, that He displays cosmic pastimes as creator (Brahma), maintainer (Vishnu), and destroyer (Shiva), enjoying the material world through these partial manifestations, and that He stands—in His fullness—before Uddhava, smiling and pleased with his devotion. With this as a backdrop, the Lord begins to address the ultimate subject of Bhakti-yoga, as His series of lessons comes to a close. The magnitude of this occurrence should not be lost on the readers of the *Uddhava Gita.*

8. **The Supreme Lord said: Now I will describe devotion to Me, the science of divine service, through which a human being can learn to conquer the unconquerable: death.**
9. **With thoughts always absorbed in Me, one should perform all his duties in My service without being impulsive. Fully offering mind and intelligence to Me, one should develop attraction to My devotional service.**

Commentary

One might think devotional service is easier said than done. In due course, it becomes obvious that a deep study of scripture and the process of surrendering to a guru are essential. The scriptures include many guidelines and recommendations for fulfilling these commands, and the guru provides practical instructions for making gradual progress on the path. Otherwise, one can legitimately ask, "How do I absorb my mind in Krishna? What does He mean by not being impulsive? How do I become attracted to His service?" Answers to these questions are found in the scriptures and in the words and personal example of the guru.

10. **Traveling to holy places where My saintly devotees dwell, one should take guidance from their exemplary activities. These devotees can be found among the demigods, demons, and human beings.**

Commentary

Krishna begins to briefly describe how one might remember Him and engage in His service. The most important principle of all is the association of devotees, which, it might be remembered, was the main teaching of the *Aila Gita*, described in Chapter Twenty. Krishna reminds Uddhava that devotees are often found in holy places, but that they cannot be judged by externals. Often they are found on higher planets, such as those of the demigods, and they also exist among humans, where we might find them engaged in the Lord's service. We can read about their activities on higher planets and search them out on our own planet, but we must remain vigilant to recognize them when we finally meet them. They do not always appear the way we think they should—they do not always look holy, nor do they always adhere to conventional methods. Sometimes, in fact, they appear in families of demons—Prahlad is the main example in the *Bhagavata Purana*—and are rebels of various kinds. One must take scriptural guidance and the advice of established saintly people to know who they are and how to take shelter of them.

11. There are specific holy days, ceremonies, and festivals established for worshiping Me. One should enthusiastically celebrate these events, whether alone or in public gatherings, with singing, dancing, and other exhibitions of opulence.

Commentary

Long-established traditions are helpful here, and to learn them, again, one must go to experienced devotees and to *bhakti* scriptures. Gopal Bhatta Goswami's *Hari-bhakti-vilasa*, especially, includes much information on Krishnaite festivals and how to celebrate them for maximum effect.

12. I am the Supreme Soul within the core of all living creatures. With a pure heart, one should see Me as being uncontaminated by anything material, not even by the bodies of all those entities in which I dwell. I am present everywhere, both externally and internally, just like the all-pervading sky.

13–14. O shining star amongst the devotees, one who consciously views all living entities with this perception that I dwell within each of them, and who, because of this realization, offers full respect to one and all, is considered a true sage. Such a person does not distinguish between the Brahmin and the outcaste; those who give charity to Brahmins and the thief; the sun and sparks of fire; the gentle and the cruel.

Commentary

Verses 12–14 express four important ideas: (1) God exists within the very essence of everyone and everything—a truth revealed several times already in the *Uddhava Gita*. (2) He is always pure, even though He exists within all aspects of everything, including matter, which is inherently contaminated. (3) A truly wise person sees all living creatures in terms of the awareness that God pervades all beings, and (4) he behaves accordingly, offering love and respect to all. Seeing the Lord in everyone's heart enables such a wise soul to move beyond the dualities of material existence, for, in essence, these dualities are not what life is all about. Rather, it is about perceiving the Lord in all things and at all times—it is this vision that allows one to move forward in self-realization. Thus, self-realized souls tend to deemphasize the distinctions found in material nature and, instead, focus on the divinity that engulfs everyone.

Of course, the truly wise can perceive the distinctions in opposites, such as those listed here by Lord Krishna. Indeed, it is a sign of the most rudimentary intelligence to know the difference between the gentle and cruel, for example. But Krishna speaks about a higher vision. While a sage may acknowledge these distinctions on a certain level, he is focused on something more substantial, that is, on how everything is one because it is interpenetrated by the same one Supreme Lord. Only sages such as he can perceive this harmony of existence—for he sees his loving Lord in the hearts of all. Such self-realized souls naturally gravitate toward others with this same vision, but they also relish associating with fledgling spiritualists who have not yet attained this ability, hoping to help them gradually achieve it.

15. How fortunate are those who consistently meditate on My mystical presence within all souls. For devotees with such vision, the inferior tendencies of rivalry, envy and abusiveness—along with any and all false conceptions of the self—are soon obliterated.

16. In all cases, one should renounce the bodily conception of life, even if one's companions criticize him for it. With this understanding, one should offer respects to all—even dogs, outcastes, cows and asses—falling flat upon the ground like a rod.

Commentary

Devotees do not bow down to all living beings because they somehow misconstrue them to be God. Rather, the respect is given because these beings *are children of God*, noble in their own right, and because God resides in their heart of hearts.

Such an egalitarian vision is often criticized by those who have not yet attained it. Krishna warns that, even if this is so, one should go on with one's practices, living in the awareness that he is not his body.

The reference to "falling upon the ground like a rod" recalls the ancient Indic tradition of *dandavat*, wherein, as a sign of humility, one bows down first partially and then completely, laying down on the ground flat like a stick. In India, this is still practiced by many saintly people as a sign of ultimate submission and respect.

17. When one has reached the point of seeing Me in all living beings—only then can he abandon worshiping Me in the usual way: with the activities of speech, mind, and body.

Commentary

Usually, people look for excuses not to follow the rules and regulations of scriptures. Krishna guards against this: If one does not see the Supreme Lord, fully and at all times, in the hearts of all creatures—and this is a vision that few attain—then one must follow the various commandments and guidelines set down by sacred texts and predecessor spiritual masters. After one achieves this high realization of seeing Him in all, such rules and regulations can be discarded—though they rarely are. A true saint usually follows them according to his own nature, which is steeped in goodness and love of God.

18. Absorbed in actual knowledge of the Supreme, seeing things as they are, one is able to perceive the Absolute Truth everywhere and at all times. Without a shred of doubt in his heart, such a devotee relinquishes the inclination to enjoy his senses.

19. Make no mistake: One should consistently use one's mind, body, and words to understand how I exist within all living beings. This method, truthfully, is the best possible way of attaining the Supreme.

20. Being established by Me, O Uddhava, this mystical process of Bhakti-yoga, devotional service, is completely spiritual and free from material contamination. Devotees never suffer any loss by adopting this process.

21. O greatest of saints, when confronted with danger, most people tend to cry, worry, or otherwise lament, even though such feelings cannot possibly change the situation. But all action performed as an offering to Me, when executed without selfish motivation—even if these acts are externally useless—will allow one to experience the goal of religion.

22. The process of Bhakti-yoga is actually the most intelligent and clever path of all, for by engaging its practices one can in this very life use the temporary and unreal accouterments of the material world to achieve Me, who is eternal and real.

Commentary

Ironically, in Bhakti-yoga one uses the senses, which are material, in the service of the Master of the Senses (God), who is entirely spiritual. In fact, Bhakti-yoga is the art of taking all matter and transforming it into spirit. In this sense, it is the ultimate alchemical process, easy to achieve and joyfully performed. It must be learned at the feet of an adept, however. This is the secret. Therefore, Krishna began this chapter by stressing the importance of holy association—only by associating with true devotees, from the spiritual master to other advanced practitioners who serve the Lord with a sincere heart, can one learn the secrets of *bhakti*, the secrets of transforming common material elements into high-potency spiritual substance, capable of bringing one into the realm of the divine.

A practical example of the transformation process is found in *prasadam* (literally, "the Lord's mercy"), or spiritual vegetarian food, as relished in the homes of all devotees, at Krishna temples throughout the world, and even at

Vaishnava restaurants. When one chants the appropriate mantras over the food, with love and devotion, Krishna Himself "tastes" these delectable preparations, thus invigorating them with spiritual potency. Once "offered" in this way, the food purifies all who prepare it, serve it out, and of course eat it. The *prasadam* factor has been documented in many religious texts of the Eastern Hemisphere and is a phenomenon well known by all Vaishnava devotees of the Lord.

23. I have therefore explained it to you, both in summary and with some specifics—and with this knowledge you can understand the Absolute Truth. Although externally simple, the intricacies of this process are difficult to comprehend. Indeed, even the demigods, exalted beings from higher planets, cannot penetrate its innermost mysteries.

24. I have used logic and reason in explaining these ideas to you again and again, hoping that you will understand it properly. Those who do, realizing its inner meaning, will eventually become free from all doubts and, in the end, attain liberation.

25. If one contemplates these clear answers I have given in response to your many questions, he will in due course comprehend the highest spiritual secrets of all, attaining the ultimate realization.

26. Anyone who freely communicates these ideas to My devotees is to be considered a transmitter of the Absolute Truth. I award My very essence to such a person.

Commentary

The glorification of "transmitters of the truth," especially those who enlighten devotees, is also found in the *Bhagavad Gita*, where Krishna tells Arjuna: "For one who explains the supreme secret to the devotees, devotional service is guaranteed, and at the end he will come back to Me. There is no servant in this world more dear to Me than he, nor will there ever be one more dear" (18.68–69). This is so because the entire world depends on devotees themselves having this knowledge of transcendence. The devotees, then, in turn, are meant to instruct all others. But if the devotees do not know the truths of spiritual life, then how will they instruct people in general? Therefore, enlightening the devotees is perhaps the greatest service one can offer to Lord Krishna. Of course, before explaining these truths to devotees, one must oneself know what these truths are.

27. Loudly proclaiming this supreme knowledge, clear and transcendent, one purifies himself in the process—for there is nothing so urgent as revealing Me to others with the shining light of transcendental knowledge.

Commentary

This is the principle of Sankirtan, which generally refers to congregationally glorifying the Lord, usually with song and dance. However, the word is sufficiently nuanced to include numerous ways of conveying the Lord's glories. Basically, it is the principle of "sharing" one's spiritual assets. This can manifest in the form of vocalizing mantras, especially in group chanting sessions (*kirtan*), where all who sing and all who hear make tangible spiritual advancement; by writing and distributing books; by conveying transcendental knowledge through lectures or multimedia; and by communicating spiritual truth in a host of other ways. Sankirtan is considered the recommended sacrifice of the current age and is therefore "urgent," as Krishna says in this verse.

28. One who consistently gives aural reception to this knowledge while engaging in My pure devotional service, with faith and attention, will never become entangled in the reactions to material work.

29. O Uddhava, do you now understood all that I have said? Is the confusion and lamentation now gone?

Commentary

The traditional commentators inform us that Uddhava, like Arjuna, is an eternally liberated soul, and his feigned "confusion and lamentation" is just to instigate Krishna's answers, so that future generations might read these dialogues and benefit from them. Vishvanath Chakravarti, one of the *Uddhava Gita*'s premier commentators, writes that Krishna is playfully asking Uddhava in this verse if his confusion and lamentation are gone, knowing full well, of course, that these lesser qualities had never really appeared in Uddhava's heart in the first place.

This being said, Krishna's question to Uddhava is not unlike two of the *Bhagavad Gita*'s concluding verses: "O Arjuna, have you heard My words attentively? And are your illusions and ignorance now gone?" To this, Arjuna answered, "My dear Krishna, O infallible one, my illusion is completely eradicated. I have regained my memory by Your mercy, and I am now free from doubt as well as prepared to act according to Your instructions" (18.72–73). Uddhava could say the same.

30. It is inappropriate to share this knowledge with those who are hypocritical, atheistic or dishonest, or with anyone who will not listen faithfully. It is additionally disadvantageous to share it with those who are not devotees or who lack humility.

Commentary

A similar verse appears in the *Bhagavad Gita*: "This confidential knowledge may not be explained to those who are not austere, or devoted, or engaged in devotional service, nor to one who is envious of Me" (18.67). The idea is that one who possesses these disqualifications can easily use the *Gita*'s knowledge for lesser purposes—to make money, to appear learned, or to exploit others. Therefore, Krishna advises against sharing this knowledge with them. However, if they express interest and show signs of sincerity, one can share certain fundamental precepts with them, hoping that these teachings will purify them of their lesser qualities and allow them to move forward on the spiritual path.

31. Rather, this knowledge should be conveyed to those who are no longer beleaguered by such inferior qualities; who are concerned about the welfare of Brahmins and other spiritual seekers; and who are kind to others, saintly and pure. Additionally, if ordinary workers, women, and anyone else are found to have devotion for Me, they can also be accepted as qualified.

Commentary

The *bhakti* tradition broke open the storehouse of love of God, allowing in anyone who was sincere and pure of heart. Traditionally, ancient Indian culture was somewhat preoccupied with patriarchy and social status, minimizing the position of woman and those of the lower castes. According to Verse 31 and others like it, however, such considerations were rendered inconsequential for devotees of Krishna. This perfectly egalitarian philosophy is based not on the body but on the soul, which is equal in all beings. Still, speaking to the society at hand, Krishna wants to assure Uddhava and future readers of the *Uddhava Gita* that anyone can hear these teachings and benefit from their content, as long as one is sincere at heart and willing to develop devotion for God.

32. If a truly thoughtful and inquisitive person avails himself of this knowledge, he has nothing further to know. All true wisdom is contained here. After all, one who drinks the most succulent nectar will not need any other drink.

Commentary

Verse 32 is similar to Krishna's statement in the *Bhagavad Gita*: "I shall now declare unto you in full this knowledge both phenomenal and noumenal, by knowing which there will remain nothing further to be known" (7.2).

33. Most people pursue religion, economic development, sense gratification, and liberation with the help of study, ritualistic work, mystic yoga, mundane business acumen, and politics. But things are easier for you because you are My devotee—you need simply surrender unto Me to achieve the same results.

34. All living beings can achieve liberation from birth and death, and share in My own opulences, simply by renouncing fruitive desire and enthusiastically engaging in My service. In this way, each living being should offer his life entirely unto Me—he will benefit from this more than he can imagine.

35. [Shukadeva Gosvami said:] Having heard Lord Krishna speak these words, which elucidate the many paths of yoga, Uddhava folded his hands with deep respect. He wanted to express his gratefulness, but his throat choked up with love, his eyes overflowing with tears. He was thus unable to speak.

Commentary

Shukadeva Goswami indicates that Uddhava was experiencing *prema*, or advanced love of God. At this stage, ecstatic symptoms take place, in which one's body becomes like a small divine vessel, hardly able to contain the bliss of love now flooding the heart. In its initial stages, *prema* is called *bhava*, and this is when the eight ecstatic symptoms (*ashta-sattvika-vikara*), such as crying, hair standing on end, and so on, begin to involuntarily manifest on one's person. When meditating on the Lord's lotus feet, for example, the heart may melt in such a way as to produce an intense crying session, in which tears spontaneously shoot from the eyes. Descriptions of such ecstatic tendencies are found in Vaishnava tantric texts and in the Puranas as well. We now hear of Uddhava exhibiting such symptoms.

The reference to Uddhava's "folded hands" indicates *anjali*, a traditional form of salutation—a gesture of respect in which one places one's palms together and slightly raises them to the forehead.

36. [Shukadeva continued:] Uddhava steadied his mind, which had become overwhelmed with divine love. Feeling extreme gratitude toward Lord Krishna, he bowed down and touched the Lord's lotus feet with his head. He then began speaking with great reverence.

37. Sri Uddhava said: O eternal, primeval Lord, although I had fallen into the illusions of this dark world, Your merciful presence has brought light to my life. Indeed, how can cold, darkness, and fear have any effect on one who is near the sun?

Commentary

In great humility, Uddhava expresses his appreciation for the Lord's presence in his life. Posing as a conditioned soul, his prayer is instructive, showing how those who are indeed illusioned should express their gratefulness.

38. **You have mercifully opened my eyes with the torchlight of knowledge, merely because I am Your surrendered servant. In light of such a bargain, what fool could ever give up Your lotus feet and take shelter of another?**

39. **Though initially bound by my affection for the Dasharhas, Vrishnis, Andhakas and Satvatas—families You tied me to for purposes of Your own—I am now detached due to the weapon of transcendental knowledge.**

Commentary

This is further proof that Uddhava poses as a conditioned soul: The families he cites are actually transcendental associates of the Lord, and thus attachment to them would be desirable in spiritual life. Nonetheless, in Verse 39, he shows how one would normally view familial attachment when it acts as an obstacle on the spiritual path.

40. **I offer You full respect, O greatest of *yogis*, as You know. But I beseech You: Please now give me any parting instruction You wish, for I am a soul surrendered unto You. These final words should specifically engage me in Your divine service, allowing me to gain undistracted attachment to Your lotus feet.**

41–44. **The Supreme Lord said: My dear Uddhava, take My order and all that you have learned to Badarikashram, enlightening those who dwell in the far north. Become purified by both touching and also bathing in the holy waters there, which have emanated from My lotus feet. The Alakananda River will free you from all sinful reactions. You may also dress in bark and eat whatever is naturally available in the forest. Thus, please live simply, remaining free from desire, tolerant of dualities, pleasant in nature, self-controlled, peaceful, and functioning according to transcendental knowledge. With intense focus, meditate upon all the instructions you received from Me, fully assimilating their essential meaning. Always talk and think about Me, thus endeavoring to enhance your realization of My sublime qualities. In this way, you will cross beyond the thre modes of nature and return to Me, reaching transcendenc**

Commentary

Basically, in these final verses, the Lord summarizes all He h from the beginning of their discussion: The devotee sho the Lord and glorify Him in every way. He should as holy place and live simply. Krishna should be his sole object of contemplation, and he should meditate on the teachings of spiritual reality.

Interestingly, Krishna begins these final verses by telling Uddhava to share this message at Badarikashram. This is significant. Krishna does not want Uddhava to merely relish these supreme teachings on his own, for this would neglect the element of compassion. Indeed, the principle of Sankirtan—of going out and giving Krishna to others, whether by singing His glories or explaining them to one and all—is the recommended process of self-realization for the current age, as noted earlier. And Uddhava is called on to do just that: To spread the word of Krishna consciousness.

45. [Shukadeva Gosvami said:] Thus hearing the final instructions of Lord Krishna, whose wisdom allows one to transcend all suffering, Sri Uddhava reverentially walked around the Lord, finally falling down in front of Him, taking His feet upon his head. Although free from the influence of all mundane dualities, Uddhava could not contain himself, and his tears literally soaked the Lord's lotus feet.

Commentary

Uddhava wept, fearful that their time together was coming to a close and grateful for all that had transpired. His tears were influenced by his ecstatic symptoms of love of God.

He now had his final instructions, clear and true, and so he enacted the customary circumambulation often performed in the presence of divinity. This is when one walks around one's object of veneration, usually three times. He then bowed to the ground, also part of the tradition, but then he broke down, crying. His love knew no bounds.

46. Experiencing relentless anxiety because of his imminent separation from the Lord, for whom he felt such undying affection, Uddhava was deeply distressed, not wanting to give up Krishna's association. Finally, feeling inner agony, he bowed down repeat- ...ly placed the Lord's slippers on his head, and quickly left

Commentary

...evotee and, as such, he experienced the top-
...ader should be aware, however, that such
...cs. It has, embedded within it, a type of
...hances pleasurable feelings of divine love.
...netimes *vipralambha*: "love in separation."

In fact, the only way to attain "union" (*yoga, sambhoga*) with Krishna is through this harsh feeling of the Lord's absence—through "the dark night of the soul" leading to the light of perfect Krishna consciousness.

When mundane lovers are separated from their beloved, the separation is painful because they are not getting what they want—their sensual interest is not being fulfilled. Interestingly, mundane union is, in its way, as painful as separation, for while it gratifies one's immediate sensual interest, it does not touch the soul. Thus, even in union, one tends to feel something lacking. In this sense, union and separation, at least in the material world, have much in common. Still, spiritually speaking, mundane separation is often more valuable than union, for if it endures, it easily can lead to detachment, as Krishna teaches Uddhava in various parts of the *Uddhava Gita*.

Spiritual union and separation are similar to each other, too. Both are joyful, since they are devoid of selfish concern. Love for Krishna is based on the desire to please Krishna's senses. Thus, when united with Him, one is happy—if this is what Krishna wants. And yet a pure devotee would gladly experience separation from Him as well—even if, in a sense, as in this instance with Uddhava, it hurts—as long as it is in pursuance of Krishna's desire. In the end, then, a devotee is not interested in union or separation: He is interested in Krishna's happiness, in pleasing the Lord. This is selflessness. This is love.

47. After this, knowing that the Lord is always with him in the core of his heart, the great Uddhava went to Badarikashram, as requested. By doing as he was told, to the letter, he attained the Lord's transcendental abode, which had been fully described to him by his dearmost friend, Lord Krishna Himself.

Commentary

Uddhava went on to attain total perfection. Moving beyond the dark night of the soul, fueled by the realization that Krishna is always with him, in his heart, he attained perfect union and the pinnacle of divine consciousness.

48. In this way, Lord Krishna, whose lotus feet the great yoga masters all aspire to serve, spoke to His devotee Uddhava, conveying the best of all knowledge—a veritable ocean of transcendental bliss. If any soul hears or reads this narration, feeling faithful wit[illegible] their heart, liberation is assured.

49. [Shukadeva concludes:] I thus offer my full respe[illegible] Supreme Lord Sri Krishna, the original and great[illegible] beings. He is the author of the original *Veda*[illegible] lected this sweet essence of all Vedic know[illegible] collects honey, to give to His devotees,[illegible]

This nectar, derived from the ocean of bliss, is only for His many devotees, and by His mercy they drink deeply.

Commentary

Thus ends the *Uddhava Gita*, which elaborates on the five items only briefly explored in its cousin-text, the *Bhagavad Gita*: The Supreme Lord (*ishvara*), the living entities (*jiva*), material nature (*prakriti*), time (*kala*), and activities (*karma*). The *Uddhava Gita* also details the interaction of these five items and how they can affect the spiritual journey. Lord Krishna had explained these things to Arjuna with self-conscious brevity, because they were preparing for an oncoming battle of extreme proportions. Indeed, tradition reveals that the Lord had just under an hour to express His transcendental truth to the legendary archer, whereas Uddhava encountered Krishna while the latter was comfortably seated under a beautiful banyan tree in a relaxed mood. This allowed for a more extensive discussion, with Uddhava asking numerous questions and the Lord taking His time to reveal confidential knowledge.

That being said, there was also a sense of urgency in the Lord's recitation of the *Uddhava Gita*, for He was preparing to leave the planet at a predetermined time. Accordingly, while the setting of this text is more accommodating than that of the *Bhagavad Gita*, it is still not ideal, and so Krishna was unable to delve into the details and specifics necessary for a complete understanding of these subjects. Therefore, say the great teachers and stalwarts of the Vaishnava tradition, commentators are necessary to enter into the inner meaning of the text, as is a bona fide spiritual master.

Index

About the Author

STEVEN J. ROSEN is the author of numerous books, including several volumes on the Bhagavad Gita, such as *Krishna's Song: A New Look at the Bhagavad Gita* (Praeger, 2007), *Gita on the Green: The Mystical Tradition Behind Bagger Vance* (Continuum International, 2000) and *Holy War: Violence and the Bhagavad Gita* (Deepak Heritage Books, 2002). He is also the author of *Essential Hinduism* (Praeger, 2006) and is the founding editor of the *Journal of Vaishnava Studies.*

PADDY

BOULEVARD
TRANSPORTATION

BOULEVARD TRANSPORTATION

OTTO

By

RUDY BURCKHARDT

AND

VINCENT KATZ

TIBOR DE NAGY EDITIONS

1997

NEW YORK

First Edition published in 1997 by
Tibor de Nagy Editions
724 Fifth Avenue
New York, NY 10019

Some of these photographs and poems appeared in *The New Censorship: The Monthly Journal of the Next Savage State*, Vol. 3, No. 2, May, 1992

ISBN: 0-9639033-9-X

Cover photograph by Rudy Burckhardt:
Sidewalk VIII, New York, 1939

FIRST EDITION
Printed in the United States of America

To

Yvonne and Vivien

WORLD-TELEGRAM

Boulevard Transportation

032 170

viii.
huge hooting honkers
i'm stacked up
grand motor rams
of seaside urge
against the big guys
i guzzle beer
nuzzle cuties

in eagerness to faint
of writing hunger
spilling beer all over me
guy helps a dame
look for something
wraiths in plaid
and nets spooned
by the light

x.
she stamps the frame
Old Joe finds her sexy
halfman is smoothly
groomed, to tie knot
they talk and face one

xiv.
it is now i see the direction
in which we are to go:
towards feigned destruction,
shiny impulse, a future
rattled in the light it sheds
on newspapers in the trash bin

xv.
young mr. fonda
fuck it he hits
the shake bar
buys gum
spits
eyes a cutie

xvii.
phallus with breasts
shoots up
near female forms
two women in
identical two-tone pumps

ix.
she steps on him
steps on herself
the light dirty balance
of balls weighs him
an impoverished way
of saying something

xviii.
presses up to her
paper bag
floppy white pant
bucks, summer
frame of granite

xx.
the beer's spilling!
i yell as andy mulrooney
and Todd Takeover murmur
distantly like calves
the Dalai Lama was discovered
1,000 miles from Lhasa

SAKS
&
COMPANY
STORE CLOSED

vii.
Saks will close
all day Saturday
during July and August.
When will you allow us
the pleasure of a visit?
The sight of you
might very well cure us.

1311 patterns Egyptian flowers
all netted with her chest
forward, case
and purse
you've lost any reason
you're in front of a temple
the patterns let her down soft

i.
feigned scents
two tone tony
steps in
four inch wide
diagonal stripe
tie, white hat
a distant stinging
day sweats
you, pumps

xxiv.
belted suit back
white shoes
plaid bolero

xxi.
funky dotted trouser, glove

xiii.
again, influence
of de Kooning dictum
related by denby
"the designs
on the sidewalk
Bill pointed out"

xxii-xxiii.
shiny mothers
ready to take on
New York
as much
as Garbo
driver mugs, laughing
The Republic movie theater
tire tracks in the gutter
in 1940
De Soto Sky-View
presents light shining
off distant car backs
tiny back window mistake

033 · 049
NY 40

xxv.

...

i had been—what the hell had I been?

xii.
a dull shoe
steps on Rudy's shoulder
27, looking down
at his surrounding
painting more
than a Magritte

v.
Paddy's Clam House
United Cigar
back to foreground
diagonal
male caucasian
points, directing
second male caucasian
KREDIT
old dead faces
blurred,
distant in thought
Teddy Two-Tone
improvises bravado
tiny, insignificant
moths attack me
faces hooked for miles
along this avenue

xxvi.
People walking.
People in motion.
Cinematic
sexiness.
3 rows
of sidewalk
skylights underlie
same separateness
then as now
(urbanity)
in the middle
this guy,
this slouching,
cigarette-smoking,
coiffed,
well-heeled
and -tied,
sensitive-lipped,
big nosed
guy.

He's probably still
around.

xxvii.
stepped outa
Rudley's
trieda fine
some money
ta call Tony
the delicate
grasp of
something, and
Daily News
SMALL STEAK
with potatoes
and toast, 30c

xxviii.
it’s all about
walking,
how
you do it
in the street
barbershop
pharmacy
fountain
service
letters “cut”
against
a butt
the words in
windows sometimes
take precedence:
Mais Oui,
Lifebuoy,
Aladdin
Lunch Kit,
Whipped Cream
and Wafers
Many Tasty
Combinations
Waffles
Manicuring
Shave 20c
man in white
shirt, trousers,
and shoes
swings by
in front of
proverbial revolving
barber pole
alien spinning
icon

xxix.
Joey Midrange
bumps past
Sunshine
Food Shoppe
Honeydew or
Canteloupe
on ice, 10c
patterned
tiles lead
him in
but he's got
his eye
elsewhere

xxx.
Sidewalk diagonals
geometric grid
within grid
of frame
containing contra-
angular flow
of bodies,
women's carefully
observed forms
great distant
range
and centerpiece
the "back-row"
but ideally
framed young
matron, with
straight husband
and two
young stud
sons, one with
unlit fag
dangling, the other
perfect haircut,
tie, suit cut,
and white
bucks

you have to
trip into
this stuff
that Rudy was
into, cause
he takes it
so far inside
you have to
be prepared
to take it

further back,
a white limo,
parked across
the street.

xxxii.
a fine spectacle
of proportion
and light
boy's step
is the pinion
and everything
breaks into
motion off
that, and if
it is a
certain type
of Spring day,
that is felt,
the women
hurrying through
the City, finger
to lip, a confident
one marches,
gloves in hand
different planes
of individuals'
path, and back
with boy, a
man in nice
wide-breasted
suit and haircut
bites a hangnail,
man in straw
boater steps
gaily into
frame

WE GIVE
Green Discount
STAMPS
Mais Oui
Yardley
Lifebuoy
SOAP
Rubbing
Alcohol
PINT
Phillips'
Milk of
Magnesia
$2.00

xxxi.
wait a minute —
back to
that butt, up
against the "cut"
she is so fine
in her fox,
jaunty hat
above luscious
locks,
a New York walk
but the focus
is on the
pharmacy
storefront
your glance
is taken
off her

ACCUSE
WRECKIN

XX
What'd Bill
Rogers get
into anyway?
He was some
kind of gambler,
wasn't he?
You think he's
noticed me?
I hope not.
I'd hate to be
found with him.

Europa Euphoria

i.
a lone woman strides
across a sea of cobbles
refracted white
in the haze
Europe's centuries
dwindle and dawdle
(before or after
the war)
narrow vertical
car front grille
door open
at the curb
cast-iron bench and
ornate lamposts:
two, on an island,
frame dapper
gent's assured
swagger, paper
in hand, limos
in front of
the Deux Magots
details of an
ordinary day
in Paris snatched
in haze

SUZY
Tartinette GRAF
Pce de la REPUBLIQUE

iii.
1934
Pce. de la REPUBLIQUE
the tram
is intersected
thrust
SUZY.
(framed)
under backwards
GRAF
from
overlapping
"Tartinette"
propaganda
and the figure
in such
demure death—
unreal figment
of illusionary
tram, doorways
cut into fronts

iv.
Napoli
1951
I am
looking
for
the punctum
Italy
has
survived
the war.
Girl's perfect
focus,
her smiling
face in
focus,
grading down
to soft
shoes.
These three
children
are actors—
they have
each hit
a mark
impeccably.
A man
in a t-shirt
looks into
a doorway,
oblivious.
She could
be a model
but for her
luck.

ii.
this is a well-
heeled community:
the girls' shoes,
and everyone else's,
particularly
the witty pair
entering left,
a mother and son
exit right,
this is
the girls'
moment, their
swinging the
rope in shoulder
and hand,
the left girl's
step, the middle
girl at her
moment of
success
performs
calmly, hands
at her side,
a tiny public
act

BIRRA

v.
Impossibilities
of space
impounded
on itself.
Simple
clarity
of
everything
in the
huge spread
where man
is dwarfed.

ii.
The people in
Antigua walk
differently
from the people
in America

Goodbye, N.Y.

xxxv.
this man has
been x'd out
of society
while people
talk on the
corner, delivery
boy forms
huge angle
with his step,
the harsh light
blinds one,
this man's gaze
is numbed,
in effect,
doesn't see

i.
great slit-eyed monster
finger hole for painter's
palette, these shapes
the muddy, mottled
shore, a great way
water collects light,
retains it, like
a photographic plate
horizon's shearing edge
several trees catch
the late, left, light
but what is really
happening is 3 men
with a boy, all
in summer white
near a dirty pond
enacting unconscious
rituals their ancestors
initiated, simple
in the summer light

iii.
great passing strides,
flats, handbags,
paper op dot bag
double-breasted
white coat
lots of handbags
the flooded street
and, centrally,
one woman's back
leg stepping off
on ball of foot,
her sandal stays,
forever stuck
to the ground

iv.
he gives you
something you see,
not something you
"should" see

v.
tiny, inconsequential
corner of the city
no big deals go
down, no divorces
announced, yet
here is an absurd,
powerful collection
of forms, it is
come out of
the artist's head,
nowhere in nature
found

MEN

Maine Street

i.
I put bare
feet to Terra
swim in the lake
all day long
there is nothing
to do
listen to wind
in the trees

ii.
ferns
ancient purveyors
of chlorophyll
tasty curls
on the
energy market
their pocked
faces demonstrate
ageless
understanding
they simply
extend fronds
if you were
to kill them
they would
understand

iii.
trees
givers of life
they arch
over, protecting
us, while
in our idiocy,
we plot
inane destruction
or if not,
distraction
so many
different kinds
of trees
and individuals,
like people,
they each have
a face
in winter,
some shed
their coats
a different
picture
blends in
ice and cold
sometimes
I think
ice is the
only beauty
only in
the ice
am I
truly alone,
to think,
to walk...
but in summer
you hear the
leaves singing
and you
find dimension
in every
sight

iv.
the cabin
slat pine walls
ribbed ceiling
primary-
colored
windowshade
walls painted
blue
loon
calls at night
with wind
the porch
hammock
you are
in hiding

v.
rocking chairs
icebox
filled with
books
aqua floor
and walls
blue ceiling
brown shingles
inside, the
floor is pink
two captain's
trunks filled
with linens
and down
old framed
magazine prints
photos of the
sisters or
Millie with
the dog
Hotel Threadgill
Oklahoma
City, an Indian
paddles a birch
canoe against
an orange sunset
pond, a tin
advert for
white enamel
shows a
classy dame
gingerly stepping
off an elegant
stair, in the
kitchen, a

Hotpoint frigidaire
and Kalamazoo
wood stove,
handmade
wooden berry
rake from
single block
herbs preserved
in sealed
jars and tins:
Bokar Coffee
Supreme, and
Red Seal
Peanut Butter,
and a large
wooden bowl
with crack
repaired by
two metal
plates

vi.
you swim across
the pond
every day
where a hazy
glaze covers
the water
and trees
in July
the day
seems it
will continue
forever
time slows
you hear
bird calls
dog bark
occasional
squirrel
scolding
hammering

vii.
there is
enough time
for everything
you can
have lunch
with friends
in a relaxed
manner
listen to the
weekly opera
broadcast:
today, it's
Prokofiev's
Fiery Angel,
a story
of sexual
obsession
and
destruction
that starts
with a
duet in a
drawing room

viii.
7 Canada
Geese share
the pond
with 4
loons
today, in
mist, they
paddle around
like scenery
in an Italian
film, the
loons remain
hidden, will
transport
their young,
later, to
another pond,
their pond,
where they
will make their
yearly home,
as their parents
do here

ix.
I try to
transcribe
the summer,
fix it in
poems or
postcards,
but it flits
past again,
brook water
through
fingers,
and I
sense
each year,
to the old
as to
the young,
is so
important

List of Photographs *(in sequence)*

Boulevard Transportation

Europa Euphoria

Goodbye, N.Y.

Maine Street

A photographer, painter, and filmmaker, RUDY BURCKHARDT has exhibited widely throughout the United states since his arrival from Switzerland in 1935. He has collaborated on books with the poets Edwin Denby (*In Public, In Private*, Dekker Press, 1946, and *Mediterranean Cities*, George Wittenborn, 1956) and Simon Pettet (*Talking Pictures*, Zoland Books, 1994), as well as Vincent Katz (*New York Hello!*, Ommation Press, 1990). He is also the author of a book of memoirs and selected writings (*Mobile Homes,* Z Press, 1979). His photographs are in the permanent collections of the Museum of Modern Art and the Metropolitan Museum of Art. He has been honored with a film retrospective at the Museum of Modern Art in 1987, and he received the Brendan Gill Prize from the Municipal Arts Society of New York in 1988. He exhibits his photographs and paintings with Tibor de Nagy Gallery.

VINCENT KATZ is a poet, translator, and critic. He is the author of *A Tremor In the Morning* (Peter Blum Edition, 1986, with linocuts by Alex Katz) and *Cabal Of Zealots* (Hanuman Books, 1988), both books of poetry. In 1995, he published *Charm* (Sun & Moon Press), a book of translations from Latin of the Roman love poet Sextus Propertius. His writing has appeared in A*perture, Art in America, ARTnews, Flash Art, Interview, and Parkett.* He has contributed music and poetry to several films by Rudy Burckhardt, including *Tree Streets* (1996).

Boulevard Transportation was designed by Vivien Bittencourt. It was printed in an edition of 1,000 copies, of which 26, lettered A-Z, are signed by the authors and contain an original print by the artist. The font is Franklin Gothic. The book was printed by Thorner Press, Buffalo, New York. Production assistance by Paul Lafortezza. Series Editor: Eric Brown.

Tibor de Nagy Editions, established by John Bernard Myers in 1951, published first books of poetry by John Ashbery, Barbara Guest, Kenneth Koch, and Frank O'Hara, among others. The series, which published regularly from 1951 to 1970, was reinaugurated in 1995 with the publication of *Two Journals,* journal entries by poet James Schuyler.